social work &
domestic violence

SAGE has been part of the global academic community since 1965, supporting high quality research and learning that transforms society and our understanding of individuals, groups and cultures. SAGE is the independent, innovative, natural home for authors, editors and societies who share our commitment and passion for the social sciences.

Find out more at: **www.sagepublications.com**

social work &
domestic violence
developing critical & reflective practice

Lesley Laing & Cathy Humphreys
with Kate Cavanagh

⑤SAGE

Los Angeles | London | New Delhi
Singapore | Washington DC

Los Angeles | London | New Delhi
Singapore | Washington DC

SAGE Publications Ltd
1 Oliver's Yard
55 City Road
London EC1Y 1SP

SAGE Publications Inc.
2455 Teller Road
Thousand Oaks, California 91320

SAGE Publications India Pvt Ltd
B 1/I 1 Mohan Cooperative Industrial Area
Mathura Road
New Delhi 110 044

SAGE Publications Asia-Pacific Pte Ltd
3 Church Street
#10-04 Samsung Hub
Singapore 049483

Editor:Alice Oven
Assistant editor: Emma Milman
Production editor: Katie Forsythe
Copyeditor: Solveig Gardner Servian
Proofreader: Anna Gilding
Indexer: Elske Janssen
Marketing manager: Tamara Navaratnam
Typeset by: C&M Digitals (P) Ltd, Chennai, India
Printed by MPG Printgroup, UK

© Lesley Laing and Cathy Humphreys with Kate Cavanagh 2013

First published 2013

Library of Congress Control Number: 2012943950

British Library Cataloguing in Publication data

A catalogue record for this book is available from
the British Library

MIX
Paper from
responsible sources
FSC
www.fsc.org   FSC® C018575

ISBN 978–1–4129–1992–7
ISBN 978–1–4129–1923–4 (pbk)

This book is dedicated to our late colleague and friend
Kate Cavanagh who envisioned and initiated the project. It is also dedicated
by Cathy to Ray and Nicky for their encouragement and support and
by Lesley to Chris for her patience and enduring support.

Contents

About the Authors

Lesley Laing is a Senior Lecturer in Social Work and Policy Studies at the University of Sydney, where her teaching and research focus on violence against women and children. Her social work practice has encompassed direct practice, policy, training, professional development and research. A core passion has been educating human service professionals about the ways in which the effects of violence against women and children are often present and influential in the lives of clients of diverse health and welfare services. This was pursued both in her role as Director of the Education Centre Against Violence (NSW Health) and later as the founding Director of the Australian Domestic and Family Violence Clearinghouse. Lesley's child sexual assault research has evaluated treatment programmes for intrafamilial offenders, victims and mothers and for young people exhibiting sexually harmful behaviours. Her domestic violence research, conducted in collaboration with specialist domestic violence services, focuses on interagency responses to domestic violence and on women's experiences of navigating complex service systems: the family law system, mental health services and the civil protection order process. With a team of colleagues and in collaboration with the NSW Police Force, she is currently researching the incidence and contexts in which women are arrested or are protection order respondents. Lesley is a member of the NSW Domestic Violence Death Review Team.

Cathy Humphreys holds the Alfred Felton Chair of Child and Family Social Work at the University of Melbourne. The Chair was established by the Alfred Felton Trust to work with community sector organizations to capacity build research in the vulnerable youth and families sector. She has a strong background in practice, research and publication in the domestic violence and child abuse areas. Her research has explored the major social problem of domestic violence through a range of different lenses: substance use; mental health; child abuse; multiagency working and reform. A three year action research project, Talking To My Mum, developed activity books to strengthen the mother-child relationship and provide support for workers engaged in intervention which crossed the silos between adult women's services and children's services in the domestic violence sector. More recently research projects have focused on the domestic violence policy reform in Victoria, Australia; the development of good practice guidelines and standards for women with disabilities living with domestic violence; and a policy critique of mandatory reporting for children living with domestic violence. Her research is international with a specific focus on the UK where she worked for 12 years at University of Warwick before returning to Australia and the professorship at University of Melbourne.

Kate Cavanagh was born in Glasgow, Scotland in 1951. She studied sociology at the University of Stirling, graduating in 1975, and then completing an MSc thesis, *Battered Women and Social Control* (1978) whilst working as a research assistant. In 1978, she began a career in social work, obtaining a second master's degree from the University of Warwick, becoming a *guardian ad litem* for Derbyshire, helping establish a voluntary hostel for women with housing needs, and becoming Leicestershire's first research social worker. In 1990, after the birth of her second child, she moved into social work education, spending the next eighteen years at the Universities of Stirling and Glasgow where she taught and researched on domestic violence, drug taking, disability, mental health, child abuse, and social work education. From 1991 to 1994 she worked with Rebecca and Russell Dobash and Ruth Lewis on the evaluation of newly established programmes for perpetrators of domestic violence for the U.K. Government, co-writing *Changing Violent Men* (Sage, 2000) and completing a PhD thesis for the University of Manchester: *Do You Live Here Too? A Study of the Intimate Relationships of Violent Men and the Women They Abuse* (1998). With the same team, she undertook an ESRC funded study of homicide in Britain. She also co-edited *Working with Men: Feminism and Social Work* (Routledge, 1996) with Vivienne Cree, and published in a number of journals including *Homicide Studies* and *Journal of Social Policy*. Kate Cavanagh was diagnosed with ovarian cancer in 2006, and died in 2008.

Preface

This book would not have been written without the vision and passion of our late friend and colleague, Kate Cavanagh. Kate identified the pressing need for a critically reflective and research-minded approach to social work practice with domestic violence. Her vision was for a book which would offer this to social workers, whatever their field of practice, since domestic violence is encountered in all fields of social work. We trust that we have honoured this vision in the book.

In writing this book we owe an enormous debt to the women and children who have shared their experiences with us in our roles as both social work practitioners and researchers. These experiences have encompassed both the pain of violation and betrayal and the courage of resistance and survival.

Each of the three authors is a social worker with extensive practice experience in addressing violence against women and children prior to becoming researchers within this field. We believe that this experience assists us to bridge what are sometimes disparate worlds of research and practice. An important part of the research base that we draw on in this book is our own research. This research includes studies of behaviour change programmes with men who perpetrate domestic violence and child sexual assault; domestic violence and child protection; domestic violence and mental health; post-separation violence and Family Law; and criminal and civil legal responses to domestic violence. Across this body of research, building collaborative, cross-sector responses, is a central theme which also is one of the organizing themes of this book.

As feminist researchers our work is characterized by a commitment to research that improves the lives of women; that is done in collaboration with survivors and specialist domestic violence workers and recognizes their unique contribution to knowledge; and that seeks to bring forth marginalized voices, for example: of women with mental health problems who are also dealing with domestic violence; women who experience racism and discrimination and who are also struggling with domestic violence; and of children who are affected by domestic violence. We draw extensively on this research base throughout the book.

1

Introduction: Key Concepts in Social Work and Domestic Violence

Jessica is a newly qualified social worker employed in a drug and alcohol service. Amongst her numerous roles is the facilitation of the women's group, a part of the service which provides follow-up and outreach to women who have experienced the residential rehabilitation service. Jessica is constantly struck by how many of the women report living with domestic violence, are concerned about their children, but worried that they are unable to tackle both their drug and alcohol problems as well as separating from the violence. Jessica previously worked in a women's refuge while she was studying and where a more holistic service to women and their children was provided. She is concerned that the focus on drug and alcohol issues for the women where she is currently working is pushing both the issues for children and the engagement with the problem of domestic violence to the background. She knows she should be working to change the practice orientation but feels constrained by her more experienced co-facilitator who has rather pointedly maintained the focus on women's engagement with their use of drugs and alcohol whenever Jessica has opened the discussion to address the other issues for children or the issues of violence.

The vignette about Jessica illustrates the way in which domestic violence emerges as an issue for social workers, albeit one which is not necessarily the focus of the service intervention. Social workers across a range of service sectors and specialist domestic violence workers have a varied and sometimes contentious history. At its best, it is a harmonious, challenging and productive relationship. As social workers with a long history in the violence against women movement, we would argue that there is more commonality than difference. The aspirations of social work and its professional and theoretical framework are congruent with the values inherent within the violence against women movement, of which domestic violence is a part. The intention of this book is to explore and support these compatibilities. In the process, we envisage that practices with children, women and men will be extended.

In this first chapter, we outline a number of key concepts to provide the framework through which the interface between social work and domestic violence can be analysed. These concepts include: **working definitions of social work and domestic violence**; an exploration of **intersectionality and the significance of social location**; attention to **knowledge to support practice**; the **role of narrative and strengths based perspectives** through which questions for students and practitioners are derived; and a discussion of **critically reflective practice**. The chapter finishes with a description of the **structure of the chapters** and **different ways in which educators, facilitators and practitioners may wish to use the book** and its presentation of the many dimensions of domestic violence.

The writing of this book arises from recognition that too often the interface between social workers and domestic violence workers has seen more disconnection than connection. Social work has not necessarily had a proud history in supporting the safety and protection of women and children and holding men accountable for their violence. In particular, the close association between child protection and social work has often placed a wedge between child protection workers and women's advocates in domestic violence services. It is one of a number of divisions which this book will seek to address.

These divisions frequently occur through the 'siloed' nature of the work in human service organizations. Drug and alcohol services, mental health services, health services, services for disabled people, children's services, youth services, services for older people and homelessness services all bring their own priorities and discourses, of which an understanding of domestic violence intervention is but one element. Social workers are present, though not exclusively employed in all these human service systems. In a parallel process, domestic violence is present, but not the exclusive problem in all these service systems. It is everywhere and too often nowhere on the radar of the workers involved. It is not the main 'business' of any of these services, yet when women, children and some men are living in fear, traumatized by violence and abuse, then their worlds, their decision making and their ability to change their lives will be severely constrained.

Engaging social workers such as Jessica in recognizing, assessing and intervening in domestic violence within diverse service arenas forms the primary motivation for writing this book. Our thesis is that an understanding of domestic violence intervention with its emphasis on safety and autonomy for victims and accountability and responsibility for perpetrators of violence should change practice in these services. It is not a peripheral problem but one which will usually require centre-stage attention when it is present. It is also not a problem which can always be referred to another, more specialized agency, though sometimes this will be appropriate.

> Emphasis on safety and autonomy for victims and accountability and respon-
> sibility for perpetrators of violence provides the foundation for all domestic
> violence intervention in all practice settings.

Key Concepts for Social Work and Domestic Violence

A Working Definition of Social Work

A commitment to social justice lies at the heart of the aspirational framework through which the international definition of social work is derived:

> The social work profession promotes social change, problem solving in human rela-
> tionships and the empowerment and liberation of people to enhance well being.
> Utilising theories of human behaviour and social systems, social work intervenes at
> the points where people interact with their environments. Principles of human rights
> and social justice are fundamental to social work. (International Federation of Social
> Work, 2000)

Other definitions of social work in England, Canada and Australia reflect similar aspirations for social work. For example, in the United Kingdom, social workers joining the British Association of Social Workers (BASW) are required to agree with the Ethical Code of Practice which reflects the basic tenets of the international definition.

While most social work definitions are aspirational, the reality of practice within bureaucracies and large community sector organizations where most social workers are employed may be somewhat different. Social workers work within the organizational and legal constraints of these large bureaucracies. Housing, income support, child, youth and family policies may not be conducive to actioning a social justice agenda except as a point of resistance within a wider, conservative realm. The role of social workers as 'agents of care or agents of control' is an ongoing professional debate (Dickens, 2012; Thompson, 2002). The aspiration of developing anti-oppressive practice which challenges the policies of the very organization in which a worker is employed may credit social workers, and particularly frontline social workers, with more power and influence than their role permits (Harris, 2003). This terrain for social work is constantly developing and changing. Its definition and its boundaries are dependent upon the weight placed along four different dimensions outlined by Dickens (2012: 34) in his analysis of the multiple ethical and practice codes in the four countries of the United Kingdom. These include an emphasis on: values or roles and tasks; an individual or social change focus; an emphasis on care or control (empowerment or protection); and whether social work is defined by the profession or other public stakeholders such as politicians and the media.

While contested, we would argue that BASW Code of Ethics and the aspirational international definition of social work are not irrelevant. In the domestic violence arena they provide an essential framework for connection to the wider violence against women movement. Anti-oppressive practice with its attention to diversity across all social divisions including gender provides an ethical basis through which progressive social workers within the bureaucracy and community sector organizations can reflect and develop their work with women and children living with domestic violence. It will be a theme developed across the book to engage with students, educators, workers and their managers who tread a fine line between aspiration and the realities of working within a legally and resource constrained environment.

A Working Definition of Domestic Violence

All definitions and terminology include as well as exclude. The terminology of 'domestic violence' is no exception. 'Intimate partner violence', 'domestic abuse', 'family violence', 'abuse by known men', 'batterer violence' are all terms that are used to explain violence and abuse in intimate relationships.

A standard definition is provided by Women's Aid, UK:

> Domestic violence is physical, sexual, psychological or financial violence that takes place within an intimate or family-type relationship and that forms a pattern of coercive and controlling behaviour. This can include forced marriage and so-called 'honour crimes'. Domestic violence may include a range of abusive behaviours, not all of which are in themselves inherently 'violent'. (Women's Aid Federation of England, nd)

This definition emphasizes the core element of coercive control and the patterned use of a range of tactics to achieve it. The following definition includes this element but also addresses its gendered nature and the effects of these behaviours. In addition, it makes the important point that domestic violence does not necessarily end with separation:

> Domestic violence is … [v]iolent, abusive or intimidating behaviour carried out by an adult against a partner or former partner to control and dominate that person. Domestic violence causes fear, physical and/or psychological harm. It is most often violent, abusive or intimidating behaviour by a man against a woman. (NSW Department of Health, 2003: 4)

The Scottish definition in the *National Strategy to Address Domestic Abuse in Scotland* provides an encompassing definition, but adds:

In accepting this definition, it must be recognised that children are witness to and subjected to much of this abuse and there is a significant correlation between domestic abuse and the mental, physical and sexual abuse of children. (Scottish Executive, 2000: 5)

Each country will tend to emphasize the issues of domestic violence emerging in that particular country. For example, in the Australian context, the complexity of Indigenous kinship relationships needs to be recognized:

For many Indigenous people the term family violence is preferred as it encompasses all forms of violence in intimate, family and other relationships of mutual obligation and support. (Laing, 2000: 1)

Within the book, definitions that are encompassing and attend to the issues for children, Black and minority women, Indigenous women and same sex domestic violence provide the necessary framework for investigating the diverse experiences and vulnerabilities of different women, children and some men. Of particular significance are the issues for disabled women where the definitions of domestic violence need to be extended to include women and men abused within an institutional setting (which is their home) and by carers who may be intimate in terms of their access to personal space but are not partners or ex-partners (Healey and et al., 2008).

> It can be helpful to reflect on which experiences are included, and which are marginalized, in various definitions of domestic violence.

An increasingly diverse approach to domestic violence highlights the close connection to the broader violence against women movement (Heise and Garcia-Moreno, 2002). The overlap of abusive experiences can be greater than the differences. It is therefore helpful to acknowledge the United Nations' definition in the Declaration on the Elimination of Violence Against Women resolution (A/RES/48/104) which sets out violence against women as:

[A]ny act of gender-based violence that results in, or is likely to result in, physical, sexual or psychological harm or suffering to women, including threats of such acts, coercion or arbitrary deprivation of liberty, whether occurring in public or in private life. (United Nations General Assembly, 1993)

The human rights frame is used to encompass the diverse experiences of women living with domestic violence and other forms of gender-based violence. It provides a significant backdrop and acknowledgement that a life free from violence and abuse is a right which places obligations on states to take proactive and direct action on the issue.

While acknowledging the broader violence against women perspective, in this book we have nevertheless chosen to stay with 'domestic violence' as our dominant frame. The term has a long association with the women's movement which recognized that domestic violence encompasses a pattern of power and control in intimate partner relationships in which gender inequality provides the social and cultural value system that can account for the ubiquitous nature of the problem. More recently the issues for children living with domestic violence have been highlighted (Mullender et al., 2002). Given that many social workers tangle with the issues of domestic violence through the destructive effects on children, focusing on domestic violence allows the issues for children to be highlighted and explored.

Contested Terminology

Language is contextual and often requires some explanation. We have already discussed definitions of 'social work' and 'domestic violence'. However, there are many other locally specific terms, some of which do not translate easily across national contexts. We have chosen to discuss some issues for clarity in reading the book, but recognize that there will remain some terminology that will be unfamiliar or possibly jarring in different national contexts.

There is contention about the use of terms such as 'victim' and 'perpetrator'. The strength of these terms is that they make clear the power relationship in which abuse occurs. While the use of the term 'victim' acknowledges the violation and oppression experienced, it can obscure the agency that the terminology of 'survivor' accentuates. We have used the terms interchangeably depending on context and at times have used 'victim/survivor' to highlight the complex coexistence of both agency and oppression. We have also gendered the use of the term 'victim' to acknowledge that women are most commonly, though we recognize not exclusively, the victims of domestic violence.

The use of the term 'perpetrator' is also problematic and some prefer to use terms such as 'men who use violence' to denote that such behaviour is a choice and/or that it is open to change. Again we have used these terms interchangeably, depending on context. In the United States, the term 'batterer' remains common. However, we have chosen not to use this terminology as it emphasizes physical assault at the expense of other tactics of control and coercion. We have generally referred to men as 'perpetrators', as this is the dominant but not the only pattern of abuse.

Defining disability is a contentious issue. Disability advocacy organizations in both the United Kingdom and Australia adopt a social model of disability that describes disability as the interaction between a person's impairment and the disabling (negative) social and physical context. Disabling environments pre-vent people with disabilities from accessing human and justice services, trans-port, housing, work opportunities and education. The United Kingdom and Australia have taken different paths in differentiating this social perspective from the medical/impairment model of disability. In the United Kingdom, the terminology of 'disabled people' is preferred to highlight the disabling social context (Hague et al., 2011), while in Australia the preference has been to 'put the person before' the disability and impairment, using the term 'people/women with disabilities'. We have tended to use the latter, or used the language of the publications cited.

One of the most difficult definitional challenges arises when talking about issues of 'race' and culture. Because these categories have commonly been used to exacer-bate inequality and to define others as different/inferior to White people, it is diffi-cult to acknowledge the disadvantage that follows without colluding in a process of 'othering'. Multiple terms have been used over time in different countries in efforts to grapple with this element of complexity. In Australia, for example, the term 'non-English speaking background' (NESB) has largely been replaced by the term 'cultur-ally and linguistically diverse' (CALD). While terminology of Black, Indigenous or Aboriginal and Torres Strait Islander is used interchangeably in different parts of Australia, the term 'First Nation' is recognized but less common. In the United Kingdom, the terminology has also changed over time. The terminology 'Black' was commonly used to describe a wide range of people who experienced discrimination on the basis of 'race' or culture in Britain. However, with new waves of immigration from Asia, Africa and Europe, the terminology of Black and minority ethnic (BME) has become more widely used. Some people prefer to designate their ethnic origin or religious background, for example, Kurdish, Sudanese, Asian or Muslim (Thompson, 2003).

In referring to groups such as these which experience significant discrimination and disadvantage, we often use the term 'marginalized' or 'minoritized' as coined by Burman and Chantler 'to highlight that groups and communities do not occupy the position of minority by virtue of some inherent property (of their culture or religion, for example) but acquire this position as the outcome of a socio-historical process' (2005: 60).

An Exploration of Intersectionality

In exploring these issues of diversity, we draw on a growing body of work from scholars and practitioners which attends to the intersectorial nature of domestic violence. This work understands women in relation not only to their experiences of gender inequality, but also the social divisions of class, 'race', age, heterosex-ism and disability (Almeida et al., 1994; Bograd, 1999; Sokoloff and Dupont, 2005). This attention to diversity speaks more directly to the experiences of a significant group of women who find themselves 'on the margins' and do not necessarily identify gender oppression as the primary frame through which they understand their lives, even when they live with violence and abuse from their partner or ex-partner.

Building on the work of Kimberley Crenshaw (1991) who introduced the concept of 'intersectionality', we find the intersectional 'turn' both enriching and challenging for the framing of domestic violence. Black and minority ethnic women have been particularly instrumental in leading this debate, drawing attention to the vulnerabilities to racism and the profound connections within extended families and communities which compound the problem of secrecy and loyalty for women living with domestic violence (Almeida and Dolan-Del Vecchio, 1999; Atkinson, 2002; Mama, 1989). The analysis of the ways in which cultural practices alongside historical experiences of colonization, war, slavery and trauma create a context in which male violence is rationalized, excused and reinforced has been the subject of continuous interrogation within this rich seam of work. In some instances, it has led to criticism of traditional models of intervention which encourage criminal justice routes as the primary response to violence. While not necessarily eschewing the criminal justice route, Black, minority ethnic and Indigenous women have been prominent in the development of community based responses, restorative justice and community prevention programmes as alternative and sometimes preferred intervention routes (Almeida and Durkin, 1999; Blagg et al., 2000; Coker, 2004).

The work of Sokoloff and Dupont (2005) is particularly helpful in extending the exploration of the intersectional frame. They draw the distinction between the objectives of giving voice to abused women from diverse, and often ignored social locations and cultural backgrounds while recognizing the structural inequalities (race, gender, class, dis/ability and sexuality) that shape and constrain the lives of abused women in different ways. The first objective, they point out, can lead down the road of 'identity politics' with every individual holding a different standpoint – a unique and different struggle. For a social movement, such individualized politics can be problematic (Nixon and Humphreys, 2010). The second frame emphasizes a more structural approach, which focuses on the interlocking systems of class, 'race' and gender that perpetuate existing hierarchies of power, privilege and domination, exploring how these hierarchies are supported and maintained. It is argued that the individual story of multiple oppressions needs to be understood within this broader analysis of interlocking systems of power and domination. In this process, a single, monolithic framing of domestic violence is challenged without losing the attention to the broader patterns of discrimination and oppression through which this destructive social problem is perpetuated.

To date, intersectionality has been most developed in the exploration of the experiences of Black and minority ethnic women. However, as with the concept of 'anti-oppressive practice', it can be used to explore diverse experiences of discrimination and oppression. It recognizes that explanations which only provide a lens to one form of structural oppression, for example gender, may be experienced as oppressive in their exclusion of a range of different forms of discrimination. In this book we have attempted to bring an intersectional lens to social work practice with domestic violence.

Knowledge to Support Practice

While we have both been social workers with 30 years of practice experience between us, we are now social work academics involved in research and evaluation in the domestic violence area. We are therefore actively involved and committed to the development of research evidence to inform practice and policy development. That said, we also have a critical approach to what counts as evidence. The domestic violence area is one in which the voice of survivors (Hague and Mullender, 2006), and latterly the voice of children and young people (see Houghton, 2006) has had a pivotal role in the development of the knowledge base for practice and policy development.

> The voices of survivors brought the knowledge of domestic violence into the public realm. This continues to be an important source of knowledge.

The 'knowledge diamond', seen in Figure 1.1, derives knowledge from survivor experience, practice wisdom, policy data and research evidence and provides a heuristic or means of framing the knowledge used to support the writing in this book. We recognize that this is not without controversy. We argue that the 'evidence debates' which continue to promote the randomized control trial as the gold standard for evidence (see www.cochrane.org) do not encompass enough of the knowledge base that informs the domestic violence arena. While such research is important, it does not acknowledge or celebrate the long tradition of survivor experience that has also informed the development of knowledge in this area. Particularly for women and children who are marginalized, the tools of empirical research may not be in their hands. Hence, an approach which recognizes that knowledge is drawn from many sources is one which is both ethical and enriching in the development of policy and practice.

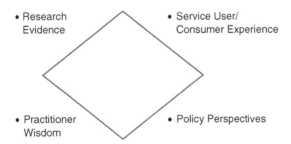

Figure 1.1 The Knowledge Diamond

Source: Humphreys, C. and Kertesz, M. (2012). Personal identity records to support young people in care. *Adoption and Fostering, 36*(1): 27–39.

At the heart of any profession are claims to knowledge and hence to power (Foucault, 1980). It is therefore unsurprising that what counts as evidence, or what counts as knowledge, is contested. In the domestic violence arena it raises the question of whose knowledge counts and who is allowed to speak and be heard. In the development of reflective practice for social work, it is clearly not a question that can be ignored and it will therefore be an important aspect of reflecting upon the connections and disconnections between social work and domestic violence intervention.

In returning to our opening scenario, Jessica, as a relatively inexperienced social worker, will need to recognize the knowledge sources that she is drawing on in order to have her voice (knowledge) heard and to engage in practice change in her organizational setting. For instance, she is drawing on her own practice experience in a different setting (practitioner knowledge) where she has observed the effectiveness of addressing the issues of domestic violence for women and their children, sometimes in the context of co-occurring drug and alcohol problems. She is also informed by the experiences of the women themselves (service-user experience). However, she would also be well advised to understand the research knowledge base in this area (e.g. Galvani, 2006), as well as excellent practice tools which have been developed (Stella Project, 2007).

Reflective and Critical Practice

The exploration of reflective practice will draw from a concept of the research-minded or knowledge-informed practitioner as a key aspect of reflection. It will also draw from narrative (White and Epston, 1989) and other strengths-based frameworks (Saleebey, 1994, 1997). These approaches support curiosity and questioning and provide a useful lens through which domestic violence intervention for social workers can be explored.

Our approach draws from the reflective practice tradition established by Donald Schon (1983) and colleagues and further developed in the social work context by those interested in critically reflective practice (Adams et al., 2002; Davis and Auchter, 2010; Fisher and Somerton, 2000; Fook, 1996). The reflective practice tradition with its attention to the significance of relationship and the acknowledgement of complexity and uncertainty in human problems stands in contrast to the increasingly technical-rational approach to practice (White et al., 2009). The latter is exemplified by the uptake of information technologies in the statutory child protection area where tools to support decision making are embedded in the response systems to vulnerable children and their families (Gillingham and Humphreys, 2010). While there is a role for structured guides to decision making, ethnographic studies of professionals using the tools report frustrations with over-simplification and 'dumbing-down' of professional judgement (Munro, 2011; White et al., 2009). Alongside these technical developments has been the dominance of the legal and administrative requirements, task and outcomes in the construction of social work practice particularly, though not exclusively in the children, youth and families arena (Howe, 1997).

Practice has become procedurally dominated in an increasingly risk-averse environment (Parton and O'Byrne, 2000).

In the face of the turn to increased technical control of social work practice and recognition that it has not solved the crises in children's services and social care, the reflective practitioner tradition is now experiencing a resurgence of interest and enthusiasm (Ruch, 2005). The seminal work of Schon (1983) remains pivotal. His respectful recognition of the way in which experienced practitioners draw on 'knowledge in action' as they work with individuals and their families recognizes the significance of tacit and intuitive knowledge derived from repeated, rich and reflective experience. He, and others (Thompson, 2002), highlight that this draws from both the ability to work with heightened awareness of the self in relationship to others while practising (What am I feeling? How am I presenting? Do I need to change my approach or focus? Do I feel uncomfortable?), as well as the reflection on these actions (What sources of knowledge was I drawing from? What previous experiences influenced me? How did my organizational and legal position affect my actions? What were the values and cultural beliefs which affected my actions and the action of the person with whom I was working?).

The more recent developments in reflective practice recognize that:

> Part of the difficulty of defining reflective practice can be attributed to its dual function as it both generates knowledge through the reflective process and is the vehicle by which it is applied in practice ... a complex concept which involves engaging in practice at a content and process level. (Ruch, 2005: 116)

Ruch (2005) goes on to identify a series of characteristics of holistic reflective practitioners which include their understanding that knowledge is drawn from diverse sources and is dynamic and specific to each situation; attention to process; the development of relationship-based, reflective support mechanisms; and the ability to engage proactively and collaboratively with risk and uncertainty. Ruch argues that the more recent developments in reflective, relationship-based practice incorporate a richer understanding of the role of research and evidence in informing practice, as well as paying greater attention to the organizational and legal context of the worker and the structural issues that impact upon those they work with.

A further development in this area has been the attention to reflexivity, defined as the reflection on reflection: 'A key aspect to reflexivity is seeing yourself as always part of, as well as responsible for the framing of, situations and acting with awareness that this is always the case' (Ison and Blackmore, 2010: 40). This book is written with awareness of this discourse. Our specific contribution is to develop questions for social workers derived from narrative and strengths-based perspectives – perspectives which we believe are sympathetic to the reflective practitioner tradition.

Narrative approaches to therapy and community work, originating in the work of Michael White (White, 2007; White and Epston, 1989) and now developed and practised internationally in many settings, have commonly been applied to work with both the survivors and perpetrators of violence against women (Denborough, 2006).

It is unique as a therapeutic approach in that it can explore both the individual and socio-political contexts relevant to experiences of abuse and trauma. This approach employs a narrative or story metaphor to explore the ways in which meaning is ascribed to lived experience. Although we all have a rich stock of lived experience, very little of this is ascribed meaning. Narrative questions are framed to explore the effects of 'problem-saturated' stories on people's lives and relationships and to explore un-storied, alternative and preferred directions for their lives and relationships.

Strengths-based approaches are widely used in social work because the key tenets are consistent with social work's value base. The strengths perspective calls on social workers to work collaboratively with clients rather than to 'diagnose' them from a position of greater power and knowledge; to assume that they have strengths and resources rather than to focus on deficits; to recognize agency and resilience, even in the face of traumatic and unjust experiences; and to recognize the importance of a sense of belonging within communities (Saleebey, 1996, 1997). This is a perspective which is very consistent with the approach to working with domestic violence survivors that is practised within the specialist domestic violence sector.

Reflective questions drawn from narrative and strengths-based traditions are included in each chapter because they can assist social workers to develop practices that are consistent with their values, such as a commitment to anti-oppressive and empowering practice. They can also assist in building awareness of the effects of our practices both from the perspective of survivors and of colleagues within our own and other organizations.

We believe that the need for a critical, reflexive and research-minded approach to practice informed by the experience of survivors of domestic violence has never been stronger, nor more widely recognized as an essential aspect of social work. The aim of this book is to encourage critical, reflective and research-minded practice in domestic violence and abuse, and to identify and reflect on some of the complexities and controversies, dilemmas and difficulties encountered by practitioners as they strive to work in constructive and creative ways with survivors and perpetrators. Our approach aims to raise awareness of the contested issues within the field and to critically evaluate (emerging) research findings and their implications for contemporary policy and practice.

How to Use this Book

We have worked to make the book and its content 'user friendly' in ways that can be helpful for practitioners, educators, trainers and students. Each chapter begins with an opening vignette to provide context, raise questions and highlight different social divisions (e.g. ability, sexuality, gender) or systems issues. This theme is used to highlight particular issues in relation to social location as well as a specific intervention area. Most of the vignettes describe client situations. For example, the chapter on practices with women places particular emphasis on the complexities associated with disability. A slightly different approach is taken in the chapter on children

(Chapter 5), where the vignette is used to highlight the ways in which current policy approaches have created challenges for social workers in developing new ways to work with children and their mothers in the context of domestic violence.

The particular issues to be addressed in each chapter are introduced at the beginning, and at the end of the chapter summary points are made. Important connections between theory, research and practice are highlighted throughout each chapter through the use of boxed material. Reflective questions are posed at the end of chapters to encourage critical reflection and further readings are recommended for those practitioners, educators and students who are keen to extend their knowledge in a particular area.

Readers may wish to engage with this foundational first chapter and then choose different chapters depending upon their particular interest and practice focus. Chapter 2 addresses the complexities of domestic violence through exploring the issues of prevalence, the historical legacy and contemporary context for responding to domestic violence, and the conceptual frameworks that we argue are 'ways of seeing' which translate into 'ways of doing'. Chapter 3 tangles with the complicated legal and policy contexts which underpin intervention. We argue that social workers can play a critical role in facilitating women's access to legal remedies for domestic violence and that social workers can also make important contributions to policy advocacy, drawing on their experience of the often unintended consequences of domestic violence policies for women and children to highlight service gaps and areas for change.

The practice context is elevated in the next three chapters. Chapter 4 focuses on working with women, addressing some issues in relation to intimate relationships as sites of struggle, patterns of help-seeking and the dilemmas of parenting when living with violence. Essential aspects of practice with women are outlined as are some frameworks for counselling practice with women that can be useful in the post-crisis stage. Chapter 5 focuses on issues for children and the context of child abuse, with particular attention to the statutory child protection context. This is the field of practice that most strongly highlights the challenges for social work in responding to domestic violence, and directions for more progressive work in this area are explored. This chapter also addresses the issue of post-separation violence and abuse. Chapter 6 addresses working with men both as perpetrators and victims of violence and abuse in intimate partner relationships. This involves differentiating the needs and responses of gay and heterosexual victims and attention to the complexities of assessment when heterosexual men present as victims of domestic violence. Although most social workers will not be working with men in specialist men's behaviour change programmes, we draw a number of key principles from the knowledge base in this field which can inform social work practices with men who perpetrate violence, whatever the setting.

Chapter 7 explores the challenges and benefits of interagency collaboration using a lens and practice example in the mental health field. This builds on the discussion in every chapter on the importance of locating domestic violence practice within a multi-agency context. We outline the essential elements of successful collaboration including establishing a shared understanding of the problem and a shared sense of purpose, before providing an example of a research project that had as its aim enhancing collaboration between workers in the domestic violence and mental health sectors.

The final chapter provides some concluding commentary on developing critical and reflective practice for social workers dealing with the complexities of domestic violence intervention. It engages with the expanded agenda of violence against women and the significant role of prevention. It is a chapter in which we reflect on the three primary themes that structure practice in this area: secrecy, responsibility and protection/loyalty.

Conclusion

The connections and disconnections between social work and domestic violence are longstanding. As the context for social work practice changes, so does the interface with domestic violence survivors, their children and the perpetrators of violence. The newly qualified social worker in a large organization may feel constrained by the policy and practice framework within the organization and under-confident in building the necessary alliances and context for a change agenda with a more holistic focus: one more conducive to addressing the issues of domestic violence. The book will draw on the research and broad evidence base to support social workers to a more reflective and effective practice in which the issue of domestic violence is bought to the foreground, recognizing the profound impact that it has on those living with its detrimental and fear-inducing tactics.

Summary Points

- While social workers and specialist domestic violence workers have a varied and sometimes contentious history, the aspirations of social work and its professional and theoretical framework are congruent with the values inherent within the violence against women movement, of which domestic violence is a part.
- Domestic violence will be present in the practice of social workers in all settings, yet rarely is it the main 'business' of these services. Recognition and action informed by an understanding of domestic violence intervention with its emphasis on safety and autonomy for victims and accountability and responsibility for perpetrators of violence should change practice across the service system.
- All definitions and terminology include as well as exclude. The terminology of 'domestic violence' is no exception. Definitions need to include: a wide range of abusive behaviours; the gendered nature of the violence which is predominantly but not exclusively men's violence towards women; and recognition that children are profoundly affected by domestic violence.
- An intersectional framework understands women in relation not only to their experiences of gender inequality, but also the social divisions of class,

age, 'race', herterosexism and disability. This attention to diversity speaks directly to the experiences of many women 'on the margins' who do not necessarily identify gender oppression as the primary frame through which they understand their lives.

- The 'knowledge diamond' which derives knowledge from survivor experience, practice wisdom, policy data and research evidence provides a heuristic or means of framing the knowledge which allows for respectful engagement with survivors, practitioners and policy workers as well as empirical research.
- The reflective practitioner tradition is pertinent to the social worker engaging with domestic violence. It draws on the notion of 'knowledge in action' (Schon, 1983) and narrative and strengths-based perspectives.

Reflective Questions for Practice

- What ideas from this chapter might be helpful in encouraging Jessica to continue to bring knowledge about domestic violence into the 'alcohol and other drugs' setting and to avoid this knowledge being marginalized?
- How might Jessica seek out support to strengthen her commitment to supporting survivors of domestic violence in this setting?
- If some of the clients of the drug and alcohol service are lesbian, how might the definitions of domestic violence used by workers obscure their experiences of domestic violence?

Further Reading

Kelly, L. (2005). Inside outsiders: mainstreaming gender violence into human rights discourse and practice. *International Feminist Journal of Politics*, 7: 471–495.

An article which addresses the human rights agenda pursued by violence against women activists, critically reflecting on both the challenges and benefits of this transnational approach.

Ruch, G. (2005). Relationship-based practice and reflective practice: holistic approaches to contemporary child care social work. *Child and Family Social Work*, 10(2): 111–123.

(Continued)

(Continued)

This is an accessible and nuanced article on developments in reflective practice in social work.

Mann, S. (2006). 'How can you do this work?' Responding to questions about the experience of working with women who were subjected to child sexual abuse. In D. Denborough (ed.), *Trauma: Narrative Responses to Traumatic Experience* (pp. 1–24). Adelaide: Dulwich Centre Publications.

This article provides an example of the use of questions by a practitioner to reflect on the challenges of working with people who have been traumatized through experiences of violation and abuse.

2

Naming and Framing Domestic Violence: Engaging with Complexity

Asmina is a South Sudanese woman who arrived in England as a refugee with her husband and two children four years ago. Following the birth of her third child, she is referred to a social worker due to concerns about postnatal depression. Asmina is tearful and appears uninterested in caring for her baby daughter. Through an interpreter, she explains that her husband is right, she is a hopeless mother who shames him in front of his friends and family, and it is her fault that he gets angry with her. She is surprised and confused when the social worker is concerned about how sad she is feeling and wants to understand her family situation and particularly whether she has ever been afraid of her husband. The social worker explains that she asks all women this question because domestic violence is common and that it is not the fault of the woman. Asmina lives with the constant fear of making her husband upset and of his rages, but is careful to be loyal to her family, particularly in front of the interpreter, and says nothing about this. However, in the days following, Asmina begins to ask her own questions about whether it is fair that she and the children should live with this fear. From her own family experience, she knows that her mother was not treated like this.

As the story of Asmina illustrates, women's naming of their experiences as 'domestic violence' is the first step in a change process. This is both a personal and a historical story. In this chapter we engage with the complexities of naming and framing domestic violence given that our conceptual frameworks or 'ways of seeing' translate into 'ways of doing'. We begin by **charting the history** of the ways in which domestic violence has been understood, leading to an acknowledgement of the need for **a more inclusive frame**. These understandings of domestic violence enrich a gendered understanding of domestic violence to take into account issues of social location such as ethnicity, disability, sexuality, class and age. Through an emphasis on 'ways of seeing', we tackle complex and contested issues such as: **coercive control; different types of domestic violence;** and the **prevalence** of domestic violence. This framing provides the basis for interventions that recognize the connection between the individual and the social and also raises issues about **research methodology**. The chapter concludes with attention to the intersection between domestic violence and **other forms of violence against women**.

Charting the History

Prior to the activism of feminists in the late 1960s and 1970s, abused women, if considered at all within the human service professions, were understood within an individualistic framework in which their victimization was attributed to their psychological pathology. Hence they were seen as 'masochistic' for seeking or tolerating violence, and, consistent with the times, the role of the perpetrator and the broader context of gender inequality were not examined. For centuries, women and children had endured the types of violence and abuse that is widely recognized as domestic violence today, but their experiences were not named. Indeed, as Evan Stark notes, 'Its ordinariness made wife-beating "just life"' (2007: 24).

The important contribution of second-wave feminists was to locate women's victimization in their intimate relationships within the broader social and political context of unequal, gendered power relationships. Rather than a matter of individual pathology, abuse of women by intimate partners and ex-partners was framed as a political issue, part of the wider issue of violence against women, affecting all women. Feminist activists argued that gender was the central and essential concept in understanding domestic violence and other forms of violence against women. They located domestic violence within the context of the historical-legal precedent of male domination of women in marriage and in society (e.g. Dobash and Dobash, 1979). Feminist theory focused on patriarchy as a form of social organization which, with its gendered imbalance of power and the normalizing of male privilege, creates the conditions for the oppression of women in all aspects of life.

A historical perspective reveals that, throughout history, the control of wives by their husbands has been accepted and even encouraged. The reasons (some) men have historically beaten their wives originates from the common-law belief that a man had property rights over his wife and their mutual children, who were regarded as his 'chattels' and over whom he was expected to exercise control. In return for economic dependence, wives were expected to obey their husband's demands. The husband had 'conjugal' rights, which meant that rape in marriage could not legally exist. In fact, laws criminalizing rape in marriage were introduced only relatively recently: in England and Wales in 1993; in Scotland in 1983; and in Australian states and territories during the 1980s (Fileborn, 2011). Upon marriage, wives lost many of their rights: to their name, to any assets they might have such as money and property, to their physical integrity, and to their children in the rare event that a woman left the marriage (Dolan, 2003; Zaher, 2002).

The marital relationship moreover was reinforced by an interconnected system of socio-legal rules and norms concerning privacy, which effectively meant that what happened between a man and 'his' wife was effectively beyond public scrutiny and therefore intervention. We argue that contemporary manifestations of this historical legacy are still with us and that current cultural prescriptions continue to contribute to the sense of entitlement of men who use violence in relation to their right to control 'their' woman.

Feminist activists in the early 1970s established emergency accommodation in shelters or refuges for women and their children who were escaping domestic violence (Saville, 1982). These were grass roots organizations, developed in the community sector as an alternative to existing social services which had failed to recognize and respond to violence against women (Gondolf and Fisher, 1988). While safety and shelter were offered to individual women, this was part of a larger feminist project of reforming gender relations and fostering women's social and economic autonomy.

A More Inclusive Frame

Second-wave feminism was important because it named what was previously un-named: violence against women. Naming oppression is a key step in social change and achieving social justice for any oppressed group. Governments responded with a raft of legislative and policy and service initiatives, which are discussed in Chapter 3. However, while framing domestic violence as grounded in gender inequality enabled many women to name their experiences in ways that opened new possibilities for understanding and action, other women located 'outside the mainstream' did not find that this framing spoke to their lived experience. Black women, such as bell hooks (1981, 1984) mounted a strong critique of second-wave feminism as reflecting the concerns of White, middle-class women, and as reproducing racist and class-based inequality. For example, bell hooks argued:

> Although the impulse towards unity and empathy that informed the notion of common oppression was directed at building solidarity, slogans like 'organize around your own oppression' provided the excuse many privileged women needed to ignore the differences between their social status and the status of masses of women. It was a mark of race and class privilege, as well as the expression of freedom from the many constraints sexism places on working class women, that middle class white women were able to make their interests the primary focus of the feminist movement and employ a rhetoric of commonality that made their condition synonymous with 'oppression'. (1984: 6)

Following challenges such as this came growing questioning of the movement's claim that domestic violence affects all women no matter what their 'race', class, nationality or sexual orientation (e.g. Kanuha, 1996; Nixon and Humphreys, 2010). While this claim had benefits in raising awareness of domestic violence as a widespread social problem, it was argued (e.g. by Burman and Chantler, 2005) that this homogenizing approach limited service access to minoritized women and obscured the greater vulnerability of some women both to experiencing violence and to secondary victimization by the intervention system. For example, Indigenous Australian women experience domestic violence at much higher rates than other Australian women and are more likely to sustain severe injury and death through domestic violence (Lumby and Farrelly, 2009). The compounding issues of poverty, colonization and discrimination create a context of profound vulnerability to violence and abuse. To give some idea of the scope of the difference, the rate of domestic-related assault for Aboriginal women in the state of New South Wales (NSW) is 1774.6 per 100,000 compared to a rate of 337.5 for NSW women as a whole (Fitzgerald and Weatherburn, 2002).

In response to these challenges, feminists have subsequently drawn on poststructuralist and intersectional perspectives to develop more nuanced and inclusive approaches to understanding violence against women. For example, understandings from a poststructuralist perspective highlight a number of points including that: meaning is not fixed; language does not just describe the world but is constitutive of it and hence shapes what can be known and spoken about; and every act of naming, including naming domestic violence, involves a process of categorization that marginalizes some experiences. An important contribution of poststructural perspectives is therefore the requirement to more fully explore what is involved in 'naming': for example, who is doing the naming (an exercise of power); whose interests are served; whose experience is excluded or marginalized through this exercise of power; and what are the material consequences of these practices? For example, in the opening vignette, Asmina was unable to name her experiences as domestic violence but instead interpreted her world through her more powerful partner's framing of her as a failed wife and mother.

Another example is provided by Sundari Anitha's research (2011) about the lived experience of South Asian women in northern England with insecure immigration status. This research demonstrated the limitations of common definitions of domestic violence. Without widening the frame beyond partners and ex-partners to include other extended family members, the nature and extent of the violence and coercive control that the women reported becomes invisible to 'mainstream' services (and also research). Anitha argues that further widening of the frame is required to reveal the ways in which the state's immigration and welfare policies are implicated in creating the vulnerabilities that can be exploited by partners and other family members, to avoid attributing abuse simply to culture or religion.

In seeking to explore the ways in which race and gender interact to shape Black women's experiences of sexual and domestic violence, Kimberley Crenshaw (1991) proposed the concept of 'intersectionality'. An intersectional perspective has subsequently been used extensively to widen the frame around domestic violence, encompassing a degree of complexity that could not be gained from a singular focus on gender.

> The essence of intersectionality, then, is that in a society marked by multiple systems of domination (based on 'race', gender and class among others), individuals' experiences are not shaped by single identities or locations (as a woman or a black person), but that the experience of each is also marked by other social divisions. Crucially, it recognises that some women's experiences are marked by multiple forms of oppression, and that single categories can be further broken down so that 'women' (for example) can be situated in powerful/less ways to one another. (Thiara and Gill, 2010a: 38)

An intersectional approach to domestic violence moves beyond additive notions of disadvantage, or solely 'giving voice' to the experiences of diverse women, to enable consideration of the complex ways in which women's multiple social (dis)locations intersect to shape their experiences of victimization and their opportunities for achieving safety and autonomy. This approach had its origins in the activism of women who experienced exclusion from early feminist approaches to violence. It is more able to acknowledge that some women are particularly vulnerable to victimization because of their social locations. A further strength of an intersectional approach is that it can explore the complex ways in which all women are situated with respect to their experiences of violence. It therefore enables attention to the specificity of women's experiences of violence through the intersection of 'race', class, ability and sexuality without attributing women's experiences of violence, for example, to their culture or disability. As with the initial feminist analysis of gender, the focus remains on historically situated social inequalities based on categories such as class and 'race'. Very importantly, the inclusion of all women within an intersectional frame has enabled feminists to tackle the issue of White privilege, defined by Donnelly et al. as 'a system of benefits, advantages, and opportunities experienced by White persons in our society simply because of their skin color' (2005: 6).

While many second-wave feminists were vitally concerned with issues of racism and class (Kelly, 2002), this more recent recognition of the privilege of White women brings with it accountability for thinking about access to services in a different way, with a focus on the privileged rather than on 'others' who do not use services, as Suchting argues:

> What if we were asking the wrong question? What if it were more important to ask what it is about 'us', rather than why 'they' don't come? Introducing 'us' into the picture (whoever 'we' are) starts a process of looking at ways in which power is enacted through everyday practice. (1999: 76)

In summary, framing domestic violence within an intersectional perspective allows more diverse groups of women and men to name their experiences and to have this recognized within the service systems with which they engage. It also provides greater scope for tackling the institutional neglect of violence against the most vulnerable women (Burman and Chantler, 2005) and militates against the 'other-ing' of minoritized women because an interrogation of White privilege is seen as essential to addressing the exclusion of some groups from access to services.

Understanding the Complexity of Domestic Violence: The Centrality of Coercive Control

From the preceding discussion it is clear that naming domestic violence and defining it is by no means a straightforward task. Yet definitions are critical: how a problem is defined determines how it is measured, how it is understood, and the types of responses that are regarded as appropriate. Physical and sexual violence are the most readily recognizable forms of abuse, and indeed, as will be discussed later in this chapter, some domestic violence prevalence studies limit their definition to these forms of abuse. Physical abuse can include hitting, slapping, punching, kicking, shoving, choking, attempted drowning, strangulation, head-butting and burning. It can also include violence and abuse towards pets or property and may involve the use of weapons. Acts of violence may cause not only immediate injury such as bruises, cuts and fractures but also a range of injury-related chronic and/or physical and mental health consequences such as acute pain, disability, miscarriage, stress and depression (Bonomi et al., 2007).

> He hit me, knocked me out, split my lip open and he had me on the floor with his steel-capped boot on my throat and I managed to get away, and I ran and locked myself in the bathroom. (Survivor in Laing, 2010: 31)

Sexual abuse and the degrading acts which are often part of it can profoundly affect a woman's self-esteem, integrity and identity. Women report being raped by their part-ners and/or with a range of objects; they may be asked to perform sex acts against their will and be physically harmed whilst engaging in sexual activity; they may be urinated upon or forced to watch pornographic videos. Some acts are sexually coer-cive but not violent, such as refusal to use a condom or refusing to use or allow birth control (de Bocanegra et al., 2010). While it is estimated that close to 50 per cent of women living with domestic violence experience sexual abuse (Campbell and Soeken, 1999), the level of humiliation that such acts of degradation produce means that many women choose to remain silent about this aspect of their experiences.

> I went to Court for one sexual assault [during a child contact visit, after separation], but during the course of our relationship, there was a lot of sexual abuse. It's like being abused all over again, when you go for a protection order because you're questioned about it. You have to relive the story again. (Survivor in Laing, 2012)

Despite the range of violent acts that women may experience, such as the examples above, women consistently report that it is the emotional or psychological impact of living with domestic violence that is most harmful, debilitating and distressing (Hegarty et al., 2005; Williamson, 2010). Informed by the lived experience of women who have sought refuge and support from feminist services and who have participated in the body of feminist research that aims to bring forth women's voices (e.g. Abrahams, 2010; Chantler, 2006; Healey et al., 2008; Humphreys and Thiara, 2003a; Kelly, 1988), feminist understandings of domestic violence centralize the concept of *coercive control* as the core dynamic of domestic violence (Dutton and Goodman, 2005; Stark, 2007). From this perspective, acts of violence are one of many tactics that the perpetrator employs in order to control and dominate his partner. The following definition by Almeida and Durkin captures the key elements of this dynamic:

> Domestic violence is the *patterned* and *repeated* use of *coercive* and *controlling* behavior to limit, direct, and shape a partner's thoughts, feelings and actions. An array of power and control *tactics* is used along a continuum in concert with one another. These tactics include: physical abuse, emotional abuse, economic abuse, threats and intimidation, isolation and entrapment, sexual abuse and exploitation, control and abuse of children, and isolation through job relocation and language barriers. (1999: 313; emphasis added)

There are myriad complex abuse tactics which are deployed by an abuser to establish a relationship of coercive control. The context of an intimate relationship enables the abuser to tailor the tactics of abuse to the vulnerabilities arising from the woman's social location (such as her immigration status or poverty), or to create vulnerabilities (e.g. financial vulnerability or forced pregnancy). Financial abuse can involve the abuser denying the woman access to sufficient money for essential food, medicines and bills, forcing the woman to fund all living expenses from her wage and accruing debts in the woman's name (Branigan, 2007). Some abusers force women to participate in illegal behaviours involving illicit drugs, prostitution or welfare fraud, deepening their control over them. This enables them to make effective threats of retaliation and to block women's access to legal redress for domestic violence. Isolation of the woman from friends and family is a common tactic that enhances the perpetrator's power and control, and the woman's entrapment. Women whose immigration status depends on their partner's sponsorship are particularly vulnerable to entrapment through threats to withdraw this support and to poverty and illegal immigration status if abandoned by their partners. Similarly, women with disabilities can be abused by the withholding of essential medications or mobility assistance by an abuser who presents to the external world as a compassionate carer (Thiara et al., 2012). These tactics of abuse commonly occur in a context of emotional abuse: abusers systematically degrade and belittle women, seeking to make them feel unattractive, incompetent and useless and slowly diminishing their sense of dignity and self-worth, including their competence as mothers (Dobash et al., 2000). The case of Asmina provides a clear example of this corrosive process.

Surveillance is a key element of coercive control. Some abusers will monitor a woman's movements not only in relation to any social activities but also in relation to basic domestic activities like shopping; and some will use mobile phones to continuously check on a woman's whereabouts. However, despite their entrapment by tactics of coercive control, women both resist as well as attempt to placate the abuser (Dutton and Goodman, 2005): this important point is taken up in Chapter 4 in our discussion about working with women.

The abuser's demands for the woman's compliance under threat range across all domains of the woman's life, including, for example, her appearance (demands to not/wear particular types of clothing), the household (demands about levels of cleanliness that must be achieved) and children (threats to report her to child protection services) (Dutton and Goodman, 2005). These elements of coercive control, integrated into the flow of everyday life and reflecting taken-for-granted gender roles, will usually be invisible to those outside of the relationship. They can only be understood within the context of the relationship and its history, where even a small, seemingly innocuous gesture on the part of the abuser can signal to the woman that she has transgressed and will be punished.

A very important point to note is that abuse does not end with separation and in fact it may escalate, including to lethal violence (Davies and Mouzos, 2007). In addition, there may be an intensification of what Frederick (2008: 525) calls 'nonviolent coercive tactics', such as financial abuse and threats of subjecting the partner to protracted litigation, also known as 'paper abuse' (Miller and Smolter, 2011). Because women who have children with their ex-partner have to negotiate parenting arrangements in a Family Law policy context that increasingly promotes shared parenting, this provides a context for ongoing abuse and control of women and children through Family Law processes and during contact.

This discussion of coercive control as the central element of domestic violence helps to explain why women report that the emotional effects of living with domestic violence are the most harmful aspect: it invades every aspect of their lives, yet it is hard to explain the corrosive effects, often in the absence of frequent or severe physical violence:

> And in all honesty, [the physical violence] is easier to get over – I know that sounds like backward, but it is easier than this sustained psychological warfare that goes on all of the time. (Survivor in Laing, 2010: 29)

Anitha's research (2011) with South Asian women with insecure immigration status identified similar patterns of coercive control. However, in the majority of cases, the partner was not the sole abuser: women living in extended families reported that control and surveillance were allocated to other extended family members to ensure that she upheld the family *izzat* (honour).

In small communities women may be reluctant to speak about their experiences of domestic violence in front of an interpreter. Family members should never be used as interpreters.

We turn now to the contested issue of the prevalence of domestic violence. As this discussion of the complex range of tactics that abusers employ to impose a regime of coercive control indicates, measuring such a complex phenomenon as domestic violence presents many challenges.

Efforts to Unravel the Complexity of Domestic Violence: Different Types of Domestic Violence?

Data from agencies that responded to the emerging social problem of domestic violence, such as shelters, medical services and police, attested to the gendered nature of domestic violence in heterosexual relationships, with women the victims and men the perpetrators in the vast majority of cases. However, two early family violence studies undertaken in the United States in 1975 and 1985 using large, nationally representative samples found that rates of 'marital violence' were similar for men and women (Straus and Gelles, 1986). These findings, in direct contrast to the findings of feminist research which identified gender as a key factor in domestic violence perpetration and victimization, have sparked an ongoing debate, often referred to as the 'gender symmetry debate' (see, for example, Dobash et al., 1992). Based on these and similar research findings, some men's groups and researchers claim that men and women are equally violent within intimate relationships and that there are vast numbers of hidden male victims of abuse who do not seek assistance for reasons such as shame.

Findings that men and women perpetrate domestic violence at similar rates do not fit with current service usage data. For example, the Australian state of Victoria's comprehensive family violence database, which holds nine years' data about family violence incidents reported to police, courts and emergency accommodation services, identifies a consistently gendered pattern of intimate ex/partner violence: men comprise 80 per cent of perpetrators and women over 80 per cent of victims (Victorian Government Department of Justice, 2009). While arrests of women for domestic violence (either as sole or dual perpetrators) have tended to rise with the increased emphasis on proactive policing of domestic violence in most jurisdictions, current patterns of police data across international jurisdictions consistently find a pattern of incidents with a female victim and a male perpetrator in around 80 per cent of intimate partner violence (e.g. Holder, 2007; Scottish Government Statistician Group, 2010).

Data on homicides also reveals a consistently gendered pattern. Women are much more likely than men to be murdered by their partners or ex-partners. For example, the 2009/10 British Crime Survey found that 54 per cent of female homicide victims aged 16 or over had been killed by their partner, ex-partner or lover, while this was the case for only 5 per cent of male victims (Smith et al., 2011). The most recent Australian data confirms a consistent trend over time with women the victims in 78 per cent of intimate partner homicides (Virueda and Payne, 2010).

How can this apparent conflict between the findings of two bodies of research and data be understood? In attempting to answer this question, it is important to recognize that ways of understanding shape the research questions that we ask and the methods that we use. The family violence studies by Straus and Gelles used an instrument – the conflict tactics scale (CTS) (Straus, 1979) – which asks respondents how often they (and their partner) use a number of responses to deal with conflict, these responses categorized as reasoning, verbal aggression and physical violence. The introduction of the survey using the following preamble clearly identifies that the focus is on ways of dealing with *conflict*:

> No matter how well a couple gets along, there are times when they disagree on major decisions, get annoyed about something the other person does, or just have spats or fights because they're in a bad mood or tired or for some other reason. They also use many different ways of trying to settle their differences. I'm going to read a list of some things that you and your (spouse/partner) might have done when you have an argument. I would like you to tell me for each one how often you did it in the past year. (Straus, 1979: 87)

Framing domestic violence as a result of conflict clearly represents a very different understanding of domestic violence to the explanations discussed in this chapter – as a *pattern* of behaviours by which the perpetrator aims to establish a regime of coercive control that instils fear and undermines the autonomy of the victim. Feminist researchers have argued that much male violence occurs in the absence of conflict and that research using the CTS (including its later revisions) is flawed because it fails to look at the context in which domestic violence occurs – including the intentions (attack or self-defence) and the effects, such as injury or fear. They argue that ranking behaviours in a linear way from least to most serious assumes that psychological abuse is necessarily less injurious than physical assault, although many women report that psychological abuse is the most debilitating effect of domestic violence. Another critique of this self-report survey is that it ignores the evidence that men under-report their violence (Dobash et al., 2000). The initial version of the CTS also did not include many types of abuse such as burning, suffocating, sexual assault and many forms of psychological, social and economic abuse (Bagshaw and Chung, 2000; DeKeseredy and Schwartz, 1998).

There are clearly very different 'ways of seeing' domestic violence that are reflected in the different findings. The focus of the family violence research is on the couple dyad; in contrast, feminist domestic violence research locates the couple within the broader context of social and historical gender relationships. Several approaches have been taken to addressing this seeming impasse. Some researchers have attempted to develop research instruments that can measure the complex dimensions, severity and meaning of domestic violence that are encompassed in feminist definitions. An example is the composite abuse scale (CAS), which has four dimensions: severe combined abuse; emotional abuse; physical abuse; and harassment (Hegarty et al., 2005), and which also measures severity. In a sample of over 2000 female general practice patients, more than one-third had experienced some form of abuse in an adult intimate relationship; just under half of these had experienced moderate to great abuse; and 28 per cent of the abused women had this experience in the past year.

Michael Johnson (2005, 2010; Johnson and Leone, 2005) addresses the dilemma by arguing that family violence researchers and feminist researchers reach different findings because they are studying different phenomena. In other words, he argues that not all domestic violence that occurs between intimate ex/partners is the same. He has developed a control-based typology of violence based on the relationship context of the violence, that is, 'based on the way in which the violence is or is not embedded in a context of coercive control' (Johnson, 2010: 214). This typology distinguishes three types of domestic violence. In the first type, 'intimate terrorism' (primarily perpetrated by men), violence is used in conjunction with a range of coercive tactics with the aim of controlling the partner. The second, 'violent resistance', is engaged in by those (predominantly but not solely women) who are entrapped in a relationship of coercive control established through intimate terrorism. Johnson argues that it is these two types of domestic violence that are seen in agency data because the impacts of intimate terrorism are likely to cause fear and injury and lead to help-seeking or to bring about the engagement of authorities. These are the types of situations that feminist research has highlighted.

Johnson's third type of domestic violence is 'situational couple violence' (initially termed 'common couple violence' but subsequently renamed). This is described as involving:

[A]rguments that escalate to verbal aggression and ultimately to physical aggression. It does not involve a general pattern of coercive control. The interpersonal dynamics that produce the escalation can differ considerably from couple to couple, variously rooted in anger management problems of one or both of the partners, couple communication issues, substance abuse issues, and so on. (2010: 213)

Johnson argues that it is this type of domestic violence, situational couple violence, that is captured by family violence research using general population samples. He asserts that population surveys using the CTS capture little of the first two types of violence, citing the 40 per cent participation refusal rate, and the unlikelihood of either the victims or perpetrators of intimate terrorism or violence resistance participating in a general survey.

Unravelling the Complexity of Incidence and Prevalence Data

The discussion of the controversies about the extent and nature of domestic violence alerts us to the challenges involved in researching the nature and extent of domestic violence. In depth, qualitative studies have proven essential in illuminating the experiences and effects of domestic violence on victims/survivors. However, ascertaining the scope of the problem in the population – not just those who seek help – is also essential if governments are to develop policies and programmes to address it. This includes preventive efforts. There are two main types of population studies using nationally representative samples that can provide an estimate of the extent of intimate partner violence in the general community: general crime surveys and specialized violence against women surveys. Each has strengths and limitations in addressing the task of uncovering the extent of intimate partner violence.

General crime victimization surveys are large omnibus surveys that were developed to identify the extent of various crimes in the community, beyond that which is officially reported to the police. While they have the advantage of using large, representative samples, they also have a number of limitations as a method to measure the extent of domestic violence. For example, it is unlikely that victims will disclose such sensitive information in response to one or two questions within a larger survey about crime because they may not classify violence occurring within their home as a 'crime'; they may be reluctant to discuss potentially traumatic experiences with a stranger; and it may be unsafe to do so depending on who else is at home. These factors result in the likelihood of such surveys underestimating the extent of domestic violence (Johnson, 1996). Over time, however, refinements in methodology (often drawing on specialist violence against women studies) have addressed some of these limitations. For example, the British Crime Survey (BCS) now uses a self-completion module on intimate abuse in recognition that this provides a context which is more conducive to disclosure of information about sensitive topics than are the face-to-face interviews used for the rest of the survey (Smith et al., 2011).

At first sight, the results of crime surveys can appear to call into question the gendered nature of domestic violence. While they generally find that more women than men experience domestic violence, they do also find a larger proportion of men reporting victimization than is identified in service usage data. For example, the 2001 BCS found that 21 per cent of women and 10 per cent of men reported ever having experienced at least one incident of non-sexual domestic violence since age 16. However, detailed analysis of the questions asked to contextualize these experiences – about frequency, duration and physical and emotional injury – does reveal a strongly gendered pattern to domestic violence.

> Social workers with a critical perspective on research methodology and statistics can be informed consumers of research in this field.

Analysis by Walby and Allen (2004) of the British Crime Survey found that women comprised 89 per cent of the more heavily abused group (measured as those who report being subject to domestic violence four or more times). Another measure of severity, being subjected to the potentially life-threatening form of violence – being 'choked or tried to strangle you' – was reported by ten times more women than men. The data on the worst incident of domestic violence experienced since 16 also revealed a pattern of gender asymmetry: women were more likely than men to sustain some form of physical injury (75 per cent women, 50 per cent men); to sustain serious injury such as broken bones (8 per cent women, 2 per cent men); to sustain severe bruising (21 per cent women, 5 per cent men) and to suffer mental or emotional problems as a consequence of this incident (37 per cent women, 10 per cent men). Different meanings of violence to men and women were reflected in very different rates of reported fear, which is associated with patterns of coercive control: 11 per cent of women reported frightening threats since 16, compared with 1 per cent of men (Walby and Allen, 2004). These findings about the qualitatively different experiences of domestic violence by men and women are also found in the most recent BCS (Smith et al., 2010) and in a large-scale study in the United States involving a representative sample of 8000 men and 8000 women on rape, physical violence and stalking by intimate partners (Tjaden and Thoennes, 2000).

One limitation of the BCS is that it measures sexual assault separately to domestic violence, thus omitting a common form of domestic violence. However, an indication of the extent of this experience for women within intimate relationships is the finding that the most common perpetrator of serious sexual assault against women since age 16 was a partner or ex-partner (Smith et al., 2011). With regard to ethnicity, the BCS finds little difference in rates of domestic violence. Anitha (2011) points out that the BCS is limited by the definition of domestic violence as violence between current or former intimate partners because it misses the pattern of violence that is common in South Asian communities of violence by in-laws or paternal family.

While they also use large, representative samples, specialist violence against women surveys have developed methodologies that address the potential barriers to disclosure and the ethical and safety issues involved in asking women about sensitive and potentially traumatizing experiences of male violence. The best contemporary example is the International Violence Against Women Survey (IVAWS), which was developed in recognition that the methodology of the International Crime Victimization Survey, a general crime survey, was inadequate to identify sexual and domestic violence against women (Johnson et al., 2008). The use of common definitions and methodology across countries enables comparison of data on women's victimization across nations and over time (see www.heuni.fi/12859.htm).

The IVAWS draws on the methodology developed for the first such study, the Canadian Violence Against Women Survey, which identified almost twice as many incidents of domestic violence as the general Canadian crime survey and four times the number of wife assaults reported to police (Johnson, 1996). Multiple, behaviourally specific questions are asked rather than a single question to determine victimization or not, providing women with multiple opportunities to disclose. Multiple approaches also are used to understand severity and consequences of the violence, such as frequency, physical and emotional effects, social and economic effects, service use and impacts on children. Specialist training of interviewers is central to the approach (Johnson et al., 2008).

Australia is one of the countries that has implemented the IVAWS using a random sample of 6677 women aged between 18 and 69 years (Mouzos and Makkai, 2004). Over one-third of women (34 per cent) who had a current or former intimate partner reported experiencing at least one form of violence – physical, sexual or psychological (controlling behaviours) – during their lifetime. In common with the findings of other, similar surveys, levels of violence experienced from a former partner (36 per cent) were much higher than from a current partner (10 per cent), and women who experienced violence from former partners were also more likely to sustain injuries and to feel that their lives were in danger. The strongest risk factors for current intimate partner physical violence were the partner's behaviour: his drinking habits (gets drunk a couple of times a month or more); his general levels of aggression (violent outside of the family); and controlling behaviour. Significantly for the theories of domestic violence that emphasize the centrality of coercive control, the strongest risk factor for physical violence by a current partner was the male's controlling behaviours (Mouzos and Makkai, 2004).

Combining the findings of both large-scale studies using representative samples and smaller studies using qualitative methods can provide important information for policy and programme development. For example, large-scale studies have identified the strong association between domestic violence and a constellation of mental health impacts for women including high rates of depression, anxiety and post-traumatic stress disorder (Rees et al., 2011). In-depth interviews with women who experience both domestic violence and mental health problems about their experiences of help-seeking provide information about the changes in service provision that are necessary to respond more effectively to this issue (Humphreys and Thiara, 2003a; Laing et al., 2010a). In a similar vein, the BCS identifies that women with disabilities and long-term illness are more likely to become victims of domestic abuse (Smith et al., 2010). However, in-depth interviews with disabled women with physical and sensory impairments identified both the commonality in abuse tactics with those experienced by many women and the specific tactics of abuse that were available to the abuser because of the woman's disability (Hague et al., 2011). For example:

> He'd turn off the wheelchair and leave me there and walk away, or—this is a good one—move it to one side just as I was shifting myself into it. (2011: 154)

The findings of this study also highlighted the need to widen the frame in order to make visible the perpetration of abuse by paid carers and other family members, in addition to partners.

Taking up the notion of the broader framing of domestic violence, it is highly unlikely that Asmina's experiences of domestic violence would be captured in a large-scale study due to language barriers, and beyond these, issues of trust of authorities, fear and myriad other barriers to disclosure, including naming her experiences as domestic violence or as a crime. The experiences of many minoritized groups are only able to be explored through smaller and targeted studies, where it is often not possible to use a representative sample.

Another example is violence in same sex relationships. Donovan and colleagues (2006) surveyed 800 same-sex respondents, recruited through community organizations in the United Kingdom. They found that domestic abuse is a sizeable problem in same sex relationships and that, while it is experienced in similar ways by those in lesbian and gay relationships, men were more likely to experience sexual abuse. They found that domestic abuse is often not recognized because of high rates of emotional and sexual abuse rather than physical abuse. Rates of reporting to authorities were low because respondents tended to see their experience as their own problem, and partly because they do not believe they will receive a sympathetic response (Donovan et al., 2006). Since this study was undertaken, the self-completion section of the BCS questionnaire has included a question asking respondents about their sexual orientation. However, the low numbers of respondents identifying as lesbian/gay or bisexual means that the BCS findings are limited and need to be treated with caution (Smith et al., 2010). At this stage, richer data emerges from the combination of survey and interview data in the targeted sample.

Further Methodological Issues

In this chapter we have explored the different findings about prevalence of domestic violence that are associated with different research methodologies. We have also identified some of the challenges in finding out the nature and prevalence of experiences of domestic violence in minoritized groups. These are two examples of the wider challenge of building a comprehensive knowledge base in the domestic violence field. As discussed in Chapter 1, the question of what constitutes knowledge is contested, as are the relative strengths of different research approaches or methodologies in producing knowledge. In this part of the chapter we look briefly at some of the issues and debates about the types of research approaches that can build the knowledge base.

One of the questions of most interest in the domestic violence field is whether programmes and interventions are effective in reducing domestic violence and in assisting victims/survivors to overcome its many effects on their health, well-being and relationships. When the effectiveness of interventions is evaluated, there is a strong body of opinion that experimental research using random controlled trials (RCT) are the 'gold standard' in research design because they provide the best evidence of 'what works' (Robson, 2002). Nevertheless, in a complex field such as domestic violence where safety must be the priority consideration, implementing experimental designs can pose significant difficulties. For example, Feder et al. (2011) note that it would be unethical to randomly allocate women to staying or leaving the relationship in a study of safety outcomes. There are many similar examples where life-threatening risks would make it unethical to withhold assistance from a control group. One way to address this is to provide a control group with 'usual services', while the experimental group also receives the intervention under study. The widely cited study of an intensive advocacy intervention with women post refuge (Allen et al., 2004; Sullivan and Bybee, 1999), discussed further in Chapter 7, is an example of this approach. Using the example of a domestic violence prevention intervention, the Enhanced Nurse Family Partnership (ENFPS) Study, which uses a RCT design and is embedded within an existing intervention, Feder at al. advocate greater use of experimental designs in building the domestic violence knowledge base:

> Although experiments may not be appropriate for all evaluations, when feasible, experiments that are conducted with a high ethical standard, full transparency, and high fidelity will help immeasurably in building the knowledge base so as to better understand IPV and, in this way, develop more effective policies and programs. (2011: 352–353)

Where experimental designs are not appropriate or feasible, quasi experimental designs provide an alternative. These also involve comparison of outcomes for different groups. While allocation to groups is not random, a number of methods are commonly used to minimize differences between the groups. A limitation of this design is that it is less clear that any changes are due to the intervention rather than to pre-existing differences in the two groups. In the evaluation of perpetrator programme effectiveness, there is currently strong debate about the relative weight of evidence from experimental, as opposed to quasi experimental, research designs. As is discussed in Chapter 6, evaluations using experimental designs have not provided evidence that these programmes are effective in reducing domestic violence reoffending. In contrast, several evaluations using quasi experimental designs have found more promising evidence of change in men attending them and in the safety of their women ex/partners. Debate centres around assertions that only the 'best' evidence – that is, evidence provided by experimental (RCT) designs – is acceptable for informing such important matters of public policy (e.g. Labriola et al., 2008). An alternative view is that experimental designs also have limitations, such as implementing random allocation in 'real world' settings (where, for example, courts may not agree to random disposition of offenders to control and experimental groups) and that they are less well suited to studying complex interventions embedded in multiagency contexts (Gondolf, 2001).

The research approaches discussed so far are both examples of quantitative research; that is, research based on a positivist world view, or the perspective that there is an objective reality that can be discovered (Alston and Bowles, 2003; Sarantakos, 1993). The starting point is a theory that is tested by the research, termed a 'deductive approach'. The researcher predetermines the categories of analysis and uses standardized measures to collect data (e.g. surveys and scales). Statistical methods are used to explore relationships between variables of interest. The collection of data from large samples enables the results to be generalized to the broader population.

Qualitative research, in contrast, is based on a world view that emphasizes interpretation over notions of objectivity. Rather than fixed and measurable, 'reality' is understood as socially constructed through our experiences and interactions. Qualitative methodology moves from the specific to the general, beginning with a set of observations and developing theory from these, in what is termed an 'inductive approach' to theory development (Patton, 1990). Data collection is flexible rather than tightly structured, and methods such as in-depth interviews are used. Smaller samples are used than in quantitative studies because the aim is not to generalize from the experiences of the participants but to generate rich and detailed data that respects the social location of the participants.

Qualitative studies have played an important role in building the evidence base in domestic violence. This approach is well suited to capturing the voices of marginalized groups, and the emphasis on the co-creation of meaning by the researchers and participants also fits with feminist research approaches. It is also consistent with social work's emancipatory tradition. It is salutary to recognize that the foundations of the knowledge base about domestic violence and other forms of violence against women were laid down by the accounts of their experiences by courageous survivors who spoke out when violence against women was seen as rare, and was not spoken about. The voices of women and children have been powerful and essential forces in the social movement that has spurred governments to begin to address violence against women (e.g. Kelly, 1988; Mullender et al., 2002). As discussed in Chapter 1, we contend that knowledge is multifaceted, and that the voice of survivors of domestic violence is a core component of this knowledge base. Research that seeks the view of survivors about the effectiveness, impacts and unanticipated consequences of policies and practices that are implemented with the aim of assisting them is essential, but often undervalued or excluded (Hague et al., 2003). Yet survivors report that participating in research that ensures their safe and confidential participation, acknowledges their unique expertise in understanding the service system, and has the capacity to assist other women, can be an empowering experience (Laing, 2010; Laing et al., 2010a).

There is no single 'right' approach to using research to build knowledge about domestic violence. In fact, much of the current research involves 'mixed methods': the use of both qualitative and quantitative research. The key issue is the research question to be answered, and the method is secondary, determined by the question and the context (Cresswell and Plano Clark, 2011; Hesse-Biber, 2010). It is a position succinctly described by Gioia:

> Conceptualizing any research problem as concentric circles of complexity invites us as social work researchers to peel back those layers and dig in with whatever methods might seem most useful or ethically acceptable to that particular layer of exploration. (2012: 222–223)

Social workers require a good understanding of the strengths and limitations of different research methodologies when assessing domestic violence research to inform their practice and when they are approached to refer clients to research studies. In the latter situation, social workers can draw on their generic research knowledge together with information about the complexities of domestic violence, such as this book provides. Attention to women's physical and psychological safety at all stages of the research and the willingness of researchers to collaborate with service providers and value their practice wisdom are important considerations for social workers in referring clients to studies (Campbell and Dienemann, 2001; Edleson and Bible, 2001).

Further Widening the Frame: Domestic Violence in the Context of Violence Against Women

Although we have chosen to focus in this book on domestic violence, we believe that as part of the efforts to 'widen the frame' that have been encouraged in this chapter, keeping in mind the intersection of domestic violence with other forms of violence against women, should form part of the critical reflection that social workers undertake in their work with domestic violence. Adopting this broader perspective, or 'way of seeing' domestic violence, has implications for how it is understood and measured. For example, we have discussed some of the different approaches to measuring incidence and prevalence between general crime and specialist violence against women surveys. Another important difference between these surveys is the conceptualization in violence against women research of domestic violence as part of a continuum of violence against women. Hence these surveys collect data about women's experiences of physical and sexual abuse in childhood, sexual and physical violence from known and unknown men, as well as their experiences of intimate partner abuse (e.g. Mouzos and Makkai, 2004). This reflects a perspective that locates gender as a risk factor for all forms of interpersonal violence, whether in the family, the workplace or in other public spaces. This is a very different perspective from general crime surveys which measure discrete incidents of sexual and physical assault that comprise criminal offences.

This 'way of seeing' the connections between different forms and contexts of violence against women has generated a broad research agenda that includes the relationship between different forms of violence against women; for example, the increased vulnerability of women who have experienced sexual assault in childhood and young adulthood to sexual re-victimization over their lifespan (Casey and Nurius, 2005; Macy, 2008). It has also generated a body of knowledge about the health impacts of violence against women (Astbury and Cabral, 2000; Bonomi et al., 2009; Ellsberg et al., 2008). This provides an important evidence base for the ongoing development of policies and practice.

> Social workers can critically reflect on their practice context to identify the ways in which domestic violence may present; for example, as depression, problematic substance use or homelessness.

Another advantage of broadening the frame to the issue of violence against women is that it avoids certain forms this violence takes, such as forced marriage and crimes of (dis)honour, being constructed as pathologies intrinsic to certain (inferior) cultures (Chantler et al., 2009), because the commonalities as well as the differences are in the frame. An intersectional violence against women approach also enables an exploration of the ways in which globalization has enabled men from advantaged economic locations to exploit the gendered disadvantage of women and children beyond their national borders, for example, through sex tourism and trafficking of women for prostitution (Radford and Tsutsumi, 2004). These issues are taken up in the final chapter.

Conclusion

The forgoing discussion of studies of the extent of domestic violence and the examples of current debates about methodological approaches to knowledge-building highlight the importance of social workers becoming critical consumers of research in this field. Statements about rates of domestic violence experienced and perpetrated by men and women need to be interrogated to identify the assumptions about the nature of domestic violence underpinning the methods used; methods need to be explored to see whether the approach simply counts incidents of violence or explores the context in which they occur through questions about frequency, severity and impact. No study alone can capture the complexity of domestic violence, and all have limitations as well as strengths.

Summary Points

- The history of domestic violence intervention has been framed over time from gender neutral/individualized conceptualizations, followed by a strongly gendered lens, and more recently by intersectionality with its attention to the diversity of social locations in relation, for example, to class, disability, sexuality and age.
- The more complex framing of domestic violence allows more diverse groups of women and men to name their experience and have this recognized within the service systems with which they engage.
- The recognition of diversity challenges social workers working in a wide range of agencies to recognize and respond to domestic violence wherever women and their children are seen.
- Different 'ways of seeing' domestic violence lead to different 'ways of knowing'. The evidence base is framed by the measurement tools that are used and whether questions and data contextualize factors such as fear, severity and frequency.
- In addition to a focus on intersectionality, other approaches to unravelling the complexity of domestic violence involve attempts to develop typologies that differentiate between the contexts of abuse.
- Social workers need to critically reflect on their organization's framing of domestic violence and how this configures their recognition and response to violence against women and their children.
- Different 'ways of knowing' frame our 'ways of doing'. Understanding the different tactics through which power and control are orchestrated enables assessments that are sensitive to the complexities of intervention which promotes safety, autonomy and accountability.
- A further element of complexity lies in the recognition that domestic violence is one form of violence against women and their children; there is a strong overlap with issues such as sexual assault, trafficking and crimes of (dis)honour.

Reflective Questions for Practice

- How might the social worker explore Asmina's abusive situation further while demonstrating respect for the particular constraints of her situation?
- What good reasons might influence Asmina's decision not to disclose more about the abuse at this time?
- In planning the next interview, how might the social worker manage the problem of finding a suitable interpreter?
- What types of research approaches could helpfully inform the knowledge base for social work in work with women from newly arrived communities?

Further Reading

Sokoloff, N. J. (Ed.) (2005). *Domestic Violence at the Margins: Readings on Race, Class, Gender and Culture*. New Brunswick, NJ: Rutgers University Press.

This comprehensive collection of papers applies an intersectional approach to domestic violence. It includes perspectives from women from diverse and often marginalized social locations.

Thiara, R. K. and Gill, A. K. (eds) (2010). *Violence Against Women in South Asian Communities*. London: Jessica Kingsley.

This book provides an excellent example of the application of an intersectional approach to understanding and responding to violence against women.

Fisher, S. (2011). *From Violence to Coercive Control: Renaming Men's Abuse of Women*. White Ribbon Research Series: No. 3 www.whiteribbon.org.au/uploads/media/449%20White%20Ribbon%20-%20Policy%20Report%20Fisher%20%28web%29%20-%20111220.pdf.

A comprehensive and clear guide to succinct discussion of issues in naming men's violence against women and of the dynamics of coercive control.

Ellsberg, M. and Heise, L. (2005). *Researching Violence Against Women: A Practical Guide for Researchers and Activists*. www.path.org/publications/files/GBV_rvaw_complete.pdf.

Provides a clear guide to addressing the complexities in studying violence against women. In the authors' words, it:

> [A]dvances an ethic of research that is action-oriented, accountable to the antiviolence movement, and responsive to the needs of women living with violence. It strongly encourages collaboration between researchers and those working directly on violence as activists and/or practitioners. (2005: 6)

3

Contemporary Legal and Policy Contexts

> *Maria and Louise have been in a relationship for 18 months. Maria has two children aged 3 and 6 from her previous relationship. Her ex-husband has care of the children every second weekend and overnight midweek, but is seeking equal time. They have been involved in family proceedings since their separation three years ago, with Dmitri taking Maria back to court with allegations that she is interfering with his time with the children. Maria and Louise are concerned about a number of issues: the disruptive, expensive and stressful court appearances which they experience as litigation abuse; Dmitri's verbal abuse and threats in front of the children, including that 'she will never see the children again', and his denigration of Louise to the children. Maria is wondering whether a protection order would help the safety of the family or make matters worse.*

Social work has a longstanding commitment to addressing both the micro and macro spheres of practice. Indeed, considerable attention has been directed to exploring how social workers can work both at the individual level to address the impacts of oppressive social structures on individual clients and at the broader policy level to promote greater social justice (Vodde and Gallant, 2002). Nowhere is attention to multi-layered practice more important than when social workers are responding to issues of domestic violence in the context of the law. The scenario of Maria and Louise highlights the complexities of legal responses to domestic violence, crossing the domains of 'private' family law, civil protections available under the law and, potentially, criminal law. It also highlights the complex and continual process of weighing up safety and risk that individual women engage in as part of the process of safety planning. In a similar way, at a systems level, analysis of policy and legal responses to domestic violence needs to appreciate the elements of both safety and risk.

This chapter addresses some of the key areas of legal and policy development that are part of the contemporary policy response to domestic violence. We begin by exploring the **historical context** in which the law became a key element in the response to domestic violence and the **challenges** that can arise **for women in their use of the criminal justice system**. We traverse **research to inform practice about the effectiveness of civil and criminal legal remedies** and note the complexities that women face at the intersections with family law, while recognizing that there are numerous other legal and policy contexts that are relevant (such as child protection, mental health, housing, immigration, income support and human rights legislation). Despite the challenges of engaging with the legal system, we note the dangers for women and their children, who find themselves 'outside the law' with few viable forms of legal protection.

We then look at some **new service approaches** that have been developed to enhance victim/survivors' access to the legal system. We argue that, while social workers are not legal practitioners, they have a critical role in facilitating women's access to legal remedies and outline **core principles of social work practice** with women in the context of the law: belief, support and advocacy; safety planning and risk assessment, including of systemic risks; avoiding and challenging victim blaming responses; and attention to evidence and documentation. We conclude with some examples of **new policy directions** that have been developed, often through policy advocacy, so that the response to victims/survivors is better co-ordinated and more socially just. These include efforts to break what is a too common link between domestic violence and women and children's homelessness and the use of Domestic Violence Death Review processes to highlight areas where systemic responses need to be improved.

A Historical Perspective

Historically, the division between the spheres of 'private' and 'public' life meant that the state was reluctant to intervene in violence against women (Fineman and Mykitiuk, 1994). This reluctance was challenged by early domestic violence activists who argued that violence perpetrated in the home should be treated in the same way as violence committed in public; that is, as criminal behaviour. Hence the criminalization of domestic violence as a key policy in Western societies over the past 35 years represents a sea change in the state's response to domestic violence; domestic violence matters now comprise a very significant amount of the police work in most jurisdictions. Prior to this, governments could be described as condoning men's use of violence to control and chastise their wives (Lutze and Symons, 2003).

The calls by activists for a criminal justice response to domestic violence were assisted by results of the Minneapolis Arrest Experiment (Sherman and Berk, 1984), which aimed to find out whether arrest deterred domestic violence offenders from future assaults. Re-arrest rates were compared following random allocation of domestic violence offenders to three police responses: arrest; advice (including in some instances informal mediation); or separation (an order for the suspect to leave for eight hours) (Sherman and Berk, 1984). Based on recidivism measured by criminal justice records and victim reports, arrest was found to be almost twice as effective as the other police responses in reducing re-offending. Despite inconsistent results from a series of studies that attempted to replicate these findings in other jurisdictions in the United States, this study was enormously influential in domestic violence policy development in the United States, and subsequently in many jurisdictions across the world. Policies of 'preferred' or 'mandatory' arrest for domestic violence offences have subsequently become common in many jurisdictions. Their aim is to remove the discretion of individual police officers, in an effort to address the historical failure of police to take domestic violence seriously.

In concert with policies of preferred or mandatory arrest, many jurisdictions have also developed prosecution policies that aim to reverse the common situation where prosecutors failed to pursue domestic violence matters because of victim reluctance and notions that victims of domestic violence were 'uncooperative'. These prosecution mandatory or 'no drop' polices are also frequently accompanied by efforts to enhance evidence collection by police at the scene of the domestic assault so that prosecution is not dependent solely on the evidence of the victim/witness. Under the most extreme form of these policies, cases are prosecuted regardless of the victim's wishes and a warrant may be issued for the victim's arrest if she fails to appear to give evidence. Other jurisdictions provide advocacy and support and encourage women to continue the legal process, but they are not forced to participate nor sanctioned for failure to do so (Hanna, 1996).

In parallel with policies that criminalized domestic violence, most jurisdictions also developed civil law protections for women living with domestic violence. Whereas the criminal law deals with behaviours that have already occurred, civil protection orders aim to prevent future violence by placing limitations on the behaviours of the abuser through the issuing of protection orders (which have various names across different jurisdictions). Civil protection orders potentially offer women a more flexible way to use the law because the conditions placed upon the man can be tailored to the woman's particular situation and the standard of proof is the 'balance of probabilities', a lower standard than the criminal one of 'beyond reasonable doubt'. However, the effectiveness of protection orders depends on the willingness of police and courts to enforce them, an issue of concern in many jurisdictions (NSW Ombudsman, 2006; Peirce, 2005; Robertson et al., 2007).

Challenges for Women in Using the Criminal Justice System

Implementing a criminal justice response to domestic violence has proved a more complex and challenging endeavour than was initially anticipated. The reasons for this are related to: the nature of domestic violence; the ways in which the criminal justice system operates; and to the complex interaction of these factors. With reference to the nature of domestic violence, this crime occurs within the context of an intimate relationship: it is perpetrated by a man against a woman whom he purports/purported to love (Cavanagh, 2003). In this sense, while comprising criminal behaviour, domestic violence is not 'just the same' as other crimes. However, in thinking about this element of complexity, it is important to recognize that a large proportion of women turn to the law for protection when they leave the relationship yet continue to experience post-separation violence and harassment (Humphreys and Thiara, 2003b; Raphael, 2004).

The consequences of criminal sanctions are different when the perpetrator is an intimate partner rather than a stranger: women whose partners are jailed or fined for domestic violence offences may face economic disadvantages that would not follow if the offender was a stranger. Further, the domestic violence perpetrator has continuing access to his victim, especially where there are child contact arrangements, making the threat of retaliatory violence and intimidation a reality for women who seek the protection of the law (Erez and Belknap, 1998; Laing, 2008).

The traditional criminal justice system is poorly suited to dealing with domestic violence. The criminal law is incident-specific, while domestic violence is constituted by an ongoing pattern of behaviours aimed at exerting coercive control, only some of which may be codified in the law as criminal acts. For example, much verbal and psychological abuse does not fall within the purview of the criminal law, but is reported by its victims as one of the most harmful and hurtful aspects of the abuse. Further, it is assumed that the interests and goals of the victim and state (which prosecutes the offender) are the same; that is, conviction and punishment (Ursel, 2002). Judith Herman eloquently describes the mismatch between the needs of victims of sexual and domestic violence and the operation and assumptions of the criminal justice system:

> Victims need social acknowledgement and support; the court requires them to endure a public challenge to their credibility. Victims need to establish a sense of power and control over their lives; the court requires them to submit to a complex set of rules and bureaucratic procedures that they may not understand and over which they have no control. Victims need an opportunity to tell their stories in their own way, in a setting of their choice; the court requires them to respond to a set of yes-or-no questions that break down any personal attempt to construct a coherent and meaningful narrative ... Indeed, if one set out intentionally to design a system for provoking symptoms of traumatic stress, it might look very much like a court of law. (2005: 574)

In essence, the criminal justice system is focused on intervention with offenders. While holding domestic violence offenders accountable for their violence is one of the goals of domestic violence policy, the challenge lies not only in ensuring convictions and appropriate sanctions, but also in achieving this goal without inadvertently re-victimizing women (Bell et al., 2011). Beyond the disposition of the case, contact with the legal system can play a valuable role in linking women into a range of support services, providing information about legal remedies available and acknowledgement that the woman has suffered harm. As the following discussion indicates, however, policies that recognize and attempt to respond to the criminal nature of domestic violence can have the unintended consequence of undermining the safety and autonomy of some women, particularly those 'on the margins'. Without information about the complex process of the legal system and without consistent support from advocates including social workers, a woman is unlikely to be able to make constructive use of the law.

Policies of preferred or mandatory arrest and prosecution continue to be the subject of intense debate. Proponents such as Hanna (1996) argue these policies take the burden of prosecution from the victim, thus removing the incentive for the perpetrator to try to intimidate her; that they treat domestic violence as a public crime; that they meet the demand by feminists that the state not condone domestic violence; and that aggressive prosecution policies have been associated with a decline in domestic homicides. Others argue that, rather than empowering women, these policies undermine women's autonomy and replicate the disrespectful, emotionally abusive and coercive behaviour of the domestic violence perpetrator (Mills, 2003).

Two major concerns are commonly raised about mandatory policies. The first is the increase in the number of women arrested in mandatory arrest jurisdictions (Raphael, 2004), despite research indicating that most women are acting in self-defence or in response to an ongoing situation of domestic violation (Miller, 2001). Arrest can make women ineligible for victim services and can disadvantage them in family law proceedings (Coker, 2004). Arrest of women who are the victims of domestic violence can compound the feelings of powerlessness and self-blame that are engendered by the experience of domestic violence and can place them at greater risk because of reluctance in future to seek the protection of the law (Rajah et al., 2006).

The second concern is the disproportionately negative impact of such policies on women who are socially disadvantaged because of class, 'race', ethnicity or immigration status (McDermott and Garofalo, 2004). Mandatory policies increase the state's control of the lives of the most vulnerable women, for example by increasing the risk of deportation for women with insecure residence status, and by exposing poor women to potentially victim-blaming intervention by statutory child protection authorities. If a victimized woman's arrest results in loss of employment, her dependence on her partner may be increased (Coker, 2004; McDermott and Garofalo, 2004). In some jurisdictions, women may be placed at greater risk of incurring harsh penalties for involvement in criminal activities, which are often related to women's victimization, such as illegal drugs or prostitution (Coker, 2001). Referring to impacts such as these, Snider charges that 'strategies of criminalization have benefited privileged white women at the expense of women of colour, aboriginal and immigrant women' (1998: 3).

Related to concerns about increasing the state's control of women is the impact of the criminalization agenda on male partners from disadvantaged and marginalized communities (Snider, 1998). In Australia, for example, Aboriginal men are disproportionately represented in the correctional system (Weatherburn and Snowball, 2006). In this context, domestic violence policies that expose marginalized men to the risk of racism within the criminal justice system have been critiqued as inappropriate solutions imposed without appreciation of the intersectionality of gender with other systems of oppression. In contrast, others argue that the high rates of violence experienced by Aboriginal women who have access to few other resources mean that the criminal justice system must be reformed to make its protections more accessible to marginalized women. From this perspective, the problem lies primarily with the failure of police and the justice system to address violence towards Aboriginal and other marginalized women (Greer and Laing, 2001; Stark, 2004).

Aside from these concerns about the consequences of mandatory arrest policies, there are more straightforward issues about the ability of the criminal justice system to provide an effective response to perpetrators of violence. The most comprehensive study of attrition within the criminal justice process is provided by Marianne Hester in a study based in Northern England. The data, based on three command units and three months of domestic violence incidents, showed the following attrition process:

- 869 domestic violence incidents were recorded by the police
- 222 incidents resulted in arrest (26 per cent of incidents)
- 60 individuals were charged for criminal offences (27 per cent of those arrested, 7 per cent of incidents)
- 31 individuals were convicted (52 per cent of those charged, 14 per cent of arrests, 4 per cent of incidents)
- 4 convictions were custodial sentences (13 per cent of convictions, 0.5 per cent of incidents). (Hester, 2006b: 81)

Hester (2006b) goes on to note that the 25 per cent arrest rate is similar or greater than in other parts of England. Moreover, a different study undertaken by the English police and Crown Prosecution Service Inspectorate sampled from a range of localities showed that 3 per cent of domestic violence incidents resulted in a conviction (HMIC and MMCPSE, cited in Hester, 2006b: 81). This is not an evidence base which leads to a high level of trust in the criminal justice system to deliver appropriate consequences for domestic violence offenders.

The lesson for social work from these debates is that engaging with the law holds the potential for both positive and negative outcomes for women. Hence advocacy that includes the provision of accurate information is important in assisting women to consider this in their safety planning. Women outside the mainstream, in particular, may be wary, with good reason, to engage with the law. Maria and Louise, for example, may fear receiving a homophobic response if they engage with the police about the threats that Dmitri has made, which in many jurisdictions could constitute criminal behaviour.

> Knowledge of the law and policy is critical for working effectively with domestic violence survivors and their children.

The other issue that the situation of Maria and Louise highlights is that women may be involved simultaneously with different parts of the legal system, where the expectations that they encounter are quite different, and indeed often contradictory (Hester, 2011). For example, a woman's call to the police for assistance from an imminent assault may trigger a report to the statutory child protection service and she may be urged to separate from her partner under threat of removal of her children. On entering the family law system, however, she is likely to encounter the expectation that she promote the ongoing relationship between the children and her ex-partner and may find it difficult to have the impact of domestic violence on herself and her children adequately considered in this context (Laing, 2010). Hunter's (2002) research on protection orders in the Australian state of Victoria provides a further example of the impact on women and children's safety of the intersections of different systems of law. She found that defendants were often encouraged to consent to the making of the protection order 'without admissions'. On the surface, this assisted women to obtain an order without being subjected to a hearing involving stressful cross-examination. However, protection orders made by consent in this way were subsequently likely to be discounted as evidence of domestic violence in family law proceedings because the evidence was seen as having been untested. This highlights the complex and perilous territory that women have to navigate when seeking to use the law to increase their safety and that of their children.

Research to Inform Practice: Effectiveness of Legal Interventions

Most of the research on legal responses to domestic violence has focused on outcomes, such as arrest and conviction, rather than on process (Cattaneo and Goodman, 2010). Typical of outcome research was the original Minneapolis arrest experiment and the subsequent replication studies. Garner and Maxwell re-analysed the data from this body of research and concluded that arrest had a 'modest but consistent deterrent effect [on re-offending]' (2000: 106). Several factors contributed to this conclusion: the effect of arrest was much smaller than that of other factors such as the offender's age and prior criminal history; 30 per cent of victims reported at least one new domestic violence offence; and the women who were re-victimized reported an average of five new incidents of domestic violence. Hence they concluded that 'However consistent the deterrent effect of arrest may be in our analysis, it is clearly not a panacea for victims of domestic violence' (Garner and Maxwell, 2000: 107).

Subsequent research moved beyond a focus on arrest to look at outcomes of the wider criminal justice system. While canvassing this vast body of research is beyond the scope of this chapter, one important and consistent finding is that, while the criminal law may contribute to women's safety in some cases, on its own it cannot provide the solution for all women experiencing domestic violence (Bell et al., 2011). Evidence from studies that look at the outcomes of the entire criminal justice process – for example, studies by

Fleury-Steiner et al. (2006) and Ford and Regoli (1993) – found that around one in five women were re-assaulted between arrest and finalization of the criminal case. Six months after their case was finalized, 38 per cent of the women in the Fleury-Steiner et al. study had experienced subsequent violence from the same perpetrator.

Research into the effectiveness of civil protection orders reveals a mixed picture, with studies finding rates of violation of orders of between 23 and 76 per cent (Humphreys and Thiara, 2003b; Jordan et al., 2010; Logan and Walker, 2009). This variation can in part be related to different measures used, such as victim reports or arrest data. Logan and Walker (2009) argue that effectiveness should be measured both in terms of violations of orders and the perceptions of the woman. Their longitudinal study found that just over half the sample, 58 per cent of the women, experienced a violation of the order. A majority of women reported that the order was extremely (51 per cent) or fairly (27 per cent) effective, and a majority felt safe (34 per cent 'extremely' and 34 per cent 'fairly'). Stalking and returning to, or resuming, the relationship were the two factors associated with increased likelihood of an order violation. Importantly for risk assessment, stalking was shown to be a critical risk factor for psychological, physical and sexual abuse and injury after the granting of a protection order.

Increasing the extent and effectiveness of civil protection orders has been a drive in some domestic violence reform agendas (Office of Women's Policy Victoria, 2005). In some Australian states, police have the power to take out intervention orders on behalf of the 'affected family member'. For instance, this third-party protection order has been used in an increasing number of family violence incidents as part of the Victorian reform to lift both the protective and the financial burden from the woman at the point of crisis. Alongside this development has also been the use of the Family Violence Safety Notice, a legislative reform which provides police with powers to remove the offender from the home for 72 hours while an interim protection order can be sought (Thomson and Goodall Associates, 2010).

Complementing research efforts focused on the outcomes of criminal and civil justice policies is a body of research that explores women's experiences of the legal process. The findings of this body of research are being used to develop policies and services that make the legal system more responsive to the needs of women dealing with domestic violence. They can also assist in shaping effective practices for social workers and other advocates who are supporting women through legal processes.

Research with women indicates that they call the police for a range of reasons and with a range of expectations. These include, for example, to stop an immediate assault on herself and her children; to (temporarily) reverse the power relationship by showing her partner that the community thinks that his behaviour is wrong; or to motivate him to seek help or to change (Hoyle and Sanders, 2000; Robinson and Stroshine, 2005). Whatever her motivation, a woman does not usually envisage becoming involved in a complex and extended legal process in which she has little control over either the process or outcome (Bennett et al., 1999). This highlights the need for social workers and other advocates to be well informed about the legal processes in their jurisdiction in order to be able to provide women with accurate information about the processes involved. Accurate information about what to expect of the system can play a vital role in reducing women's anxiety and restoring a sense of control.

In a similar vein, research on women's decisions about prosecution (Ford, 1991) sheds light on what is often seen by players in the legal system as the apparent problem of women's 'non-cooperation' with the legal system. Women may pursue criminal action up to the point at which they achieve their goal (such as agreement to divorce, or the abuser entering substance abuse treatment), leading Ford to conclude that 'What is troublesome to prosecutors may be a rational use of criminal justice by victims' (1991: 316). This mismatch between women's efforts to use the law as a resource in dealing with domestic violence, and the focus of the criminal justice system on holding the offender accountable through the legal process, underlies the all too common negative and judgemental attitudes that women report encountering in their interactions with criminal justice personnel (Baker, 1997; Erez and Belknap, 1998). There has been a tendency for women who are reluctant to follow through the criminal justice process to its conclusion to be judged as 'uncooperative' and their choices about continuing with the criminal justice process attributed to psychological conditions such as 'learned helplessness' (Goodman and Epstein, 2008; Walker, 1977–78). This is not supported by the research evidence. Situational factors, such as the severity of abuse and level of tangible social support (e.g. help with transport, emergency money and child care) rather than psychological variables (e.g. depression) predict women's completion of the prosecution process (Goodman et al., 1999). Similarly, situational factors, most commonly being prevented by the offender from calling the police or believing (often based on prior unsatisfactory experience) that police would be either ineffective or would make matters worse, influence women's decisions to call police to a much greater extent than intrapersonal reasons such as embarrassment, shame and love (Fleury et al., 1998).

Studies that explore women's perspectives have also identified a number of systemic barriers to women's participation in the legal system. These are: the confusing nature of the system; the lack of accurate and timely information; frustration at the slowness of the system; the proceedings being cancelled at least once; experiencing pressure rather than support by legal personnel; and feeling silenced or alienated from the process (Bennett et al., 1999; Fleury-Steiner et al., 2006; Lewis et al., 2000).

Bell and colleagues (2011) explored what severely abused, low-income Black women found helpful and harmful about their encounters with the civil and criminal justice systems. While the women mentioned aspects of court outcomes, such as how effectively sanctions were enforced, they spoke more about aspects of the court process in their assessment of helpfulness or otherwise. Aspects of the court process that shaped women's positive or negative experiences were their treatment by court personnel, whether supportive and inclusive of their views or cold and impersonal; the length of the process and its impact on child care and work commitments; the quality of information provided about other resources; and the public exposure that comes with court involvement.

The strong message from this body of research is that women's decisions about using the law are shaped by the complex interaction of the oppression exerted by the abuser, the contexts of their lives, and their experience with the legal system. Legal remedies for domestic violence hold both potentially positive and negative effects, summed up in the following way by Coker: 'A woman who opposes prose-cution is taking a calculated risk, as is the woman who actively pursues prosecu-tion' (2001: 826). Too often women are blamed for failing to participate in or complete the legal process. Blaming women for failing to co-operate and attributing their decision to women's inferred psychological state shifts responsibility away from focusing on the risk that the abuser poses, the consequent responsibility of the criminal justice system to attend to women's safety throughout the legal process, and the system's responsibility to examine those aspects of the criminal justice sys-tem itself that may constitute barriers to women's attempts to use the law to increase their safety.

Social workers can play an important role in advocating for individual women, bringing their voice and some understanding of the complexities they are dealing with into the legal process. In their work with women, they can ensure that safety planning (discussed in detail in Chapter 4) incorporates the elements of safety and risk that legal remedies might hold. Through the multi-agency approach to domestic violence social workers can also play a role in systemic advocacy to develop policies and services that facilitate women's access to the protection of the law.

New Service Approaches to Enhance Access to Legal Remedies

Over time, new approaches to service delivery have been implemented in efforts to reduce the barriers to women's participation in the legal system and to support their ability to access legal remedies. Some of these initiatives focus on policing, recognizing that a positive police response – a woman's first point of contact with the criminal justice system – needs to be conceived of more broadly than simply as constituting arrest (Holder, 2001). In the Australian state of Victoria, for exam-ple, the police code of practice requires that police take action in every case of domestic violence. Based on risk assessment (including independent risk assess-ment of any affected children and young people), police manage identified risk through the selection of one or a combination of three options for action: referral, criminal and civil law (Victoria Police, 2010). This police policy is embedded within the state's integrated domestic and family violence strategy. It stresses the importance of developing effective partnerships with specialist services and the responsibility of police, in addition to their role in investigation and ensuring safety, of 'facilitating access to specialist services for additional and ongoing assis-tance' (2010: 43).

> In addition to individual advocacy, systems advocacy is an important aspect of social work with domestic violence.

Other efforts to enhance legal access have focused on reducing the coercive elements of 'pro' or mandatory prosecution regimes. Epstein et al. (2003) exemplify this more nuanced approach when they argue for what they term 'prosecution in context', in which the prosecutor retains discretion about the decision to prosecute but the complex context of women's lives is taken into account in decisions about proceeding. Key to this approach is the provision of intensive advocacy/support services that are independent of the prosecution, and can thus offer advocacy that is both long-term and much broader than focusing purely on navigating the legal system. The goal of this approach is the long-term safety of the woman, beyond the immediate goals of prosecuting the offender for a particular incident.

A further important development is that of specialist courts which are:

[S]pecially convened or courts scheduling a specially allocated list day – to remove domestic violence cases from the mainstream of day-to-day court processes by identifying them and tagging them for streaming for improved legal processes and expedition ... [the specialist court] operates with the intention of providing better outcomes for victims and perpetrators, while operating within the precincts of [existing] courts. (Stewart, 2005: 4)

Such courts can include a number of core elements such as specialist personnel (e.g. prosecutors); ongoing training for key participants; procedures for case tracking and monitoring; intensive women's advocacy; protocols for assessing risk and ensuring victim safety; victim-friendly environment; consistent sentencing; and location within a multi-agency approach to tackling domestic violence (Cook et al., 2004; Stewart, 2005).

Evidence is building about the effectiveness of these efforts to facilitate women's access to justice, on legal outcomes (e.g. case disposition and reduction of attrition), on women's experiences of the process and on women's well-being. For example, the provision of independent legal advice to women seeking civil protection orders has been found to increase women's access to this form of legal protection (Durfee, 2009) and their satisfaction with the process (Hester and Westmarland, 2005). Women who received intensive legal advocacy over a six-week period between the granting of a temporary and final protection order, compared with women who received usual services (brief contact at court with a volunteer advocate) reported significantly less physical and psychological re-abuse and marginally better emotional support (Bell and Goodman, 2001). The initial evaluation of five specialist courts in England and Wales found that the effectiveness of court and support services for victims were enhanced by both the 'clustering' and 'fast-tracking' of domestic violence cases; that these arrangements facilitated advocacy and information-sharing; and that victim participation and satisfaction increased (Cook, et al., 2004). A major evaluation of 27 projects funded by the Home Office to reduce domestic violence (Hester and Westmarland, 2005) found the projects that achieved an increase in reporting to police were those which also had specific advocacy interventions geared to supporting women in relation to the criminal justice system, such as legal and court support; support workers based in a police community safety unit; or police based in a one-stop shop. Projects that had an increase in arrests were those employing specific interventions to provide women with legal support in order for them to engage with the criminal justice system. The findings of this meta-evaluation support earlier research which indicates that women are more likely to continue through the legal process if they are provided with support and liaison with the criminal justice system (Hester et al., 2003; Robinson, 2003). Indeed, a recent study highlighted the potential of the justice system to contribute to women's well-being and recovery, finding that 'an empowering experience in court predicted even greater improvement in both depression and quality of life, above and beyond experiences of reabuse, the outcome of the criminal case, and expectations about the court' (Cattaneo and Goodman, 2010: 497).

Principles of Social Work Practice

We contend that the centrality of legal responses to domestic violence policy requires social workers to have a good understanding of the legal remedies to domestic violence in their particular jurisdiction. Women whose first encounter with the legal system is to seek redress or protection from domestic violence need social workers who can provide them with accurate information about the legal system and about the strengths and limitations of the law in dealing with domestic violence. Some women may be unaware that the law is an option for dealing with domestic violence, while others may have received an unhelpful response when they tried to access legal protection.

Belief, Support and Advocacy

The preceding discussion about the challenges of developing legal remedies for domestic violence highlights the importance of bringing the voice of women into the legal process so that a woman's efforts to use the law constitute an empowering experience, rather than perpetuating the sense of loss of control that has been fostered through the perpetrator's tactics of coercion and control. As the evidence indicates, a supportive and validating contact with the legal system can give a woman a powerful message about her capacity to act to increase her safety and that of her children, even in situations where the legal outcomes cannot be guaranteed. Naming her experiences of abuse as criminal acts for which the offender is solely responsible is a powerful antidote to the isolation and messages of self-blame that she has experienced as part of the abuse. Social workers, who believe women when they disclose abuse, offer support, advocate for them with justice system personnel and link them into the supports and resources within the multi-agency approach to domestic violence, can play a vital role in shaping a positive experience of help-seeking. The evidence base about the barriers to women's participation in the legal system provides guidance about the types of support that are most helpful. This speaks to the importance of emotional support provided by the social worker's stance of belief and validation, together with practical support such as accompanying her to court (or linking her to services that provide this specialist support) and providing material resources (e.g. assistance with transport and child care).

Some social workers may be uncomfortable with the strong advocacy role that we argue is essential in working with women seeking legal redress for domestic violence. It may appear to be at odds with a social work commitment to a holistic approach to working with families. However, when issues of violence and abuse are involved, a stance of 'neutrality' is not only inappropriate, but can also be dangerous and can place women and children at risk of serious harm. As discussed in detail in Chapter 6, working with men who perpetuate violence is a specialist field of work, underpinned by principles of practice that place women and children's safety at the forefront of the work and a value position that does not excuse violence and respectfully challenges men to address their harmful behaviours. Often this work needs to be underpinned by legal mandate and always with arrangements in place to monitor the safety of women and children.

Social workers who do not have experience in domestic violence work may be unaware that the perpetrator's tactics of control often extend beyond the relationship with his ex/partner to the service system and the personnel within it, particularly when the abuse is disclosed to people outside the family. Men who have terrorized their partners and children can present very calmly and rationally in their interactions with human services and criminal justice personnel. They may seek to reduce support for and belief of the victim/survivor; for example, by labelling her as mentally ill or as having issues with substance use. This can be confusing to workers because living with violence can result in compromised mental health and use of substances to cope. As a result of these perpetrator behaviours, social workers supporting women experiencing domestic violence may have to negotiate conflict with other professionals in the multi-agency system. A good understanding of the dynamics of domestic violence and of the evidence base for effective intervention provides social workers with a sound basis for advocacy that prioritizes the safety of women and children.

Safety Planning that Includes Assessment of Systemic Risks

In all work with women, risk assessment and safety planning is an ongoing process. As has been discussed, no legal remedy on its own can guarantee women's safety and each poses potential risks and benefits. Social workers need accurate information about the legal processes in their jurisdiction in order to assist women to incorporate this knowledge into their safety planning. For example, women who have had no previous contact with the law may not realize that the legal process can take considerable time and that they may need to attend court on a number of occasions. One of the most common barriers for women seeking protection orders is fear of retaliation by the abuser (Jordan et al., 2010). Engaging in risk assessment with the woman can assist her to think through the risks and potential benefits in her particular situation, taking into account both the risks posed by the offender, by her particular social situation and by the ways in which the legal processes operate in the jurisdiction. Risk assessment and safety planning are essential to mobilize resources within the multi-agency response to domestic violence to attend to issues of safety throughout and after the legal process. This may include 'target hardening' measures such as panic alarms and enhanced home security (Women's Health Goulburn North East, 2011). Safety planning is discussed in detail in Chapter 4.

Avoiding and Challenging Victim Blaming Responses

It is important to guard against blaming women who are reluctant or who choose not to take up recommended actions and referrals, including legal remedies for domestic violence.

As discussed in Chapter 4, women are involved in a continuous process of weighing up the protective and risk elements of a range of strategies in response to changing levels of risk posed by the perpetrator's behaviour and the additional challenges arising from her social location, such as being a mother, her immigration status and access to economic resources. From this perspective, a woman's use of the law can be seen as one of many ongoing strategies she may take in order to increase her safety (Lewis et al., 2000). Understanding her assessment of risk underpinning decisions about using the law is more productive than blaming a woman for reluctance to embrace worker-led solutions. Social workers can contribute valuable information and advocate for the woman in multi-agency contexts to reduce the risk that she receives a response which deters her from seeking legal assistance in the future and so puts herself and her children at increased risk of harm.

Attention to Evidence and Documentation

Accurate documentation of women's experiences of domestic violence can be crucial in facilitating their access to legal protections from domestic violence. Historically, many cases did not proceed through the criminal justice system because of reliance on the woman's testimony alone. Enhanced evidence collection in many jurisdictions (e.g. photographic recording by police at the crime scene) has been introduced in efforts to enhance the quality of evidence available to the courts and to encourage early guilty pleas by offenders (Hester and Westmarland, 2005; Humphreys and Holder, 2004). Social workers should accurately document disclosures and details of domestic violence, whether or not the woman is seeking legal redress at that time. Care should be taken in recording to link the documented effects of abuse to the domestic violence, rather than to record them in ways that may be interpreted as evidence of the woman's problems out of the context of her living with fear and coercion. For example, issues of women's mental health, substance use and parenting struggles can be used to disadvantage women and children in certain legal settings (such as child protection and family law) if they are not placed in the context of the effects of living with violence. Equally, it is important to record the fact that the woman is working on protective strategies within the constraints of her particular situation. Extreme caution needs to be taken in determining the risk that these records may be made available to the abuser in certain legal contexts. For this reason, details of safety plans should not be recorded if the abuser may be able to access these records.

Recording the evidence of domestic violence may prove to be critical in the safety and protection of both women and children.

New Policy Directions

Advocacy at the policy or systems level is an important aspect of the practice of social workers and other domestic violence advocates in legal contexts. They bring to the multi-agency context understanding of the ways in which the social contexts and complexities of survivors' lives can be barriers to legal participation. For example, they may advocate for specialist advocacy services that reach out to communities which have low rates of engagement with the law. Domestic violence advocates have also made important contributions to policy review and improvement, as shown in the following examples.

In many jurisdictions, systemic advocacy has been successful in highlighting the injustice that often requires women and children to become homeless in order to escape domestic violence. Measures to provide legal support to oust the perpetrator of violence from the home rather than the women and children are increasingly being developed in both Australia (Crinall and Hurley, 2009) and Europe (Haller, 2005). For example, in the Australian state of New South Wales (NSW), a study of protection orders in two local courts highlighted the low rates of orders that included the provision to exclude the perpetrator (Edwards, 2004b). A subsequent study into the factors that can enable women and children to continue to live safely in their homes (Edwards, 2004a) resulted in the funding of a state-wide network of advocates who work with women within the multi-agency context to facilitate women's ability to remain in their homes where they wish to do so. The Staying Home Leaving Violence programme is 'based on the values of women's empowerment, decision-making and choice' (Edwards, 2011: 2). Evaluation of the programme from the perspectives of women found that the role of the domestic violence advocate was essential in providing support and in advocating for a consistent multi-agency response that is focused on safety for women and children and accountability of perpetrators, particularly when violations of protection orders are reported (Edwards, 2011).

Domestic Violence Homicide Reviews represent a new approach to identifying systemic problems and policy gaps in responding to domestic violence:

> A Domestic Violence Death Review is a process of examination carried out by a multi-disciplinary board/team to examine a number of deaths over a defined period of time looking for common traits, trends and missed opportunities for intervention. The identification of patterns or trends or traits can then assist with the development of improved responses to domestic and family violence. (Taylor, 2008: 14)

Following advocacy from the domestic violence sector, such review processes are now established in legislation in the United Kingdom (Home Office, 2011) and in some Australian States (e.g. NSW Government, 2009). The primary aim of these reviews is to 'Establish what lessons are to be learned from the domestic homicide regarding the way in which local professionals and organizations work individually and together to safeguard victims' (Home Office, 2011: 6). Most importantly, from these lessons, is the identification of policy and practice gaps and the formulation and implementation of recommendations to improve the multi-agency response to domestic violence. While the scope of reviews varies across jurisdictions, the focus is on deaths that occur against a background of domestic violence. They can include, therefore, not just deaths of former and current intimate partners and children, but also people such as new partners, bystanders, police officers and work colleagues. The role of domestic violence advocates in this process is crucial in challenging victim blaming that may occur during this process (Hobart, 2004). Some review processes, such as the NSW Domestic Violence Death Review Team, have the capacity to review the suicides of victims of domestic violence and 'accidental' deaths where there is a history of domestic violence. Domestic violence death reviews also assist in developing the knowledge base for practice, for example, though the identification of common or new risk factors that emerge from examination of both individual cases and trends across multiple cases (Taylor, 2008).

Conclusion

From this discussion it is clear that each policy and legal remedy offers both strengths and limitations for addressing domestic violence. This awareness means that social workers can assist women to incorporate systemic risks and protections into their process of safety planning. The law can be a powerful weapon in holding abusers accountable and in sending a strong message to the community that violence against women and children is not tolerated. Social workers are also well placed to advocate for continuing reform of legal processes so that legal protections are more readily available to women, including to the most marginalized. Despite its limitations, the potential of the law comes more sharply into focus when we work with women who, for a variety of reasons, are 'outside the law' (e.g. asylum seekers) or women in certain relationship statuses that may be excluded from protection order legislation, such as same sex couples in some jurisdictions. Social workers need to engage with the legal system to advocate for reforms that make its protections available to all women.

Summary Points

- The history of domestic violence interventions indicates that practitioners need to be aware of both the strengths and limitations of the law and policy initiatives to support safety and accountability.
- Women may be involved simultaneously in multiple legal systems, each of which has different foci and expectations. Criminal law sanctions criminal behaviour that has already occurred; the civil law can be used to prevent future violence; Family Law deals with parenting arrangements after separation; child protection legislation intervenes in issues of child abuse. Social workers need to be well informed about the operation of each legal system so that they can provide women with support, legal referrals and accurate information.
- Since every policy and law will carry elements of both risk and safety, it is important to guard against blaming women who are reluctant or who choose not to take up recommended actions and referrals.
- Risk assessment and safety planning go hand in hand. The risks to women and their children emerge and change over time. Each new strategy, including the use of the law, needs to be assessed in relation to whether it increases safety or brings new risks.
- Women and their children from minority groups who experience themselves outside the mainstream of the society may be appropriately wary of engaging with the law.
- Generally, women living with domestic violence will need significant support, either formally or informally, to be able to use the law constructively.
- At every step along the way women will need evidence and documentation from professionals, including social workers, that domestic violence has occurred.
- Unlike some other areas of social work, domestic violence work requires belief, support and advocacy that may sometimes position the social worker in conflict with other family members and other professionals in the multi-agency system.
- Social workers need to advocate for socially just domestic violence policies, such as the conditions that can enable some women and their children to remain in their homes safely rather than being made homeless to escape violence.

Reflective Questions for Practice

- If Maria seeks assistance with her decision about whether or not to apply for a protection order, what questions could be asked by a social worker that could help her to make the decision with attention to risk and safety considerations?
- What particular barriers and concerns might be influencing Maria's decision about how she uses the law? How could these be addressed?
- What enablers within the intervention system (legal and social) need to be present to provide women such as Maria and Louise with access to the protection of the law?

Further Reading

Goodman, L. A., and Epstein, D. (2008). *Listening to Battered Women: A Survivor-Centred Approach to Advocacy, Mental Health, and Justice.* Washington, DC: American Psychological Association.

This book provides an incisive analysis of the ways in which policy and practice have moved away from the foundations of women-centred work and suggests ways to re-think our approach to policy.

Hunter, R. (2002). Border protection in law's empire: feminist explorations of access to justice. *Griffith Law Review,* 11(2): 263–285. Available at www.austlii.edu.au/au/journals/GriffLawRw/2002/15.html.

This paper explores the challenges of law reform in providing access to justice for victims of violence against women. The author suggests that insufficient attention has been paid to the challenges of implementing law reform.

Hester, M. (2006). Making it through the criminal justice system: attrition and domestic violence. *Social Policy and Society,* 5(1): 79–90.

This article is drawn from a comprehensive study of the criminal justice response to domestic violence. Its multiple lenses on attrition in the criminal justice system highlight both the strengths and problems for women engaging in this complex pathway.

4

Practices with Women

Madeline has been married for 10 years and has a daughter aged 6 years. She was diagnosed with multiple sclerosis (MS) six years ago and due to the degenerative nature of MS now uses a wheelchair. Madeline has limited vision and her speech has also been affected by MS. The family home has been modified to accommodate wheelchair and vision impairment issues. After two years of waiting Madeline has finally been given a community care package which assists her with personal care, shopping, meal preparation and house cleaning. Throughout her marriage Madeline has often experienced controlling and abusive behaviours from her husband and as her MS progresses and becomes more debilitating, the abuse has become more frequent. Her husband often threatens to have her removed to a nursing home because she is 'hopeless, pathetic and cannot even do the simplest of things' for herself, him and their child. He refuses to assist with the child at night and often 'accidentally' leaves things just out of Madeline's reach, such as the air conditioning controls (heat intolerance is a major issue for people with MS). He controls the finances and thus her social life and appointments with health professionals are 'managed' by him. Madeline had previously spoken to her GP regarding her husband's behaviour and was met with 'Look, he loves you; he's probably doing his best. You know it must be really hard for him....'. During her last health check at the hospital MS clinic Madeline tentatively spoke to her specialist about feeling depressed and anxious and her specialist said he could write her out a prescription. It was at this point Madeline decided to ask to see a hospital social worker.

The authors acknowledge the expertise of Karen Jordan in assisting us to develop this scenario.

Practices with women who have experienced violence in their intimate relationships have reflected shifting assumptions about the nature of domestic violence and about women's responses to it. In this chapter, we address a range of issues that underpin the work with women living with domestic violence. We begin by placing this work in its **historical context,** leading into the **evidence base** that informs current practice approaches. The chapter then moves to a discussion of **essential elements of practice with women** that differentiate this work from other forms of counselling or case-work practice before outlining some **current practice approaches.** As the case of Madeline indicates, all social workers need to understand the principles of this work, whether or not they are in specialist domestic violence agencies.

The Historical Context

As discussed in Chapter 2, the activism of the second-wave feminist social movement transformed the ways in which women experiencing domestic violence were under-stood. Until this time, abused women had been framed through individual/psycho-logical ideas as somehow bearing responsibility for their own victimization (e.g. through 'masochistic' personalities). The alternative framing of domestic violence as grounded in gendered inequality opened up new ways of seeing and new possibilities for action against domestic violence. The emphasis of intervention now turned to enhancing women's safety and the provision of support and the resources – such as housing, income and child care – to enable women to establish violence-free lives. Violence against women was understood as a crime rather than as a problem requir-ing counselling. 'Consciousness-raising' groups were an important part of the wom-en's movement and group work was an early approach to working with women. Groups provided a context for sharing women's experiences, reducing isolation and self-blame because the commonalities of women's lives were exposed and validated.

   This history of feminist activism has shaped contemporary intervention with women and their children and has been essential in developing practices that reflect the nature and complexities of domestic violence. While the value of counselling in assisting women to deal with the effects of living with violence and abuse is now rec-ognized, reflection is required to ensure that frameworks adopted do not separate the experiences of individual women from their social context. Some of these frameworks are discussed later in the chapter. While gender was highlighted initially as the core element of this social context, contemporary approaches need to include not only gender but also other aspects of women's social location; for example, age, ethnicity, access to economic resources, sexuality and immigration status. Madeline's story reminds us that (dis)abilities are an important aspect of women's social location that shape both their experiences of abuse and responses to it, and the responses they receive from others (Hague et al., 2011). Group work, initially with women and more recently with women and their children, continues to be a common and an effective approach to intervention (Cohen and Mullender, 2003). The unique aspects of prac-tices with women who have experienced domestic violence are outlined later in this chapter, after a consideration of the evidence base that informs this practice.

The Evidence Base: Practices with Women

Two key issues emerge as significant in the knowledge base informing practices with women. The first involves understanding women's responses to domestic violence;

the second explores what is known about women's help-seeking. This knowledge base is foundational to effective intervention in the domestic violence sphere.

Women's Responses to Domestic Violence

Until relatively recently, views of women's responses to abuse within their intimate relationships have tended to be sharply dichotomized, with the women seen as either 'victims' or 'survivors'. As understandings of domestic violence have more thoroughly appreciated its complexity, such dichotomized views of women as either victims or survivors are increasingly seen as unhelpful in shaping policy and practice responses (Lewis et al., 2000). This has parallels with the focus on women either staying in or leaving the relationship, another dichotomy that fails to capture the complexity that women are managing and that can result in women being blamed or stigmatized for their decisions around staying or leaving.

Nevertheless, the interest in researching factors that are associated with staying or leaving the relationship has contributed to the evidence base for contemporary responses. One strand of this research involves quantitative studies that attempt to identify the factors that predict women's leaving the relationship. In a review of these studies, Anderson and Saunders (2003) identified two broad categories of factors: material resources (income and employment) and social/psychological factors. When the relative influence of these two groups of factors is studied, income variables have been found to more strongly predict leaving than psychological ones. A comprehensive Australian study that examined the impact of domestic violence on women's economic well-being and the intersection of this with their recovery overall found that 'for women experiencing domestic violence, financial security goes to the heart of not only their freedom from abuse, but also their recovery and capacity to (re)gain control over their lives, now and in the future' (Braaf and Barrett Meyering, 2011: 3).

Another strand of this research comprises studies of how women respond to and manage violence in their intimate relationships (e.g. Landenburger, 1989; Lempert, 1996; Merritt-Gray and Wuest, 1995; Patton, 2003). Typically qualitative in nature, these studies explore women's lived experience of domestic violence, and have helped to shape more nuanced understandings of the complexities that confront women. This body of research indicates that dealing with domestic violence is a complex process in which women are not passive victims in the face of their partners' abusive and controlling behaviours; rather, they exercise agency in employing a range of strategies to deal with their partner's behaviour. These strategies are varied and may change over the course of the relationship in response to the level of danger and the abuser's responses to them (Cavanagh, 2003).

Women's protective strategies can include, for example: efforts to protect themselves and their children from immediate physical violence, such as leaving the house or going to another room, calling police or others to assist and fighting back; strategies to protect their children, such as putting them to bed when violence from the abuser seems imminent; becoming engaged in activities to maintain their self-esteem in the face of living with degrading abuse; pursuing education to increase their employment skills; opening a bank account and saving money; and seeking help from informal networks or from services (Hamby, 2009; Keys Young, 1998). Feminist in orientation, much of this research attempts to unsettle the preoccupation with why women stay by exploring how, given the many constraints they are confronted with, women manage to leave a relationship in which they experience violence and coercive control. The case of Madeline provides an excellent example of the complex decision making required for a woman with disabilities who faces risks including and beyond domestic violence.

Considerations about children can play a large role in shaping women's strategies and decisions. For example, Ursula Kelly's (2009) research highlighted the ways in which being a mother shaped immigrant women's decision-making processes; they prioritized strategies that would protect the psychological well-being and safety of their children, responding both to changing and terrifying tactics of abuse and a precarious social location where deportation and poverty were active risks. For older women, difficult decisions about staying and leaving can have lasting effects on their relationships with their adult children, some being angry that she left, others angry that she stayed – a 'no-win' situation for many (Morgan Disney and Associates, 2000).

> The decisions to stay and leave are complex and change with social and personal circumstances.

Building on this body of research, the process of women leaving violence has frequently been conceptualized as a series of stages. Anderson and Saunders summarize these stages as: '(a) endurance of and managing the violence while disconnecting from self and others; (b) acknowledging the abuse, reframing it, and counteracting it; and (c) "breaking free," disengaging, and focusing on one's own needs' (2003: 164). However, as they note, most conceptualizations of the stages in the process of leaving violence fail to include a further post-separation stage. This involves women building a new life, often while dealing with the effects of the violence on their mental health, post-separation violence and abuse (frequently associated with child contact arrangements) and difficulty in accessing material resources. A further criticism of this literature is that in the effort to redress the emphasis on women as victims, it risks a return to earlier approaches that emphasized women's internal psychological processes as the key area of focus by implying that the key to change lies in women's cognitive and emotional processes. This ignores the broader socio-political context and the importance of factors such as access to material resources (Anderson and Saunders, 2003) and the woman's social location. It also underplays the important interactional context between the woman and the perpetrator (Cavanagh, 2003) and between the woman and potential sources of formal and informal supports (Hegarty et al., 2008).

The complexity of these processes is captured diagrammatically in a model (see Figure 4.1) that was developed from a participatory action research project in which women and service providers worked together to develop a way of understanding women's journey away from violence (Community Care Division Victorian Government Department of Human Services, 2004). Research participants included both women who had left the relationship as well as women who remained or returned and the violence had ceased.

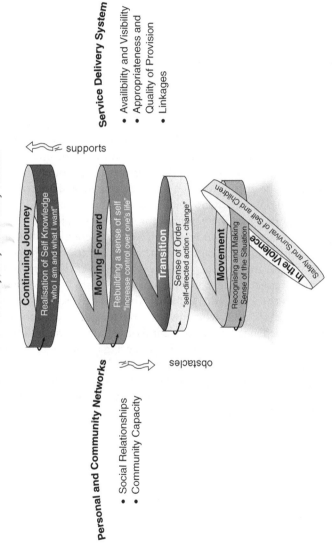

Figure 4.1 Women's Journey away from Violence (Community Care Division Victorian Government Department of Human Services, 2004: 17)

© State of Victoria, Australia. Reproduced with the permission of the Secretary to the Department of Human Services. Unauthorised reproduction and other uses comprised in the copyright are prohibited without permission.

Based on the women's lived experience, this journey is represented as a series of interconnected spirals, rather than as linear, sequential stages. This allows for the possibility that women may both move upward, integrating and learning from their experiences and the responses of the perpetrator and others, or 'recycle' back to another level in response to these complex interactions. For each 'spiral', the research drew on the women's narratives to describe common experiences and the key themes. In the first spiral, *in violence/movement*, the key theme is safety and recognizing the need for change; during *transition*, it is safety and developing a sense of order and self-directed action; during *moving forward*, it is rebuilding a sense of self and increased control over life; and during *continuing the journey*, the key theme is realization of self and increased participation in community life (Community Care Division Victorian Government Department of Human Services, 2004: 17).

The threat posed by the perpetrator is shown by the dark pyramid structure in the centre of the diagram, almost all-encompassing when the woman is *in the violence* and diminishing as she moves forward. Of key relevance to service providers such as social workers are the obstacles and supports (shown with upward and downward arrows at the side of the diagram) that the woman may encounter in her help-seeking, since the responses she encounters can either enable forward movement or send her spiralling backwards. Women who remained in the relationship in the final stage of the 'journey' recognized that the potential for violence would never be eliminated and had identified the unique ways in which they could recognize when the perpetrator's behaviour was curtailing their rights in the relationship. For this group of women, support of family and friends was vital in monitoring of the perpetrator's behaviour. The additional systemic barriers and prejudices faced by women from marginalized social locations were significant. Lesbian, Aboriginal, disabled and 'culturally and linguistically diverse' (CALD) women were over-represented 'in the group of women who remained trapped in the continual spiral of *in the violence* and *movement*' (2004: 16): they moved between 'surviving' and attempting to 'manage' the violence and taking the first steps towards regaining some control in their lives.

The participatory action study is one of only a small number of studies that have included women who were still in relationship with their partners. The findings of Campbell et al.'s (1998) longitudinal study challenge dichotomous notions of women being 'in' or 'out' of the relationship. The researchers found that categories such as these could not capture the fluidity of the women's relationships. In contrast, the study illuminated how 'most women initiated a process of achieving nonviolence rather than necessarily leaving the intimate relationship' (1998: 751). This study is particularly important in highlighting that leaving the relationship and ending the violence are often independent. That is, some women remained in the relationship and had been free of both physical violence of coercive control for a year, while others who left were subject to continuing violence. Cavanagh (2003) interviewed women whose partners had been convicted of at least one violent offence against them. Three-quarters of the women were still married to or cohabiting with their partners, and, as with the Campbell et al. (1998) study, many of the women wanted the relationship to continue but the violence to stop. The women worked to stop/prevent violence and this work included the following elements:

'defining and redefining the violence; protecting the integrity of the relationship; employing strategies for avoiding violence or "doing gender"; [and] deploying responses which challenged men's use of violence' (Cavanagh, 2003: 235).

Madeline's physical impairment clearly imposes severe constraints and provides her partner with many avenues through which to exert control, including controlling her access to others who may be in a position to help. Nevertheless, the research on women's responses to violence suggests that Madeline will have been adopting strategies to manage the situation and to increase the safety of herself and her daughter, including asking to speak to a social worker when her partner is not present at the clinic. If her disclosure is met by a response that suggests that leaving is the sole or best solution, this may well be experienced as failing to appreciate the complexity of her situation – both her unique protective strategies and the fact that the supports that are crucial to her mobility are tied to her home. Responses such as these can shame and further isolate women who do not follow worker-led solutions.

In summary, much of the difficulty in recognizing the possibility of women's coexisting agency and oppression is related to the common tendency to equate agency solely with leaving the relationship. This renders invisible both the woman's resistance to the perpetrator's abuse and control and the increased risk to her safety that leaving may well pose. However, women's strategies of resistance (often not visible to outside observers) are constrained by factors that include the coercive control which the perpetrator strives to impose, her access to resources, the quality of the responses she receives from formal and informal supports and her social location (e.g. her age, 'race', immigration status, poverty and disability) (Baker, 1997; Cavanagh, 2003; Dutton, 1996; Schneider, 1992). For older women, considerations of resources are particularly salient because they may have limited opportunities to re-enter the workforce and face the prospect of losing financial security that has been built up over a lifetime (Morgan Disney and Associates, 2000). Many have little or no superannuation and recognize the risks of poverty and homelessness that can attach to leaving the relationship (McFerran, 2009).

Help-seeking

Included among the strategies that women adopt in response to violence is seeking help from others. This can be from informal sources such as friends, family, neighbours and work colleagues and from formal sources such as police, counsellors, doctors and other professionals. The former is also referred to as 'social support' and the latter 'institutional support'. Providing social and institutional support is crucial because it directly counteracts the isolation that the abuser imposes as part of the pattern of domestic violence. Higher levels of social support are also associated with better mental health, one of the most severe impacts of domestic violence (Belknap et al., 2009).

Data from the New Zealand Violence Against Women Study (Fanslow and Robinson, 2010) provides useful information about women's help-seeking because the findings are based on a representative general population sample, in contrast to many other studies that have surveyed only women who have contacted services. Approximately three-quarters of the women surveyed had told someone about the violence. The previous discussion of women's responses to violence provides some understanding about that proportion of women who do not tell anyone about the abuse. They may be attempting to 'manage' the violence and may not yet have named their experiences as abusive, or they may be constrained by shame from telling anyone about what is happening:

> I felt I couldn't tell them [family and friends] about it [violence] . . . I was ashamed . . . Everyone had told me that it would never last and I was determined to prove them wrong. So I had to sort of take the good with the bad. I just thought it would work out, I thought I could change him. (Cavanagh, 2003: 236)

Three types of factors precipitated women's help-seeking. The first were related to the severity of the abuse (the woman 'could not endure more'; threats or attempts to kill the woman; fear of being killed or sustaining serious injury); the second were related to concerns for children suffering or being harmed; and the third was being encouraged to leave by family and friends (Fanslow and Robinson, 2010). However, over 40 per cent of the respondents who sought help also said that no one had helped them. This emphasizes the point that disclosure in and of itself is not enough to assist women: a consistently supportive response is required (Coker et al., 2002).

Consistent with other studies, this study found that women were more likely to turn to informal sources of support: 58 per cent told only family or friends about the abuse; 36 per cent had turned to both formal and informal sources of support; while only 5 per cent turned solely to formal support. The potential for family and friends to provide support and information highlights the importance of broad education campaigns that inform the community about domestic violence and about how to support a friend, work colleague or relative who is living with domestic violence. When women turned to institutional sources of support, only a small proportion sought help from specialist domestic violence services (refuge), although this type of service was universally reported as being extremely helpful. Women were more likely to seek help from generalist services, including general practitioners, health services, counsellors and police. Approximately three-quarters of the women reported helpful responses from these formal sources of support. This again highlights the fact that social workers in many settings may be called upon to respond to domestic violence and the importance of an informed and supportive response.

A study of institutional and social support in a sample of women whose cases had reached the criminal courts (Belknap et al., 2009) found that few demographic factors other than age were associated with the level of support that the women received (older women reported receiving higher levels of support). However, the status of the women's relationship with the perpetrator was associated with the level of support received. Women who were still in relationship with the abuser at the time of his arrest reported lower levels of institutional support from prosecutors, victim advocates and refuge staff. This suggests that beliefs about staying/leaving remain powerful in influencing the responses of many who work with abused women. Holding up leaving as the 'gold standard of good coping' (Hamby, 2009: 3) can create a barrier to women seeking further help. For example, in this study, women who were still with their partners at the time of the research (at the conclusion of legal proceedings) were less likely to report that others knew of the abuse, and also reported lower levels of social and institutional support.

> Since dealing with domestic violence is a complex process, single interventions are unlikely to be effective.

Chantler's (2006) study with African-Caribbean, Irish, Jewish and South Asian women in the United Kingdom provides another example of the ways in which unhelpful responses can fail women. Consistent with other studies of how women respond to domestic violence, Chantler found that the women employed many resistance strategies, even in the face of retaliation by the abuser, counteracting the stereotype that certain groups of women are particularly passive because of their cultural backgrounds. However, in seeking help, these women had to contend not only with pressure to leave the relationship, but with additional expectations reflecting ignorance of their social location: 'Looking through a minoritized lens, not only is there an imperative to "leave your man", but there is also an implicit message to "leave your oppressive culture"' (2006: 30).

> Shaming women (e.g. with heavy handed warnings about the effects of domestic violence on children) is likely to exacerbate the self-blame that has been encouraged by the perpetrator and inhibit further help-seeking.

Essential Elements of Practice with Women

In working with abused women, social workers' generic skills in engagement and non-judgemental, relationship-based counselling and support provide a strong foundation. However, the nature of domestic violence as outlined in this book, and the evidence base underpinning practice with women who experience violence within their intimate relationships, point to some ways in which practice with women in the context of domestic violence needs to include some specific elements. The elements outlined below pertain regardless of whether social workers are engaged in specialist domestic violence work or come into contact with abused women as part of their practice in other settings.

Risk Assessment and Safety Planning

Because domestic violence can result in severe physical injury and even death, assessing the risk of harm to women and children is central to intervention. Prior to formal research into risk factors, women's advocates identified a number of risk factors on the basis of their experience in working with women escaping violence, such as threats of homicide or suicide, obsessive jealousy and highly controlling behaviours, escalation of abuse and a context of separation. Over time, research has confirmed many of these factors and has identified others, such as attempted strangulation and post-separation sexual assault. In a major review of research on risk factors for intimate partner homicide, Campbell et al. (2007) identified prior domestic violence as the key risk factor, followed by access to firearms, estrangement, threats to kill and threats with a weapon, non-fatal strangulation, and presence of a stepchild in the home.

The use of structured risk assessment models or 'tools' plays an increasingly important role in enhancing policing and multi-agency work with domestic violence. These have been developed by drawing on evidence from reviews of intimate partner homicides, reviews of policy and agency data and from analysis of perpetrator characteristics and contexts. Some employ actuarial tools to calculate relative risk; others combine this with professional judgement. The benefits of using risk assessment models include: providing police with a structured guide to collecting relevant information when called to an incident; enhancing the ability to provide appropriate risk-management strategies; and improving the multi-agency response, since the collaborating agencies have a common understanding of risk. An example is the common risk-assessment and risk-management framework adopted across all domestic violence organizations in the Australian state of Victoria (Department of Human Services Victoria, 2007).

One of the best known tools is the Co-ordinated Action Against Domestic Abuse (CAADA) Domestic Abuse, Stalking and 'Honour'-based Violence (DASH) Risk Identification Checklist, which identifies high-risk cases for referral to a Multi-Agency Risk Assessment Conference (MARAC) (see www.caada.org.uk). Initially developed in Wales, MARACs are now being extended across England. This approach combines an actuarial 'threshold' for referral with professional judgement and the victim's perception. This reflects understanding that tools based on the current evidence base cannot accurately predict risk in every case and research which identifies the importance of taking into account the woman's own assessment of the risk that she is facing (Weisz et al., 2000). However, while women rarely over-estimate their risk, they may under-estimate it (Campbell, 2004). Another widely used risk assessment tool, the danger assessment scale (DAS) (Campbell, 1986; Campbell et al., 2009) involves the practitioner and woman together completing a diary of abusive incidents over the past 12 months, together with a 20-point questionnaire. Participating in this process can assist women to become more aware of the danger that they are facing (e.g. of escalating violence). This emphasizes that risk assessment is not something that the practitioner does *about* a women, but *with* her. This participatory approach to risk assessment between the woman and worker is commonly referred to by advocates as 'safety planning' (Davies et al., 1998).

The second essential component of risk assessment is risk management: that is, efforts to reduce the risk factors that have been identified. In the example of the MARACs, the risk assessment process identifies cases that are referred to the MARAC so that a plan for managing the identified risks can be put into place. An evaluation of the Cardiff MARAC found that six in ten women referred to the MARAC process were not re-victimized following this intervention (Robinson, 2006).

Initially the term 'safety planning' was used in a limited fashion to refer to developing plans to help women to escape from situations of physical threat, with an emphasis on leaving the relationship safely. Contemporary understandings of safety planning are broader, draw on the evidence base about the complex ways in which women manage the violence that they encounter in their intimate relationships, and do not assume that leaving is the best option for all women (Davies et al., 1998). Fundamental to this approach is the recognition that, long before formal help-seeking, women are already assessing risk and implementing protective strategies to increase safety for themselves and their children (Davies et al., 1998; Hamby, 2009). Hence safety planning is a women-centred, collaborative and dynamic process between a woman and an advocate or other support worker. The focus on woman-centred practice, however, does not mean that the worker does not offer information that the woman can incorporate into her safety planning (e.g. about resources, options and high risk factors).

> Woman-centred practice that seeks to understand the ways in which the woman understands her situation in all its complexity will avoid imposing inappropriate, worker-led solutions.

Consistent with the approach of this book, safety planning needs to address the diversity among women who experience domestic violence and the complexity of their lives. This means that risk assessment and safety planning encompass more than the risks that arise from the controlling behaviours of the abuser, termed 'batterer-generated' risks by Davies et al. (1998: 22). They also identify a second type of risk that abused women include in their safety planning: 'life-generated' or social risks. A limitation of many risk assessment models is that they focus predominantly on the perpetrator and pay less attention to the risks posed by women's diverse and intersecting social locations, which can mean that 'Efforts to seek safety in the domestic sphere often entail profound social risks beyond retaliation by the batterer' (Bograd, 1999: 281). Australian Indigenous women, and BME women in the United Kingdom, for example, may hesitate to use legal protections because of their own or others' previous experiences of racist and discriminatory responses from the criminal justice system. Indigenous Australian women may also hesitate to use domestic violence support services because of concern that the risk of losing community and family support may not be appreciated by non-Indigenous service providers (Blagg et al., 2000).

In addition, abusers may use social risks such as these to maintain or increase their coercive control. For example, the perpetrator of abuse in a lesbian relationship may threaten to 'out' her partner if she ends the relationship, or the perpetrator of violence against an immigrant woman may threaten her opportunity to achieve permanent residency. Older women may be threatened with placement in an aged care facility by their abuser. In the case of Madeline, she would be concerned that her partner's threats to take the child and put her into a 'home' will be realized.

Women's safety planning also takes into account the risks that are posed to them by the service system, legislation and policy. For example, the increasing emphasis in Family Law in Australia on shared parenting and the difficulty of achieving post-separation parenting arrangements that protect women and children from ongoing violence and abuse (Laing, 2010), may strongly influence a woman's decision to stay in a relationship if she judges that her children will be safer with her present to protect them than if they are ordered to spend long periods of time alone with the perpetrator of abuse.

Given this complexity that women are facing, advice to 'just leave', or heavy handed warnings about the effects of domestic violence on children that fail to explore how the woman is already attending to their safety, are unlikely to be experienced by a woman as helpful and may lead the woman to decide that formal help-seeking is not a useful protective strategy. In Madeline's case, the social worker's response to her initial attempt to disclose the abuse needs to appreciate the constraints that Madeline is taking into account in her safety planning (e.g. the risk of losing her home and the supports to her mobility and parenting available within it), the level and types of abuse she is subject to and the protective strategies that she is already implementing.

Partnering with Women

In the light of the preceding discussion, practice with women in the context of domestic violence needs to attend to the operations of power within the relationship between the woman and those working with her. This is because the experience of domestic violence subjects the woman to a range of tactics aimed at exerting coercive control over every aspect of her life, including how she experiences herself and her capacities. An empowering approach to practice can redress the impact of this pattern of coercive control by positioning the woman as the 'expert on her own life'. This is consistent with social work values such as self-determination and practices of critical reflection that encourage social workers to be aware of power relations (Fook and Askeland, 2007). Partnering with women also involves transparency about any legal or organizational requirements on the social worker, such as requirements to report children at risk of harm to statutory child protection services, what sorts of concerns may lead to this response and how this would be handled.

Nevertheless, in situations where women and children are being subjected to severe and damaging abuse, it can be difficult to patiently work alongside the woman and the urge to 'rescue' by imposing solutions can be strong. A difficult aspect of this work is the need to recognize that 'even the best plan cannot ensure women's safety' (Seeley and Plunkett, 2002: 24). Clearly, access to good supervision is important in this work. A further challenge is that intervention by agencies such as the police or child protection may take the timing and decision making out of the woman's hands and over-ride her safety planning. An important part of safety planning involves thinking through the likely responses of agencies if they become involved and incorporating these in safety planning. This highlights the important point that the social worker or advocate cannot work alone to increase the safety of women and children, but must work within a multi-agency context. Nor is counselling or casework alone sufficient: advocacy is a core component of practice with women. These two specific aspects of work with domestic violence are discussed next.

Working in Multi-agency and Legal Contexts

The work with women and children in the context of domestic violence must also involve systemic advocacy, which 'aims to redress the barriers, disadvantage or discrimination experienced by women or children' (Grealy et al., 2008: 35). Systemic advocacy is essential because services are not always adequately responsive, and this can jeopardize the safety and well-being of women and their children. There is a strong evidence base that work with women which involves advocacy to increase women's access to services and resources has long-term effects on both the safety of women and children and on women's mental health (Allen et al., 2004; Howarth et al., 2009; Sullivan and Bybee, 1999).

In addition to case-by-case advocacy, good practice also involves policy advocacy. Social workers and others who recognize persistent systemic failures or gaps can use the knowledge gained from working with individual women to work for broader policy change. For example, we discussed in Chapter 3 how recognition by advocates of the injustice of women and children becoming homeless to escape domestic violence has led to policy initiatives to support women and children to remain in their own homes where this can be done safely.

Practice with individual women and their children needs to be embedded in a network of services that can respond to the complexity of domestic violence, including, for example, police, courts, health, housing, child protection, family support, immigration, alcohol and other drug (AOD) and income support services. Some multi-agency arrangements specifically co-ordinate risk assessment and safety planning in high-risk situations, such as the Multi-agency Risk Assessment Conferences (MARACs) in the United Kingdom (Robinson, 2006). Increasingly, governments are taking up the challenge of promoting integrated responses through strategic efforts (e.g. developing national and state plans that involve all agencies with endorsement at the leadership level), and service-level integration through protocols that formalize agreements on how agencies will work together, based on shared definitions of domestic violence, agreed principles and arrangements for sharing information. Approaches to multi-agency work are discussed in detail in Chapter 7.

Accurate documentation of women's experiences of domestic violence is crucial because the protection of women and children may well depend on the availability of evidence of their victimization. Women dealing with domestic violence are often involved with multiple legal systems – civil, criminal, child protection, Family Law – in which protective action depends on the availability of evidence. This is discussed in more detail in Chapter 3.

Strengthening the Mother–Child Relationship

One of the most devastating tactics of power and control employed by perpetrators of domestic violence is the deliberate targeting of the woman's mothering (Bancroft and Silverman, 2002; Radford and Hester, 2006). These tactics include a range of behaviours that undermine the woman's mothering and damage the mother–child relationship, such as contradicting the mother's rules, rewarding children's disrespectful behaviour towards her, denigrating her as a mother and in some cases, directly involving children in the abuse (Bancroft and Silverman, 2002; Irwin et al., 2002). Domestic violence during infancy can also affect the child's development through disruption of the mother–child attachment process (Buchanan, 2008). These are very significant effects of domestic violence, and it has been argued that strengthening or recovering the mother–child relationship should be a priority of post-crisis work (Humphreys et al., 2011), particularly when the evidence base through a control trial suggests that this approach is significantly more effective than individualized work with women or children (Lieberman et al., 2006). While some examples of this type of practice are emerging, the historical separation between services for women and for children creates challenges for workers and organizations to develop new practices that address the impacts of domestic violence on mother–child relationships. Social workers with understanding of the importance of this work in different settings can advocate for reshaping services so that this aspect of recovery from violence is not neglected.

Some Current Approaches to Intervention

In this section, we briefly describe some frameworks for counselling practice with women that can be useful in the post-crisis stage. Each of them is characterized by: their attention to social justice in recognizing that women's difficulties are a response to their victimization, rather than a reflection of individual pathology; the capacity to incorporate broader social factors into the work with individual women; attention to the power relationships between the woman and social workers; a collaborative partnership with women; and a focus on safety.

Attention to Trauma

A trauma framework provides a way of understanding and responding to the longer-term mental health impacts of domestic violence while maintaining the social justice and advocacy focus that underpins good practice in this field (Warshaw et al., 2003).

From this perspective, problems such as dissociation or numbing and reliving the trauma through flashbacks and nightmares can be understood as the effects of abuse rather than as manifestations of women's internal psychological problems.

Initially, the concept of trauma developed in psychiatry as a way of understanding the impacts of 'acts of nature' such as floods or earthquakes, events that were catastrophic, terrifying and that overwhelmed people's usual coping capacities. It was then applied to understand the experiences of war veterans and torture victims and subsequently, influenced largely through the work of Judith Herman (1992), has been applied to understanding the traumatic effects of abuse that occurs in the 'domestic sphere': that is, abuse of children and of women by intimate partners. More recently, children's exposure to domestic violence has also been conceptualized within a trauma framework (Van Horn and Groves, 2006).

Herman outlines a three-stage model of therapy with women based on the three unfolding stages of 'recovering safety, reconstructing the trauma story, and restoring connection between the survivors and the community' (1992: 3). She pays particular attention to the relationship between the therapist and the woman, in which the inherent power imbalance is acknowledged and the importance of an empowering approach is identified: 'No intervention that takes power away from the survivor can possibly foster her recovery, no matter how much it appears in her immediate best interest' (1992: 133).

Clearly a trauma framework offers much strength to underpin counselling with women post the crisis stage of intervention. It recognizes that healing from trauma can only occur when safety has been established. It also offers the woman validation, the cornerstone of healing, through the process of naming and acknowledging that she has suffered harm. This validation is a powerful beginning to the survivor feeling reconnected with others, when the abuser has fostered isolation. It also speaks to the issue of responsibility for the abuse, acknowledging the accountability of the perpetrator and in this way reducing the guilt and self-blame that can be legacies of abuse. The growing field of trauma studies also provides counsellors with a range of techniques for working with women to reduce the traumatic symptoms that can otherwise undermine their well-being and impede their capacity to rebuild their lives.

However, it is important to keep in mind that trauma inflicted in domestic contexts is different from other types of traumatic experiences. It is commonly an ongoing situation of abuse rather than a circumscribed, traumatic event, the latter having shaped the development of the psychiatric diagnostic category of post-traumatic stress disorder (PTSD). In recognition of this, Herman proposed a new diagnostic concept – 'complex post-traumatic stress disorder' – to more accurately capture the experience of those exposed to prolonged, repeated trauma, but this is less widely recognized than the diagnosis of PTSD.

Importantly, the trauma arising from domestic violence is inflicted by someone from whom the victim expects love and care, a confusing betrayal which can lead to women having mixed feelings about the perpetrator since the abuse often does not comprise the entirety of their relationship. This confusion and mixed loyalties can be felt even more strongly by children who may have strong attachment to the perpetrator and who may well have been shielded from experiencing the full effects of the violence by their mothers. This is a dynamic that is absent in work with survivors of most other forms of trauma. In addition, women and children are frequently required to have ongoing contact with the perpetrator of abuse through contact arrangements, potentially subjecting them to ongoing re-traumatization. This means that in many situations, the foundation of safety is not in place and the assistance that children require to heal from trauma cannot be safely offered (Cooley and Frazer, 2006).

Women who have experienced this form of trauma are also more likely than those who have experienced other types of traumatic events to experience negative and victim-blaming attitudes from service providers, in a process that is referred to as 'secondary' victimization. Activities such as community education campaigns that inform the community about the nature and prevalence of violence against women and children form an essential part of prevention activities since they can reduce this type of harm. Indeed, Judith Herman argues that it is only possible to believe, support and assist victims of gender-based violence in the context of a strong social movement that names and condemns all forms of violence against women and children. Engaging with this movement (e.g. through participation in activities such as 'Reclaim the Night' and the White Ribbon campaign) is consistent with social work's commitment to promoting social justice and human rights.

Despite the potential benefits of a trauma framework for informing work with women, some argue that the use of any mental health framework risks pathologizing women and has the potential to create further injustice; for example, by disadvantaging women in Family Law matters or by echoing messages by the perpetrator that she is, in fact, 'crazy'. This reinforces the importance of critical reflection by social workers on their practice to identify the underlying assumptions about women and about violence and abuse and to test the ways in which these fit (or not) with the principles for working with women that have been outlined earlier in this chapter.

Group Work

Group work has been a preferred form of intervention both historically, with roots in feminist activism, and currently because it provides a powerful antidote to the isolation experienced by women as a result of the perpetrator's tactics, inappropriate service responses, fear and shame. Participation in a group can powerfully counteract notions that an individual woman is 'sick', 'mad' or responsible for the abuse because she sees that the problem is not hers alone but is shared by other women in the group and beyond. As a forum in which women are encouraged to share experiences, information and resources, the group is a potentially powerful medium through which women can recognize and reclaim their strengths. For some women who have participated in support groups, the group becomes a springboard to taking up an activist role to educate the community about domestic violence and to advocate for better systemic responses (Hester and Westmarland, 2005).

This approach to group work is effective because it is grounded in belief in women's strengths and acknowledges that they have developed unique expertise in understanding domestic violence because of their lived experience. It has a strong social justice agenda and links the experiences of the individual participants with the wider political issues of gender and other social inequalities. However, the use of groups per se does not necessarily constitute empowering practice. For example, if the focus is on the characteristics of women which are deemed in need of change (such as 'passivity' or 'co-dependency'), removed from a context that acknowledges the responsibility of the perpetrator for the abuse and the social conditions of inequality that enable the abuse of power with intimate relationships, it is unlikely to be experienced as empowering and could reinforce unjust notions of the woman's pathology and culpability.

A more recent development is the use of group work as an approach to strengthening the mother–child relationship in the aftermath of domestic violence (Humphreys et al., 2011). In particular, the use of parallel groups for children and women provides both separate spaces and linked agendas for mothers and their children in the aftermath of domestic violence (Bunston and Heynatz, 2006; Loosely et al., 2006). The randomized control trial by Sandra Graham-Bermann and her colleagues (2007) demonstrated significant effects in recovery for children and their mothers through group work relative to other individualized interventions.

In contrast to approaches to the issues that women may have in parenting after domestic violence which assume that women are deficient in 'parenting skills', this group work approach draws on the evidence base that identifies the many ways in which domestic violence constitutes an attack on the mother–child relationship. It encourages workers and agencies to step aside from traditional, separate modes of service delivery to women and children and challenges the patterns of secrecy that are common between mothers and children who have lived through traumatic abuse. It builds on the consistent research finding that children identify their mother as the most important source of assistance when living with domestic violence.

Narrative Approaches

Narrative approaches to therapy use a text or story metaphor to explore the ways in which meaning is ascribed to lived experience (White, 2007; White and Epston, 1989). Narrative questions are framed to explore the effects of 'problem-saturated' stories on people's lives and relationships and to explore un-storied, alternative and preferred directions for their lives and relationships. Problems are 'externalized' so that the person can explore the effects of the problem on their lives and relationships, with the problem, rather than the person, becoming the problem. For example, while some therapies might talk about a person having 'low self-esteem', as though this is an intrinsic aspect of the person, narrative approaches might explore the ways in which a person has developed 'habits of self-doubt' or who has coached or encouraged these habits, and explore the ways in which this habit has affected the person's life and relationships. The therapist works with the person to identify those occasions in which the problem has not completely overtaken them. These experiences, or 'unique outcomes', often unnoticed and un-storied, become the starting point for a complex process of 're-authoring conversations'. This is not a case of merely pointing out the person's strengths in the face of adversity, but an exploration of previously un-storied experiences and their meanings for the person's future life and relationships.

This approach can clearly be beneficial in working with women on the effects of having lived with domestic violence. Issues such as guilt and self-blame and the effects of these on the woman can be explored, including the ways in which they have shaped her view of herself and her ideas about the future. Questions about the contexts that have contributed to the influence of these problems in her life can expose the role of the perpetrator in co-authoring a story of the woman as deficient and responsible for the abuse that she has suffered. Narrative approaches have also been used to assist women and their children to re-story their relationships in new and preferred directions following the damage and division inflicted by an abuser.

Narrative approaches also address the isolation, which is a common outcome of many problems, through the use of carefully selected audiences. People who have dealt with similar problems are invited to participate as 'outsider witnesses' to therapy sessions. This does not involve their evaluation of the person's progress in dealing with the problem, nor the mutual sharing of experiences. Rather, the outsider witness is an audience to the therapy session and is then interviewed by the therapist about the aspects of the person's story that had salience for them, or that resonated with their own experience, or that were particularly emotionally moving (White, 2007). This aspect of narrative practice is a powerful way of deepening alternate stories and is very relevant to domestic violence practice because of the importance of women reconnecting with others and with their own capacities and strengths.

Narrative therapy developed in the era when the prevalence of gender-based violence had been established. It therefore acknowledges the gross abuses of power to which women can be subjected through the perpetrator's tactics of control, violence and denigration. Hence violence and abuse themselves are never 'externalized', only their effects. In addition, narrative therapy draws on postmodern understandings of power to assist women to explore the socio-political contexts relevant to experiences of abuse and trauma. Through a lens that understands the operations of power through dominant discourses that establish 'normalizing truths' (White and Epston, 1989: 26), against which all women are encouraged to judge themselves, questions can be asked that assist women to challenge these. An example is the gendered discourse that women are primarily responsible for the well-being of families and relationships, and hence are culpable when these relationships 'fail'. The capacity to deconstruct dominant discourses is not limited to those associated with gender but includes discourses associated with contexts of colonization and all forms of discrimination (Tamasese, 2003).

A key concept in understandings of power as enacted through normalizing discourses is that it is never total: that is, there are always points of resistance. This enables narrative approaches to tackle the women's co-existing agency and oppression in situations of domestic violence. From this perspective, a narrative therapist would operate on the assumption that, however severe the domination and abuse to which a woman has been subjected, in some ways she has resisted total domination.

These aspects of lived experience that lie outside the dominant story of the woman as a victim represent the beginning of an alternative story about the woman, her capacities, and about the possibilities for a different future that narrative questions can enable her to explore.

Readiness for Change

Motivational counselling and 'readiness to change' approaches are pervasive in counselling practice. These are based on the transtheoretical model of behaviour change (Pochaska and DiClemente, 1983) that identifies a number of common cognitive and behavioural 'processes of change' which individuals employ to move through five stages of change: pre-contemplation, contemplation, preparation, action and maintenance. It has been suggested as a potentially useful approach to working with women dealing with domestic violence.

This approach was developed to understand the process of change for individuals (e.g. in efforts to stop smoking). However, women living with violence are acting in a relational context in which the perpetrator rather than the woman has the issue requiring change. Given the unpredictability of the perpetrator and the unique combination of tactics that he may employ to impose coercive control, there are no common behaviours of the woman that can be targeted for change (Chang et al., 2006). The research cited earlier has identified the many and varied protective strategies that women employ, depending on the context, and attest that no strategy is universally effective. Research by Chang et al. (2006) with women in the health system found that women's experiences and behaviours were more complex and less linear than suggested by the transtheoretical model. Some stages were missed altogether, for example, in response to life-threatening violence. Factors external to the woman's motivation to change also impacted on movement between stages, such as the abuser's behaviour, the type of response received from formal and informal supports and life stressors such as pregnancy and financial worries. In responding to domestic violence, a broader model of 'psycho-social readiness' (Hegarty et al., 2008) has been proposed as better able to incorporate the intersection of internal and external factors that influence the change process, which were represented graphically in Figure 4.1.

> Making negative judgements of women who do not accept 'solutions' may close off possible sources of assistance to the woman at a later time.

The concept of a continuum of readiness for change can also be applied to the process of change in service responses to domestic violence. For example, the research by Humphreys et al. (2011) into the challenges of overcoming the traditional boundaries between women's and children's services in response to the evidence base about the harm caused by domestic violence to the mother-child relationship, highlights that organizations and workers are significant aspects of the change context. Reflective practice needs to take into account the readiness to change of the service environment rather than focusing solely on the woman. In the area of disability, a matrix for a policy and practice audit has been developed (Healey et al., 2013). The matrix identifies eight different areas of practice and policy development which mainstream agencies need to address in order to respond sensitively to women with disabilities. This provides a tool which social workers can use to authorize and support practice change in their organizations.

Conclusion

It is sobering that a significant proportion of women report that they received no help, given the severe threat to women and children's safety that typically propels women's help-seeking. As outlined in this chapter, an effective social work response to Madeline needs to offer belief; an approach to risk assessment and safety planning that acknowledges and builds on her existing protective strategies for herself and her daughter; accurate information about services and resources; and willingness to advocate within a multi-agency context.

Summary Points

- Attention to the social, political and cultural contexts of women's experiences of domestic violence has framed effective work with women, both historically and currently.
- Group work and more recently parallel groups for women and children are both a preferred and an effective form of intervention.
- Practice that recognizes agency and victimization as well as the complexities/intersectionality of women's lives ensures that woman-centred practice leads the intervention.
- The knowledge base highlights ways in which aspects of practice with domestic violence differs from counselling and casework in other contexts.
- Practice will be characterized by an emphasis on: safety planning, risk assessment and risk management; advocacy; multi-agency working; strengthening the mother–child relationship; and attention to case recording and documentation.
- Counselling approaches that can incorporate these elements include: attention to trauma; narrative therapy; and 'readiness to change' models.

Reflective Questions for Practice

Think back to the vignette about Madeline at the opening of the chapter. If you were the hospital social worker to whom Madeline was referred:

- What factors might Madeline be weighing up in her decision about what to tell the social worker?
- How might the tactics of abuse used by her partner be shaping her view of her situation and the possibilities for action?
- In what ways could the social worker explore the protective strategies that Madeline is already employing to keep herself and her daughter as safe as she can?
- What systemic barriers could be explored with Madeline which might affect her decisions?
- In what ways might her thinking about her daughter affect her decision making?

Further Reading

Davies, J., Lyon, E., and Monti-Catania, D. (1998) *Safety Planning with Battered Women: Complex Lives/Difficult Choices.* Thousand Oaks, CA: Sage.

This is a classic text that makes the connection between safety planning and risk assessment in nuanced and rich ways.

Breckenridge, J. and James, K. (2010). Thinking about homicide risk: a practice framework for counselling. *Stakeholder Paper 9.* Australian Domestic and Family Violence Clearinghouse. Available from www.adfvc.unsw.edu.au/PDF%20files/Stakeholder%20Paper_9.pdf.

This provides a multi-systemic practice framework for generalist counselling agencies to aid in identifying and responding to safety issues for women who present with a range of presenting issues but who may be experiencing domestic violence.

Grealy, C., Humphreys, C., Milward, K. and Power, J. (2008). *Urbis, Practice Guidelines: Women and Children's Family Violence Counselling and Support Programme.* Victoria: Department of Human Services. Available from

(Continued)

(Continued)

www.cyf.vic.gov.au/__data/assets/pdf_file/0005/238550/practice-guidelines-women-and-children-fv-counsell-support.pdf.

These provide a clear framework for organizations, managers and workers to inform working with women and their children where domestic violence is an issue.

Thiara, R. K., Hague, G., Ellis, B., Bashall, R., and Mullender, A. (2012) *Disabled Women and Domestic Violence: Responding to the Experiences of Survivors.* London: Jessica Kingsley.

This book is an important addition to the knowledge base for domestic violence which centralizes the issues for disabled women.

5

Children and Domestic Violence: Complexities in Responding to the Statutory Duty to Protect

Child protection systems everywhere are overwhelmed with referrals. A major factor in these referrals is the shift by the police to notify statutory children's services when attending a domestic violence incident where there are children. The data from both England and Australia shows that there is a lower rate of investigation and assessment of these referrals than for other categories of abuse and neglect, but a higher rate of re-notification due to further incidents of domestic violence. A major Australian Inquiry in New South Wales in 2007–08 showed that of 76,000 reports where a risk of harm from domestic violence was the primary reported issue, only 5000 (6.5 per cent) were substantiated and this did not necessarily result in the family receiving a service (Wood, 2008). A major question arises about how to provide a more proactive and appropriate response to children living with domestic violence.

In every sector where there are vulnerable children there will be domestic violence. It is therefore an issue for social workers in mental health services, family services, social work hospital services, drug and alcohol services, disability services, specialist services for Aboriginal and Black and minority ethnic families, and housing services. While framing this chapter around the specific issues for safeguarding or child protection services, the issues more generally for social work should not be overlooked.

This chapter will provide a brief canter around **the evidence base that places children living with domestic violence onto the child protection agenda** and will then explore three key policy and practice **issues for child protection workers: the problems of mandatory reporting** or widespread referral of children living with domestic violence to child protection; **the problems of the 'failure to protect' lens**; and the issue of **post-separation violence and abuse**. Finally, the **directions for more progressive work** in this area will be explored.

The most contentious area for social work practice lies in the interface between statutory child protection and domestic violence. Paradoxically, it is both a very old area of intervention by voluntary sector organizations concerned for children (see Gordon, 1988) as well as a relatively new arena for state child protection, surfacing onto the agenda in about 1994 with new books and articles (Abrahams, 1994; Mullender and Morley, 1994). Addressing the issues in child protection will also have ramifications for social work intervention in other service sectors.

The context for the chapter is set by engaging with some confronting findings from England which contrast the results of two different approaches to attending to the safety and well-being of children living with domestic violence.

The first is drawn from a study by Stanley et al. (2011b). This study involved several stages of research including a retrospective review of police and children's social work services records that tracked a cohort of 251 incidents of domestic violence cases over 21 months. In the sample, injuries to adults and children were recorded in just under one-third of incidents. The study found that the notification system acted to draw a large number of families who had had no or little previous contact with children's social workers to the attention of children's services. However, only a small proportion of families notified received a service from children's social workers and most of these were already open cases. Police notifications triggered an intervention at the level of an initial assessment from children's services in only 5 per cent of cases. A high rate of repeat notifications indicated that domestic violence continued to be an issue in these families. Where families did receive interventions, it was likely to be at the safeguarding rather than family support level (Stanley et al., 2011a). The NSW study outlined in the opening scenario showed similar findings with these children less likely to be investigated but much more likely to be re-notified (Wood, 2008). These findings were consistent with those from an earlier study in NSW when exposure to domestic violence became grounds for mandatory notification to the statutory child protection service (Irwin and Waugh, 2007; Irwin et al., 2002).

The second English study evaluates the impact of providing an intensive case management service by Independent Domestic Violence Advisors (IDVAs) to women who were seriously affected by domestic violence (Howarth et al., 2009). The study followed 2500 women with 3600 children over a two-year period. Only women experiencing serious domestic violence were offered the service. It found that women with children experienced more severe abuse than those without children. The findings showed clearly that attention to the safety of women also impacted children's safety: direct threats to children's safety between Time 1 (at intake) and Time 2 (4 months later or at case closure) markedly decreased; conflict around child contact improved by 45 per cent; victim fear of harm to children improved by 76 per cent; and perpetrators' threats to kill children changed by 44 per cent.

The two studies, one with a statutory child protection focus and one with a focus on an independent service for women experiencing serious domestic violence, suggest, paradoxically, that the service that focused on women's safety had a greater impact on children's safety than the service which was actually set up to attend to children's safety or safeguarding issues. These studies set the context for the exploration of the interface between child protection and domestic violence. Their findings challenge notions of how best to protect children and raise many questions about our current approaches to intervention.

The Evidence Base: Domestic Violence and Child Abuse

It is unsurprising that children living with domestic violence have surfaced as an area for child protection concern. The prevalence of children living with domestic violence, the links to physical abuse, sexual abuse and child homicide, and the negative impact on children's safety and development provide a convincing rationale for concern. This well established knowledge base needs to be held up against the more recent data on resilience and the countervailing data on poly-victimization and cumulative harm.

The Prevalence Data

The most significant challenge in responding to children and young people affected by domestic violence lies in recognizing that this is a widespread, chronic and serious social problem. It is worth casting back to the introductory chapters to revisit the data. The numbers are alarmingly high. While prevalence and crime surveys are not consistent in the way that they respectively define and ask about experiences of domestic violence, when taken together they reveal a pattern of gender-based violence in which large numbers of children are also embroiled as victims of abuse.

As discussed in Chapter 2, large-scale surveys in Canada (Johnson, 2006), the United States (Tjaden and Thoennes, 2000) and Australia (Australian Bureau of Statistics, 1996, 2005; Mouzos and Makkai, 2004) reveal rates of domestic violence which cluster around one in four or one in five women victimized across a lifetime. Based on the British Crime Survey of 23,463 men and women (Walby and Allen, 2004), the Department of Health estimated that at least 750,000 children in England and Wales were living with domestic abuse (Department of Health, 2002), while an English national prevalence study of 2869 young adults indicated that 26 per cent had witnessed violence between their parents at least once, and for 5 per cent the violence was frequent and ongoing (Cawson, 2002). These figures reflect closely the Australian population-based study of 5000 young Australians which showed that 25 per cent reported witnessing violence against a parent (Indermaur, 2001).

Taken together, the empirical data continue to show that domestic violence is widespread. However, a dominant gendered pattern is most graphically established through examining the issues of frequency, injury and living in fear (Walby and Allen, 2004). A gendered pattern emerges in which male violence to women is the dominant though not exclusive pattern. This pattern is significant for workers in the child protection context who have been consistently criticized for failing to grasp the gendered nature of domestic violence and the consequence that effective intervention will need to respond to both an adult and a child victim.

The Co-occurrence of Abuse

Children's safety and well-being is rarely threatened by one form of abuse. Children's experiences of living with domestic violence are compounded by the increased vulnerability to many forms of abuse which heighten the concerns about the risks for children living with domestic violence.

Initially, in drawing attention to the connection between domestic violence and child abuse, the destructive impact of children 'witnessing' domestic violence was highlighted. However, there are problems which arise from drawing 'false' distinctions between exposure to or witnessing domestic abuse and direct abuse, rather than responding holistically to the child's experience (Edleson et al., 2003; Mullender et al., 2002). Research is now showing that children are involved in myriad ways when they live with domestic abuse. For instance, they may be used as hostages (Ganley and Schechter, 1996); they may be in their mother's arms when an assault occurs (Mullender et al., 2002); they may be involved in defending their mothers (Edleson et al., 2003). Describing this range of violent experiences as 'witnessing' fails to capture the extent to which children may become embroiled in domestic abuse (Goddard and Bedi, 2010; Irwin and Waugh, 2007).

Children living with domestic abuse are also more likely to be directly physically or sexually abused. The early meta-analysis by Edleson (1999a) of 31 high-quality research studies showed that between 30 per cent and 66 per cent of children who suffer physical abuse are also living with domestic abuse. The variation is largely dependent upon research site and methodology. It is an association which continues to emerge with later studies (Osofsky, 2003; Zanoti-Jeronymo, 2009). The severity of violence is also relevant though somewhat equivocal about the impact on children. Ross (1996), for example, found in an American study of 3363 parents that there was an almost 100 per cent correlation between the most severe abuse of women and the men's physical abuse of children. Other studies also indicate this trend: the more severe the violence towards the child's mother, the higher the risk of the domestic violence offender physically abusing the child (Hartley, 2004; O'Keefe, 1995). In tandem, with these studies, though contested (Holden et al., 1998; Mullender et al., 2002; Radford and Hester, 2006) is that it is not only men who are more physically abusive to children, but the more severely victimized mother may be more prone to physically abusing the children as well (Hartley, 2004; Kelleher et al., 2008). The data is clearly drawn from different studies and suggests that social workers need to be vigilant in their assessments of the child abuse issues when they are aware that the level of violence is severe and chronic.

Studies of child sexual abuse are less common, as discussed in an overview by Holt et al. (2008). However, clear evidence is emerging that between 40 and 70 per cent of child sexual abuse occurs against a backdrop of fear created through domestic abuse (Farmer and Pollock, 1998; Hester and Pearson, 1998; Kellogg and Menard, 2003; McCloskey et al., 1995). The study by Hester and Pearson (1998) drew attention to the fact that the rate depended markedly on whether mothers of sexually abused children or their children were systematically asked about domestic violence. In their sample at a specialist counselling centre for children who had generally (but not exclusively) suffered child sexual abuse, the rate shifted from one-third of cases where there was co-occurrence of child abuse and domestic violence to two-thirds of cases once systematic assessment (screening) for domestic violence occurred. In an area prone to secrecy, such findings throw into question much of the data about co-occurrence and prevalence, particularly in studies based on data mining case files and administrative data from child protection services. It is also a finding that directs social workers to sensitively explore the issue of domestic violence and never assume that it is not present.

> When issues of child abuse are evident ask sensitively about the presence of domestic violence, and when domestic violence is present ask about the issues of child abuse.

Other issues are now emerging about the co-occurrence between domestic violence and other forms of child abuse. Hartley (2004) points out that the co-occurrence of domestic violence and neglect has been overlooked. Her study drew attention to the fact that the more severe the violence, the greater the lack of supervision and neglect of children in the family. She raises the issue that it is usually mothers rather than fathers who are held responsible by child protection workers for neglect of children, and there are problems with understanding the exact nature of the overlap when drawing such an association from quantitative data.

While constructed as neglect in the child protection data, other studies have drawn attention to the way in which domestic violence directed at the child's mother is a direct and indirect attack on the mother–child relationship, effectively disabling the mother (Humphreys et al., 2006; Radford and Hester, 2006). Both mothering and fathering may be compromised by domestic violence. When women are traumatized by their own abuse, suffering from depression and post-traumatic stress, they may be less available to their children and attachment relationships may be compromised, particularly with infants and toddlers (Levendosky et al., 2003; Osofsky, 2003). The relative lack of attention to the impact on fathering when men are domestically violent is an emerging research gap (Guille, 2004).

Their lack of impulse control, inability to understand the impact of their violence, and their modelling of physical abuse and threat as means of negotiating conflict are emerging as issues of grave concern (Bancroft and Silverman, 2002; Margolin et al., 2003).

The evidence on co-occurrence of different forms of child abuse and neglect where there is domestic violence suggests that there needs to be a move away from 'silos' created by different categories of child abuse and neglect. More recent work by Finkelhor et al. (2009a) suggests that there is a group of vulnerable children who live in environments in which poly-victimization is prevalent and where certain forms of abuse such as child sexual abuse and domestic violence markedly increase the risks that they will be involved in other forms of violence and abuse. The literature on poly-victimization shows a linear relationship between the number of childhood adversities (domestic violence, peer bullying, property crime, child physical and sexual abuse) and the level of adverse outcomes for children (Finkelhor et al., 2009b: 404). Domestic violence leads to the largest increase in lifetime victimization scores for children under 18, though issues such as child sexual abuse are weighted more heavily in terms of their impact on the child's future emotional well-being.

At its most extreme, children (Jaffe and Juodis, 2006; O'Hara, 1994) or their mothers (Hendricks et al., 1993) may be killed. Child death reviews of children known to child protection services consistently indicate that domestic violence is a factor in a high proportion of cases, often in conjunction with other parental problems such as mental health or substance use issues (Brandon et al., 2008a). It may also occur in the context of separation and divorce in which children are murdered as part of retaliation towards the child's mother or as part of murder/suicide, most commonly though not exclusively of men and their children (Kirkwood, 2012). Frequently this is in the context of previous domestic and post-separation violence (Saunders, 2004).

The Impact and Resilience Issues for Children Living with Domestic Violence

It is now evident that there is a group of children living with domestic abuse who may be at risk of significant harm (Holt et al., 2008). Throughout the 1990s, these risks to the well-being of children living with domestic abuse began to be documented and a comprehensive body of knowledge started to develop with substantial overviews provided in the United Kingdom (Hester et al., 2006), Canada (Ministry of Children and Family Development, 2010) and Australia (Laing, 2000). While there are some inconsistencies in the evidence, the research shows that children living with domestic abuse have much higher rates of depression and anxiety (McCloskey et al., 1995) and trauma symptoms (Graham-Bermann and Levendosky, 1998). While emotional problems are significant, data from a large UK study suggests that of more significance are behavioural problems (conduct disorders), which are three times more likely to occur for children living with severe domestic violence (Meltzer et al., 2009).

While some studies show that children who are directly abused are more likely to show more severe impacts on their health and well-being (Carlson, 2000; Crockenberg and Langrock, 2001; Edleson, 1999a; Hughes et al., 2001), other research shows little difference between witnessing domestic abuse and actual abuse (Mertin and Mohr, 2000). In this latter study, the experiences of 56 children living with domestic abuse were divided according to children witnessing abuse; being involved in the violence; and being a target of the violence. Little differentiation was found. Perhaps the most substantial evidence is provided by the meta-analysis of 118 studies by Kitzmann et al. (2003), which evaluated the psychosocial outcomes of children living with domestic abuse. It showed significantly poorer outcomes on 21 developmental and behavioural dimensions for children witnessing domestic abuse than those not witnessing abuse. However, the witness outcomes were similar to those where children were also directly physically abused.

Other research shows that problems for children can compound over time as they live with the multiple problems associated with the destructive effects of domestic abuse. A summary is provided by Rossman:

> Exposure at any age can create disruptions that can interfere with the accomplishment of developmental tasks, and early exposure may create more severe disruptions by affecting the subsequent chain of developmental tasks. (2001: 58)

The impact on children at different developmental stages shows the broad range of ways in which children react to their environments. Babies living with domestic abuse are subject to high levels of ill health, poor sleeping habits and excessive screaming (Jaffe et al., 1990) and disrupted attachment patterns (Quinlivan and Evans, 2005). While children of pre-school age tend to be the group who show the most behavioural disturbance (McFarlane et al., 2003), older children and young people are more likely to show the effects of disruption in their school and social environments, particularly if they are the ones who are constantly 'on the move' (Mullender et al., 2002).

An approach which takes into account developmental stage and vulnerability is compatible with the emerging evidence on the interaction between the child's environment and their neurological development (Teicher, 2002). This research draws attention to the vulnerability of babies in utero and infants to the effects of trauma. Potent chemicals are released in the brain as a response to fear, which creates an over-active stress response. This over-arousal interferes with the development of other parts of the brain that mediate the development of more reflective emotional responses (Schore, 2003). It is important to note that, in spite of these early biological effects, these 'baby' studies also suggest that development is recoverable with early intervention in which babies are no longer in such a stressful environment (Perry, 1997).

The evidence of the negative effects of living with domestic violence can seem overwhelming. However, within the evidence base, studies are emerging that also highlight children who are doing as well as other children in spite of living with the serious childhood adversity created by domestic abuse. Sometimes this is referred to as 'resilience' (Margolin and Gordis, 2004). Such terminology suggests an individual trait and hides rather than elucidates the fact that children live in different contexts of both severity and protection. Laing (2000) in her overview of research draws particular attention to the incomplete state of our knowledge of protective contexts for children. Higher rates of distress shown across a range of clinical measures should not be conflated with the notion that *all* children show these elevated levels of emotional distress and behavioural disturbance. It highlights the maxim that 'correlation is not causation' (Magen, 1999: 130).

The point is exemplified by research that shows that in any sample of children exposed to domestic violence there are generally about 50 per cent who do as well as the control group (Edleson, 2004; Magen, 1999). This is a slightly different proportion from Kitzmann et al. (2003) who, in a meta-analysis of 118 studies, showed 63 per cent of children witnessing violence doing worse than those who do not witness violence, but 37 per cent whose well-being is comparable or better than other children'. The study by Hughes and Luke (1998) of 58 mothers living in a refuge showed 26 per cent of children with few behavioural problems, high levels of self-esteem and no anxiety recorded. There was also a group (36 per cent) who had mild anxiety symptoms and above average self-esteem. Other research studies point to similar findings (Hughes et al., 2001; Margolin and Gordis, 2004; Sullivan et al., 2000).

This research data seriously challenges over-pathologizing all children living with domestic violence. There is a substantial proportion of children who are managing in a situation of adversity. This *must not be read* to mean that children do not have a right to live free from violence or need a service in these circumstances. However, it does raise questions about whether all children need a statutory referral.

There are many factors which moderate the risks and experiences of children. Children will be affected by the severity of violence with which they are living and for a particular group of children, whether they are being directly abused (Edleson, 1999a), as well as by the extent to which their needs have been neglected (Hartley, 2004). 'Resilience' may be strongly influenced by the level of family and community support which children experience, and this factor is particularly evident for Black and minority ethnic children who potentially (but not always) draw on a wider range of extended family and community relationships (Blagg et al., 2000; Mullender et al., 2002).

A number of studies point to the mother's mental health as a source of resilience for children (Moore and Pepler, 1998). For example, an overview of three studies of children's resilience when living with domestic abuse showed that the children of women who did not experience moderate or severe depressive symptoms showed much fewer emotional problems (Hughes et al., 2001). However, it may be that it is the severity of men's violence which is the intervening variable, not the mother's mental health. Both women and children will be impacted in similar ways by the severity of violence and hence both the women's mental health as well as the children's will be affected (Sullivan et al., 2000).

Like their mothers (Radford and Hester, 2006), many children will recover their competence and behavioural functioning once they are in a safer, more secure environment (Mertin and Mohr, 2000) and with support have even proved to be effective social and political actors in securing resources for similarly affected children and young people (Houghton, 2006). In particular, children who are not continually subjected to post-separation violence (Mathias et al., 1995) and protracted court cases over child contact (Buchanan et al., 2001) show a much stronger pattern of recovery.

Issues for Child Protection Workers

The complex link between children, domestic violence and child abuse has thrown up an equally complex series of problems for appropriate intervention. Simply 'adding' domestic violence as an issue of child abuse to the current intervention model is generally proving to be unsuccessful. New thinking, or at least the development of strategies which are on the margins shifting to the centre of practice, may be required. We have chosen to briefly raise three issues of concern in the current practice and policy response.

The Problems of Mandatory Reporting

This chapter began by looking at the data from studies which tracked child protection referrals that arose from police attendance at domestic violence incidents in England (Stanley et al., 2011b) and Australia (Irwin and Waugh, 2007; Wood, 2008). The data highlighted the ineffectiveness of the response. Children living with domestic violence were less likely to be investigated by child protection workers but more likely to be re-notified. Very few families experienced enhanced services. The data from these smaller case tracking studies are also reflected in the broader notification data, which shows dramatic increases in notifications/referrals to statutory child protection services but little investigation or service response. An enquiry into its child protection system in one Australian state made the following finding:

> While introduced in Tasmania and elsewhere to increase the referral net for child protection referrals and improve child safety, mandatory reporting has had the unintended negative consequences of overloading the statutory system without necessarily improving child safety. (Jacob and Fanning, 2006: 59)

The costs of this shift in reporting have been raised both in Australia (Ainsworth and Hansen, 2006; Mendes, 1996) and in the United States (Edleson, 2004). The thought-provoking article by Edleson et al. (2006) draws on Minnesota as a case example. They point out that the changes to the Minnesota Reporting Act 1999 resulted in a 50 to 100 per cent increase in child protection reports for domestic violence exposure:

This seemingly simple and unfunded change in the law created the need for over $30 million in expanded services to newly identified families. The experience was so overwhelming for child protection agencies that the Minnesota Legislature repealed the change in April 2000. (2006: 8)

The Minnesota change points to the fact that the lack of resourcing to child protection agencies can have a further unintended consequence which contributes to only high-risk cases being provided with services, and that screening and investigation does not help to strengthen the families involved (Edleson, 2004). In fact, the response may undermine the help-seeking behaviour of women living with domestic violence who become concerned about state intervention and the loss of their children (Irwin and Waugh, 2007). Statutory intervention generally shifts the emphasis of work from services *for* families to investigation *of* families (Scott, 2006) as the National Society for the Prevention of Cruelty to Children (NSPCC) (Stanley et al., 2011b) and the NSW study (Irwin and Waugh, 2007) showed so graphically.

The research about both the impact and the resilience of children living with domestic violence suggests that practitioners need to be highly aware of the needs of children in these families. However, managing this highly prevalent social problem through increasing the notification of *all* children affected by domestic violence to the statutory child protection system raises serious questions about efficacy (can the system manage the notifications appropriately?), efficiency (is this the best use of resources?), effectiveness (are children safer?) and ethics (is 'net widening' ethically defensible when such a high proportion of these families are not investigated or abuse substantiated?). In other words, the functionality of the statutory child protection service to manage the weight of notifications of children living with domestic violence requires interrogation and new policy and practice development.

The 'Failure to Protect' Lens

The ethics of net widening, the cost, and the effectiveness of notification and investigation are not the only contentious issues when the statutory response to children affected by domestic violence is considered. Other issues also create difficulties in developing a sensitive child protection response as exemplified in a paper by Douglas and Walsh (2010) in which at least 10 different aspects of the unsatisfactory interface between child protection and its work with women and children living with domestic violence are discussed. The same stories, dominant patterns, tales of mistrust and poor practice are depressingly consistent with previous research in this area stretching back to Linda Gordon's examination of Boston child protection files in the 1860s (Gordon, 1988) through to more recent work (Holt, 2003; Lapierre, 2010; Stanley et al., 2010). They include: the failure of child protection workers to understand the gendered nature and the power and control issues at the heart of domestic violence; holding women living with domestic violence responsible for the protection of children rather than the perpetrator of violence; lack of education and training for child protection workers; providing inappropriate ultimatums to women to leave and keep their children or stay and lose their children; poor collaborative relationships; and an inability to grapple with the complex issues for Black and minority women (Humphreys and Absler, 2011). The repetitive nature of these themes points to the structured nature of the problems which clearly go beyond the intentions and practices of individual workers. It is therefore a sensitive area for child protection workers struggling to shift a century of organizational culture.

Perhaps the greatest problem is the failure to recognize and respond to the woman as a victim of domestic violence as well as a mother of children (Radford and Hester, 2006). Some would suggest that it is not the role of statutory child protection services to respond to adult victimization, but that the organizational remit is set through legislation and must, by definition, focus all attention on the child. The needs of adults are secondary. This is perhaps the nub of the problem and one of the structural issues which sits at the heart of the inadequate child protection response. By definition, domestic violence has both adult and child victims. A response which cannot respond equally to both will fall short. The same, of course, may be said of the community based domestic violence response which may privilege adult women over their children, though the long history of services for children associated with refuges and outreach services belies some of this criticism.

> The most effective way of creating safety for the child is usually to increase the safety of their mother. This will always require complex multi-agency work.

Nevertheless, this recognition of the child protection remit heightens the problems of mandatory reporting of children living with domestic violence to statutory child protection services. It is not an agency which has been established to intervene with an adult and child victim. To do so will always push the boundaries of the intervention response. The problem is compounded rather than alleviated by the positioning of child protection towards a forensic response of investigating and substantiating abuse (Scott, 2006). Victim support for either children or their mothers is not the primary focus even though it may be the primary need in the majority of cases.

Related to this issue is the longstanding focus of child protection intervention on women rather than men (Featherstone et al., 2010). While not all perpetrators of domestic violence are men, there is a very strong gendered pattern which highlights the significance of the intervention with men who are violent. It is not an area of expertise for most child protection workers in spite of its prevalence within their caseloads. It does require excellent collaboration with police; attention to the issues of violence against workers; knowledge of the laws that relate to domestic violence; and a capacity to engage men and their family networks about the impact of violence and abuse on both women and children (Wade, 2007). It is not an easy task. Without this focus, however, the slippage onto other issues that retain the focus on women as mothers rather than men as perpetrators of violence will remain and undermine the safety and well-being of children and their mothers (Humphreys and Stanley, 2006).

The issues of cumulative harm are also a significant aspect of the assessment of the issues for each child in the family (Bromfield and Miller, 2009; Finkelhor et al., 2009a). Understanding the range of abusive events and their impact on the child, alongside the range of protective factors involved, highlights the complexity of the lives of many children living with domestic violence. Many children are living with mothers and fathers who may also have substance use and mental health problems (Forrester and Harwin, 2006). They may also be impacted by neglect, sexual and physical abuse and other forms of violence outside the family which create fear and compromise their health and well-being. For children living in Black and minority ethnic communities these assessments may be particularly complex given the interplay of protection and harm, particularly where poverty and homelessness may undermine the family and community resources available.

In short, individual social workers may make a difference to the experience of women, children and men where there is child protection intervention. However, the organizational culture has not been well structured to work with both women and child victims, or to intervene with violent men. Significant policy and practice shifts are required to support major changes which would ensure a more sensitive response is consistently available.

Post-separation Violence and Abuse

The earlier discussion of the research findings on domestic violence and children highlights the problems attending a narrow focus on a siloed issue within a focus on the nuclear family. Children are no safer if separation allows ongoing and unsupervised access to violent fathers (Radford and Hester, 2006). Too many women are now finding themselves shifting from being designated as 'the failure to protect mother' to that of the 'alienating mother' (Laing, 2010). The children and the risks are the same or higher, but the legislative arena is different. The study by Stanley et al. (2011b) found that 50 per cent of the referrals to the statutory service were for post-separation violence: circumstances in which child protection traditionally takes little interest in spite of the dangers. This is, in fact, a system's problem.

Urging women to separate from violent men is totally ineffective, if not dangerous, unless careful planning to create a tight network of safety and support is provided alongside careful documentation which outlines the child protection concerns about the father and his violence. It is an arena in which careful investigation and assessment skills are required, as most violent fathers will argue that the mother is either as violent as he is or the instigator of the violence (Bancroft and Silverman, 2002; Jaffe et al., 2003b). While the evidence suggests that this may be true for a small minority of women, the gendered nature of domestic violence (outlined earlier) in which the dominant pattern is of male violence towards women suggests that these 'family law arguments' are structured to gain strategic legal advantage (Laing, 2010). They may even be part of litigation abuse (Frederick, 2008; Miller and Smolter, 2011). They are rarely in the interests of children.

The documentation required by child protection workers to outline the evidence and their concerns about the impact of domestic violence on children must be readily available and accessible in private law proceedings. It requires that child protection workers are able to assess domestic violence and understand its impact. It would also require child protection workers to be available to provide assertive testimony to support the ongoing protection of both women and children (Humphreys, 2010). In many areas this would represent a significant change in practice and policy.

Directions for More Progressive Work

The critique of child protection intervention in the research literature has been matched by an equally wide range of recommended strategies for change. There is, in fact, almost as much commonality in this area as there is in the critique of child protection practice, with much of the research reporting on initiatives that are being implemented and evaluated and which point to both the challenges and the enablers of more progressive intervention (Banks et al., 2008; Edleson and Malik, 2008; Shephard and Raschick, 1999; Stanley et al., 2010). It is clear that much of the change initiative needs to occur at the level of policy rather than at the level of frontline social work practice. This recognition is needed if there is not to be a shift from mother-blaming to worker-blaming.

A primary issue to address is shifting the bulk of notifications out of the statutory child protection system. This requires opening up alternative services and pathways for children so that only the most serious and chronic cases of children living with domestic violence are referred to child protection, rather than the current practice of notifying huge numbers of children into a statutory service in which they and their mothers and fathers receive no effective intervention (Humphreys, 2008).

Good examples are provided in many of the London Boroughs which are now working with clearer thresholds for risk assessment for children living with domestic violence (see Bell and McGoren (2003) cited in Stanley et al., 2010). The matrix that is being used assesses: perpetrator risk factors; risk factors and protective factors for women; and risk and protective factors for children. It then maps these factors against whether children and their mothers should be supported by: non-specialist agencies; workers who are required to engage with secondary specialist consultation; enhanced family support services; or a child protection response. While the assessment is complex, so are the issues of domestic violence, and this response allows for a much greater number of mothers and children to have their issues addressed in situ rather than through ineffective notifications.

> Creating safety for women and children will mean actively taking action on the adult violence – usually men's violence towards their partners or ex-partners. Again, this will always involve a multi-agency response.

The primary intervention recommended across every article and intervention in this area is specialist training in domestic violence, with a preference for joint training between different professionals involved in the child protection and domestic violence intervention. As this area of work develops it is clear that training which engages with the issues of mental health and alcohol and substance use alongside domestic violence is also necessary (Arney and Scott, 2010; Brandon et al., 2008b). At the most serious end of domestic violence, and where an active child protection response usually occurs, is where other adult issues are involved for either the child's mother or father.

Experienced trainers are needed who don't simply shift the focus to 'multi-problem' or 'complex' families, but who understand the dimensions of gender, power and control which are live wherever domestic violence is present. The specialist focus on domestic violence brings a lens which attends to safety and recognizes the needs of the adult (usually woman) victim as well as the child. There are problems if, in tackling complexity, a shift occurs which diminishes the impact of violence. For instance, it is very easy to focus on alcohol problems (not male violence) and neglect (inadequate parenting) and lose the focus on the impact of trauma and fear and its gendered dimensions.

One of the strongest themes for change across all areas of the research and practice literature lies in the need to improve cross-agency co-operation and co-ordination. This includes the development of effective policies, interagency guidelines and treatment approaches, protocols and good practice guidelines between: domestic violence advocates and child protection workers; child protection, the police, the courts and domestic violence agencies. Champions are required to engage with these change processes (Edleson and Malik, 2008; Shephard and Raschick, 1999). In particular, if the issue of an adult victim and child victim is to be addressed, then co-locating workers or tight referral pathways between the specialist women's agency and child protection workers may provide the most appropriate intervention pathway (Banks et al., 2008). Similarly, the attention to men who use violence will require clear protocols with police and accredited men's behaviour change programmes. The engagement of social workers with these adult issues of both perpetration and victimization will assist in shifting the child protection culture of mother-blaming to a more effective engagement with domestic violence. The outcomes for children's well-being and safety are then much more likely to be safeguarded (Howarth et al., 2009).

Other issues arise for the development of good practice which are more within the grasp of direct social work practice. Asking in sensitive and ongoing ways about the presence of domestic violence is critical if the continuing secrecy and the shadowy presence of perpetrator violence is to be understood and addressed (Hester, 2006a). The evidence of co-occurrence and the ability to 'see double' (Fleck-Henderson, 2000) is essential for effective intervention.

Of equal significance is the attention to safety planning and case management. In any situation where domestic violence is present, safety planning will be essential. However, this should not be only a crisis plan undertaken separately and together with women and children (dependent upon age), but also a plan that interrogates a complex understanding of risk assessment and risk management. Such a plan assesses the risks and opportunities of separation, the way in which legislation can be used, and the extent to which the woman can expect any support from the interagency network, including with family/private law issues (Davies et al., 1998). The extent of risk and danger to both women and children emerges over time and once relationships of trust are established (Humphreys, 2007).

The role of child protection workers may be to ensure effective and assertive advocacy for the appropriate range of services. The safety in numbers evaluation (Howarth et al., 2009) pointed out that the wider the range of services actively engaged with women, children and men, the greater the safety of the women and children. The complex needs of women and children living with domestic violence may require a wide range of interventions: counselling, legal services, health and housing services to mention a few. Children and women's needs are connected but also separate where there is domestic violence, and bringing in the appropriate support without overwhelming the relationships is critical. Similarly, intervening with male violence will not only involve police but also an array of other service provisions including drug and alcohol agencies. This is difficult territory for workers, but many women, particularly when they hold close community connections, will be unable to make decisions about their safety unless they are convinced that the man has been treated with respect and also given help-seeking opportunities (Wade, 2007).

While safety planning for both women and children will be essential, recognition that domestic violence also constitutes an attack on the mother–child relationship opens up a further area for exploration. The issue is highly sensitive. Many women are devastated at the extent to which domestic violence has traumatized their children (Mullender et al., 2002). Working on strengthening the mother–child relationship may be difficult but necessary territory to explore in the aftermath of violence. Similarly, the undermining of the relationship between men and their children may be the greatest point of leverage for change. A number of men (particularly when they are the father of the children involved) may not wish to repeat the cycle of fear and alienation which many of them experienced (Wade, 2007).

> Active work is required to strengthen the relationship between women and their children in the aftermath of violence.

In short, the intervention strategies required to engage in more sensitive child protection practice require shifts at both policy and practice level and at every stage of the intervention from initial engagement through to complex case planning and intervention.

Conclusion

Blaming women for their failure to protect their children is part of a statutory child protection discourse which has been established for well over a century (Humphreys and Absler, 2011). Unsettling entrenched practices requires champions for change who are willing to treat domestic violence as more than an 'add on' to current child protection practice.

There are adult and child victims whose needs have to be addressed. Gendered patterns of intervention which ignore men and only engage with mothers need to be shifted. The boundary of intervention needs to be expanded to include the needs of children where post-separation violence occurs. The process of notifying/referring *all* children living with domestic violence to statutory child protection needs to change so that children and their families receive a service but not necessarily a statutory intervention. The siloed intervention that categorizes abuse into particular abuse types and fails to recognize cumulative harm needs to be rectified. The profound need for intensive collaboration with other services with a history of engagement with women, children and men to address the separate and interconnected nature of domestic violence provides the platform for change.

It is a challenging agenda which requires dedicated champions for change. Many examples now exist (Edleson and Malik, 2008; Stanley et al., 2010). Propelling these innovative changes into the mainstream will require resources and a broader recognition of the complex needs of children living with domestic violence. The field initially took 'a wrong turn' in hitching the needs of children living with domestic violence to the child protection juggernaut (Featherstone and Trinder, 1997). A group of highly vulnerable and distressed children need this protection. Most do not. They do, however, need a service, as do their mothers. It will be a sad indictment if these needs return to invisibility if they are not framed within the high-risk category of child protection intervention.

Summary Points

- Children living with domestic violence will be found in every sector of social work, not only in relation to safeguarding children.
- The presence of domestic violence is an indicator of heightened risk of physical or sexual abuse of children and child neglect.

- In any study there will be a very significant group of children who, in spite of living with domestic violence, are managing as well as other children in the community.
- There is little to suggest that referring *all* children for statutory intervention results in an effective service.
- Interventions which focus on the mother's 'failure to protect', particularly when no effective action is taken in relation to the perpetrator of violence, perpetrates both a poor response to domestic violence survivors as well as undermining multi-agency working.
- Post-separation violence is frequently present, and the safety and well-being issues for women and children do not cease at separation.
- Many of the directions for more progressive social work practice lie in the domain of policy, including: joint training initiatives, co-location or tight procedures for referral between adult and children's services; and the development of sophisticated safety planning and risk-management work which involves a wide range of agencies.

Reflective Questions for Practice

- What might a woman who is a victim of domestic violence notice about a child protection worker's approach which would indicate to her that the social worker has some understanding about her dilemmas and fears?
- In what ways could a child protection worker explore the efforts that a woman is already making to keep herself and her children safer?
- What child protection practices might ensure that the perpetrator of domestic violence is held accountable for the violence and its effects?
- What approaches could facilitate the identification of domestic violence in assessments of post-separation parenting arrangements?

Further Reading

Holt, S., Buckley, H. and Whelan, S. (2008). The impact of exposure to domestic violence on children and young people: a review of the literature. *Child Abuse and Neglect*, 32: 797–810.

This article provides an important literature review on the effects of domestic violence on children.

(Continued)

(Continued)

Howarth, E., Stimpson, L., Barran, D. and Robinson, A. (2009). *Safety in Numbers: A Multi-site Evaluation of Independent Domestic Violence Advisor Services*. London: The Hestia Fund, The Sigrid Rausing Trust and The Henry Smith Charity.

This study demonstrates the effectiveness of interventions that support women's safety in ways which also reduce the level of harm to children.

Radford, L. and Hester, M. (2006). *Mothering Through Domestic Violence*. London: Jessica Kingsley.

An important book that highlights through research and practice the significance of concurrent support for women and children in making an effective response to domestic violence.

6

Practices with Men in the Domestic Violence Context

Tom is a 40-year-old man who presented to his GP with severe facial bruising and dizziness. When questioned about the source of his injuries, Tom was hesitant and gave a vague history involving a fall down stairs. His GP noticed that there was a history of 'accidental' injuries and in this current situation the injury did not appear to match the account that Tom had provided. The GP is also the doctor for Tom's partner, Daniel, who usually accompanies Tom to the surgery, appears concerned for his well-being, but speaks for him. The doctor takes this opportunity to ask some more questions about what happened in this instance. Tom becomes distressed and describes living in fear of Daniel's 'temper', his jealous accusations of infidelity and the threats by Daniel to 'out' him to his family and work colleagues. Tom doesn't want to end the relationship and wants to get help for both himself and Daniel. The GP feels unprepared to recommend services and interventions that might be appropriate. He refers Tom to the social worker at the local family counselling service.

As the scenario with Tom and Daniel highlights, the issues for men as victims and as perpetrators are complex. Issues of power, control and secrecy and a limited service system are pervasive. The issues of intersectionality are significant, not only for gay men but also for men within different cultural and social contexts. The added and most contentious issue in practice with men in the domestic violence context is that it is often unclear who the perpetrator is and who is the victim. It is easy for the inexperienced (not to mention experienced) worker to be drawn into collusion with the perpetrator in ways that undermine the safety of the victim.

Just as workers grapple to find clarity in the face of ambiguity and limited information, we have similarly been challenged in an area where there are contradictions and overlapping issues. We have chosen to tackle the issues of men as victims and perpetrators in the same chapter because the assessment of men as victims and perpetrators needs to draw on a common knowledge base. While this facilitates the attention to the overlapping issues of perpetration and victimization which are prevalent in working with men, we recognize that there are limitations in this approach for men who are solely victims or solely perpetrators of violence. However, our approach emphasizes the importance of assessment because critical issues of safety and social justice are at stake.

We begin this chapter by briefly reviewing the knowledge base that can inform practice through understanding **gendered patterns of perpetration and victimization**. **Risk assessment and management** is then discussed as a pathway to untangle the issues of victimization and perpetration. We then shift to discuss the **essential elements of practice with men who use violence: focus on safety and the victims; fathering issues** for men who use violence; the **role of men's behaviour change (perpetrator) programmes**; and **attention to diversity and cultural location**. The focus of the chapter then changes to consider **working with men as victims**, looking at both the commonality and differences in working with gay men and heterosexual men.

Gendered Patterns of Perpetration and Victimization

Revisiting some of the data about prevalence and patterns of domestic violence is the starting point for this chapter. The area is contested and discussed in more depth in Chapter 2. Service usage data overwhelmingly indicates that men are primarily the perpetrators of domestic violence while women are predominantly the victims. For example, the gender breakdown of the most serious domestic violence cases which are referred to the Multi-Agency Risk Assessment Panels (MARAPs) in England and Wales show either no female perpetrators (Robinson, 2003) or very small numbers. The South Yorkshire MARAC evaluation indicated that 2 per cent of 1160 referrals involved female perpetrators (Wilkinson and Davidson, 2008).

It is not in the reported domestic violence where the area of contestation lies. Men's groups and some academics (e.g. Archer, 2000) argue that the violence and abuse of men by their female partners is under-reported. They argue that prevalence data shows a different pattern from the reported data. Undoubtedly, and as highlighted in Chapter 2, an initial reading of prevalence and incidence data taken from population-based studies shows a very significant group of men who are victims of violence. For instance, the British Crime Survey (BCS) based on a nationally representative sample of 22,463 men and women (aged 16–59) showed

---

*Other terms include batterer programmes, perpetrator programmes, or more broadly men's healing centres.

significant numbers of both women (13 per cent) and men (9 per cent) subjected to at least one incident of domestic violence in the past year (Walby and Allen, 2004). However, the further analysis of the self-completion section on interpersonal violence showed that when the frequency of attacks, the level of fear, the range of forms of violence and the severity of injury are considered, women are overwhelmingly the most victimized (Walby and Allen, 2004).

The application of this knowledge to practice is far from straightforward. Work with men in the context of domestic violence is complicated by the characteristics and tactics of perpetration. Avoidance and projection of responsibility onto others, particularly the victim, is a central rather than a marginal aspect of domestic violence perpetration. It casts the man as victim rather than perpetrator as a means through which responsibility and culpability for abuse can be avoided. From their interviews with men mandated to attend a behaviour change programme by the criminal justice system, and their partners, Cavanagh and colleagues concluded that 'Men's accounts are riven with evidence of the ways in which they deny, minimize and blame others for their own use of violence' (2001: 696).

Definitions of violence and abuse may also be different for men and women. A study of experiences of violence and abuse reported in an online survey of 913 divorced or separated men and women showed that whereas women reported high levels of fear, threat, physical and sexual abuse in their experience of violence and abuse, men were more likely to report verbal and emotional abuse from women and to construe the woman's failure to function in a stereotypic family role as being abusive to them in a way that women did not (Bagshaw et al., 2010).

The process of minimization can be particularly complicated by men who, in other aspects of their lives, experience significant levels of powerlessness and trauma. For example, the experience of colonization is a systematic abuse particularly when accompanied by dislocation from family, culture and the land (Murray and Powell, 2011). Disaggregating such experiences from men's own perpetration of abuse towards others, particularly the women and children in their families, is critical. It ensures that ongoing domestic violence is not rationalized as an aspect of cultural and colonial violence and discrimination, even if the overall intervention engages with, and is set in, understandings of a wider cultural context (Wade, 1997).

The Dyn Project

Perhaps the most detailed analysis of men as victims and/or perpetrators is provided by the evaluation of the Dyn Project in Wales (Robinson and Rowlands, 2006). The strength of this analysis lies in the fact that the Dyn Project was established to support men experiencing domestic abuse as part of a wider suite of domestic abuse services in Cardiff (see www.dynproject.org). It provides a specific safety planning and advocacy service for gay, bisexual, transgender (GBT) and heterosexual men who have experienced domestic abuse. It is also operationally linked to the Cardiff Women's Safety Unit (WSU) as a precondition of the operation of the men's service and an invaluable enhancement to initial assessment for men accessing the service.

The analysis of the referral data provides a nuanced picture of men's perspectives on victimization and is drawn upon at some length to shed light on this complex issue. From the specialist assessment that was developed for the service, different patterns of victimization/perpetration emerged. Four categories were established:

- MV1 – Men in *same sex* relationships (24 per cent of 171 men).
- MV2 – Heterosexual men with *no known history* of abusive or violent incidents as either a victim or a perpetrator (30 per cent of 171 men).
- MV3 – Heterosexual men with a *known history* of abusive or violent incidents (i.e. they have been identified as the [alleged] perpetrator of domestic abuse towards a former or current intimate partner); however, they have no record of any High or Very High Risk incidents within the last four months, and any *current incidents are medium risk or for information only* (33 per cent of 171 men).
- MV4 – Heterosexual men with a *known history* of abusive or violent incidents (i.e. they have been identified as the [alleged] perpetrator of domestic abuse towards a former or current intimate partner). *Currently they are known or alleged to be perpetrating domestic violence* (e.g. partner referred to a High Risk MARAC panel or repeat incidents) (12.8 per cent of 171 men). (Robinson and Rowlands, 2006: 5–6)

The evaluators concluded that the most frequent type of referral was a heterosexual man involved in '"common couple violence" … Therefore, the violence is at least bi-directional, and in a substantial proportion of cases there will be evidence that he is the primary aggressor' (Robinson and Rowlands, 2006: 59). A small group of these men, all drawn from MV3 and MV4, were considered as high risk and referred to the high-risk panel (MARAC). In most cases their female partners were also referred. Both the gay men and the heterosexual male victims (MV2) reported moderate forms of abuse when the standard risk assessment was applied and none were in the high risk category. The complexity of assessment when heterosexual men present as victims is shown by the finding that it was in precisely those situations when the identification of victimization and offending was most difficult that risk was highest. This may also be an issue in gay relationships.

The extent to which this pattern of victimization/perpetration in the Dyn Project would be replicated elsewhere is unknown. Other research which has explored men's reports of victimization (Gadd et al., 2002) also suggests that more than half the men would have partners who would report a history of being abused.

Taken together, the data points clearly to the fact that 'male victimization' is complex and that workers need to begin their work with men with a comprehensive assessment and, wherever possible, triangulation with data from other sources. While recognizing that there are both gay and heterosexual men who are the victims of domestic violence, the data suggest that more than 50 per cent of heterosexual men who perceive themselves as victims will be involved in perpetration of abuse, some of which also involves physical violence from their partners or ex-partners. Some, but not all, of this latter group will involve women who are long-term victims acting in the context of self-defence.

Risk Assessment and Risk Management

The complexities in understanding the context and the patterns of abuse highlight the significance of the initial assessments undertaken with men or their partners and ex-partners. Risk assessment, risk management and safety planning provide the foundations for working with men in the context of domestic violence. There are a number of dimensions to this work. Primarily the work will involve perpetrator risk assessment and risk management in relation to partners or ex-partners and their children. However, there is also risk assessment for men as victims (Robinson and Rowlands, 2006).

Perpetrator Assessment and Risk Management

Most social workers work in organizations in which specialist risk assessments for domestic violence are not systematically undertaken either for men or women. Nevertheless, most social work occurs in settings where domestic violence is ubiquitous but often not identified. Recommendations have been frequently made to overcome this lacunae in practice through supporting routine questions about domestic violence as part of initial assessments for both men and women in the mental health area (Riggs et al., 2000), drug and alcohol services (Stella Project, 2007) and child protection arena (Humphreys, 2007) to mention just a few. In each of these areas there are high rates of co-occurrence with domestic violence.

When domestic violence is not the presenting problem for the work with men, workers may come to know of the domestic violence through a number of different avenues: disclosures by victims which are not shared with the man; disclosure by victims where the man knows this has occurred, for example in some child protection investigations; incidents of domestic violence which become known to the police or other service providers and where the man may be referred, not only for his violence but also for other issues such as mental health or drug and alcohol problems; and self-disclosure.

Each of these cases will require different approaches from workers in exploring and assessing issues of violence and abuse. The principle of safety is the foundation of practice in the domestic violence area and may over-ride issues of confidentiality, particularly when children are involved. However, in these circumstances basic safety considerations still apply, and a great deal of care and skill will be needed to set the 'ground rules' about how such a risky issue can be discussed safely.

The complexity of working with a 'hidden issue' highlights how useful domestic violence screening questions can be for both men and women at initial assessment. While many people will choose not to discuss their experience of either being victims or perpetrators of violence, screening questions place the issue routinely 'on the table', open for discussion and not hidden as a secret which is only secondary to 'the main service'. An example is provided through the 'Toolkit' provided by the Stella

Project (2007) which supports the development of shared practices between domestic violence and drug and alcohol agencies. Their domestic violence screening form provides the following statement:

> As part of our interview with everyone who comes to us for help, we always include questions about other issues besides substance misuse. We feel it is really important to help you with as many of your problems as we can. We understand that sometimes in order to help with one problem other problems must also be addressed. In most homes where there is substance misuse, families have other problems too. I'm going to ask some questions to see whether any of these things have happened to you or your family. If we find that you need help, we will take whatever actions are necessary to ensure your safety and recovery, if you wish. (2007: 279)

While the approach and the questions that follow are 'victim' rather than 'perpetrator' orientated, they can be shifted to also explore and assess aspects of the abuser's role. Interestingly, the research would suggest that risk assessment yields greater disclosure when undertaken through self-completion questions rather than face to face (Kapur and Windish, 2011; Walby and Allen, 2004).

The process of exploration and assessment is more straightforward when the violence and abuse has become visible through a police report or other formal avenues. While the report may then be subject to minimization, dismissal or avoidance, there is nevertheless the opportunity to explore the man's narrative and views about the incident without breaching or jeopardizing confidentiality with the victim. Issues to explore include: his version of the history of domestic violence; his attitude towards it; his perception of the impact on both himself and others, including his children. He can also be involved in the assessment of his own risk, and work can begin to develop his motivation to seek help (Radford et al., 2006: 178). In the case of Tom and Daniel in the opening vignette, the approach of the social worker would depend on Daniel's willingness to acknowledge the abusive behaviours.

When men upon initial assessment perceive the violence and abuse as 'mutual', the early role of the worker is to establish whether there is a predominant or primary abuser, whether both parties are equally involved in the violence, or whether there is only one abuser using the language of victimization to obscure his culpability. This step is significant given that a major injustice is perpetrated if a victim becomes constructed as a perpetrator of abuse by the formal intervention system.

> Many men who are perpetrators perceive themselves to be victims. Working with men where there are issues of domestic violence therefore requires a careful assessment of the context of violence, including other sources of information.

A number of issues need to be taken into account when making the initial assessment. First, when a man is claiming that the violence is 'mutual' and he is equally or more victimized in a relationship than his partner or ex-partner, then permission is needed for further checks to occur within the formal system (police checks, checks with the women's services in the area, checks with child protection) and to interview his partner separately. Whatever the work setting, the process is ideally undertaken as part of a formal assessment contract to provide the authorizing environment for exploration.

Second, a wide range of factors are relevant in the assessment (Radford et al., 2006). These can include:

- the history of abuse and some understanding of who does what to whom and under what circumstances with particular exploration of the issue of self-defence
- the severity of the injuries and the impact both physically and emotionally
- the extent of fear and threat which is experienced and by whom
- the power relationship between the different parties including issues of authority, fearfulness and vulnerability in the relationship and the inequalities associated with social location not just of gender but sexuality, class, ethnicity, age and (dis)ability
- an understanding and assessment of a wide range of tactics of abuse which go beyond physical violence.

While the assessment is gender neutral, it takes into account the operation of gender within the context of personal and structural power relations and paves the way for an assessment of the needs of and risks posed by each person, including in relation to children (Radford et al., 2006: 180). Recognition is needed that even in those cases where both parties are involved in the violence this may be particularly dangerous: an indicator of high risk which will need to be managed, rather than lowering the risk (Robinson and Rowlands, 2006).

Chapter 4 outlined the important role that risk assessment and safety planning plays when working with women. Much of the risk assessment and the management of that risk occurs between the woman and her worker or the police. Work with men in relation to their use of violence and abuse in their relationships can only begin when there is recognition by the man that the violence has occurred. Sometimes this will be in the context of an arrest or the application for an intervention order. Minimization, denial, avoidance and blaming will be an expected initial reaction when violence and abuse is first discussed. Skilled work with men that engages them with an assessment of their own risk factors and any formal or informal consequences they have experienced as a result of their violence can be explored. In particular, any steps that were taken in the past to attempt to stop their behaviour and the results they have experienced need to be examined. In this process, the man's motivation to change can also be assessed.

There has been some controversy about engagement with techniques of 'motivation to change' in the men's behaviour change area where there has primarily been a focus on psycho-educational approaches (Day et al., 2009). However, particularly when social workers are working in other settings such as drug and alcohol services where such approaches are common, there is some compatibility with this work. Examples are beginning to emerge of 'pre-treatment' programmes that engage men who have been arrested, charged and convicted in a 'motivation to change' assessment of their goals, strengths and perceptions and any changes they had already made prior to entering a men's behaviour change programme (Curwood et al., 2011).

Essential Elements of Practice with Men Who Use Violence

While most social workers are not working with men's behaviour change programmes, a number of principles for working with men who use violence can be drawn from the depth of experience that has developed in this specialist field. These include: a focus on safety and keeping the victim(s) in mind; attention to worker safety; gaining a detailed account of the violence and abuse; engaging the man in taking responsibility; collaboration with the criminal and civil justice system; collaboration with domestic violence multi-agency forums; and assessment and engagement with men as fathers.

Focus on Safety and the Victim(s)

In most social work practice, the client is usually the person who presents to the agency. However, when working with men who use violence, a double lens is needed. It is not only the man who is the focus of attention, but a duty of care also lies towards those whom he has victimized (Day et al., 2009). Evaluation of the success of the work with the man is not only about his well-being, but also the safety and well-being of his partner or ex-partner and children (Westmarland et al., 2010). While this focus on the safety of others may make evaluation difficult, it also is a clear reminder to workers that there are other lives involved. Safety planning for those who are affected by his violence will need to be negotiated and is part of the work with the man at the outset of intervention (Jenkins, 2009; Paymar, 2000).

> When working with men who use violence, safety and sources of support for women and their children need to be held at the forefront of practice.

A controversial area in relation to safety lies with the issue of couple counselling and assessment. Traditionally, the work with men and the work with women has been separated because safety must be the central consideration (Bograd and Mederos, 1999; Lipchik et al., 1997). A number of issues inform this safety strategy and include:

- minimization by victims due to the fear of the consequences of disclosure and the hope that it is possible to save the relationship
- the ineffectiveness of the work when one partner is fearful about how much they can disclose about the relationship (an issue for children as well)
- the problems with joint review of the violence and abuse which may then result in retaliation
- the inability of the worker to 'read' the subtle and exclusive methods of communication – including non-verbal – which may signal threat
- research evidence from mediation, couple counselling and court welfare work that points to women or children doing poorly in negotiations where they are fearful of the consequences of openness and therefore reach 'agreements' which are not in their best interests. (Stella Project, 2007: 189)

While these are foundational principles for working in this area, nevertheless attention needs to be given to exceptions to this basic 'no joint counselling' principle. A significant group of men and women stay together in spite of the history of domestic violence, or though separated need to continue to negotiate child contact and property arrangements. As outlined earlier, some violence and abuse is also reciprocal involving both partners. Joint counselling as an adjunct or complement to men's behaviour change programmes and individual counselling for men focused on their use of violence and abuse may have a role to play.

Again, comprehensive assessment is crucial. While primarily addressing the context of marital and family therapy, Bograd and Mederos (1999) have developed a comprehensive screening and assessment framework to assist in decision making about whether couple therapy can be safely considered. They specify three preconditions for conducting an assessment possibly leading to couple therapy. These are: first, voluntary participation by the man, thus excluding, except in exceptional cases, court mandated men or men referred by child protection services; second, specific agreements regarding confidentiality to ensure that the woman's safety is not compromised either by therapist disclosure or pressure to disclose in joint sessions, information discussed in individual sessions; and third, a therapeutic stance involving clear location of responsibility for the abuse and clear limits. They outline a structured and focused process of assessment, including an assessment of violence and lethality (risk), where the presence of a single risk factor rules out conjoint therapy. The assessment must include individual sessions with each partner. This would be an important aspect of the assessment of Tom and Daniel, irrespective of whether they have a view that they should be seen together.

One of the most experienced practitioners and writers in this area, Alan Jenkins (2009), argues that much of the danger of couple counselling arises from apolitical counselling which fails to fully address the safety issues for women, and concentrates inappropriately on 'communication problems' and relationship dysfunction rather than situating the violence in the context of power and control and the structural inequalities which are played out through the domestic violence.

Both Bograd and Mederos (1999) and Jenkins (2009) suggest criteria to assess readiness for joint counselling. Of crucial importance is whether each person can freely agree to couple counselling. This will not be the case where there is a significant imbalance of power and privilege; high levels of fear, intimidation and entrapment; and the need of one person to accommodate to the needs and demands of the other. Each person must also feel sufficiently safe to participate in couple counselling. For Jenkins, this means that hopes, fears, expectations and experiences of violence can be spoken about and listened to. Bograd and Mederos limit consideration of joint work to situations involving a few incidents of minor violence and where psychological violence is infrequent and does not terrify or immobilize the woman.

In exploring the extent of safety, inequality and desire for change from both parties, Jenkins also suggests the importance of the counsellor/facilitator to considering the following:

- Is there an open commitment to a concept of partnership with privileges equity and entitlement?
- Does the person who has been subjected to violence feel they are entitled to feel safe and free from violence in the relationship?
- Is there an expressed commitment to partnership regarding relationship and family responsibilities? This parameter includes acknowledgement of responsibility for the violence and a concept of sharing responsibility for the development and maintenance of a respectful emotional climate in the relationship and family.
- Is there an expressed commitment to a concept of partnership with a balance between a sense for togetherness and belonging and a sense of separateness and independence in the relationship? (2009: 148)

In most cases these criteria will not be met. Couple counselling is not recommended for first contact in situations of abuse. This discussion highlights the complex and thorough assessment that must be undertaken to assess risk and safety.

Worker Safety

The risk assessment and plan for risk management informs not only the work with men, women and children but also the practice of workers and the strategies which are needed to create as safe an environment as possible. Workers have a right to feel safe and protected in their work environment. It is also clear that workers who feel unsafe and threatened will have difficulty working effectively.

This is not only the responsibility of individual workers, but also of the organization and managers who need to ensure that worker safety is prioritized (Littlechild and Bourke, 2006). Poor and potentially dangerous practice occurs when workers do not feel safe. Workers who are fearful can make accommodations that mirror the process by which survivors can underestimate the level of danger and abuse they live with. Minimization, avoidance, rationalization and denial may all feature as responses from workers who lack adequate supervision and are expected to engage in contexts in which their safety is inadequately addressed (Stanley and Goddard, 2002).

In many ways, referral of men to specialist men's behaviour change programmes can be seen as a worker safety strategy. The contained environment in which there is authorization for assessment, protective legal interventions (intervention orders) or probation orders, and where men monitor the behaviour of other men who use violence and abuse provide aspects of safety not available to social workers in non-specialist domestic violence agencies. However, comparatively few men attend these programmes.

Workers are generally reliant upon a range of other strategies for which they will need management support and an organization culture amongst colleagues which values and supports safety. Strategies can include: mobile phones; seeing men in the office rather than in the man's home; working in pairs; notifying and working with police where necessary; judicious attention to where workers are going and when they will be returning from appointments; checking in with managers on leaving a home visit; active use of risk assessment; recognition of signs of immediate mental health problems and evidence of current alcohol and drug intake; and prior checks of the man's criminal or agency history.

The critical issue is not whether there is policy and guidance on safety issues, but whether there is active implementation and a supportive organizational culture. A sign of such a culture is where workers are actively and routinely supported in supervision to disclose any fears they hold and that these are responded to appropriately. Any violent and abusive incidents are appropriately responded to by management and reporting is encouraged (Littlechild and Bourke, 2006).

Fathering Issues for Men Who Use Violence

The role of domestic violence abusers as fathers is both highly controversial and neglected. A number of issues highlight the reasons for concern about men who use violence against their partners as fathers. Chapter 5 in this book has highlighted the damaging effects on children of living with domestic violence. The majority of children show that their cognitive functioning and emotional well-being is significantly negatively impacted when compared to other children who are not living with domestic violence (Holt et al., 2008; Kitzmann et al., 2003). The co-occurrence with other forms of child abuse such as physical abuse (Edleson, 1999b; Ross, 1996), sexual abuse (Hester and Pearson, 1998; Kellogg and Menard, 2003) and neglect (Hartley, 2004) heighten the anxiety about the fathering capacity of domestic violence perpetrators. Also coming to light are the ways in which domestic violence undermines and attacks the relationship between mothers and their children (Bancroft and Silverman, 2002; Radford and Hester, 2006). Based on this evidence, child protection authorities are consistently recommending or demanding that women separate from violent men to protect their children (Humphreys and Absler, 2011).

Notwithstanding these issues, men who use violence in the home continue to have a significant fathering role with their children or step children. An American study of 3824 men who had attended court-ordered evaluation after a conviction for assaulting an intimate partner showed that 65.5 per cent of these men had a fathering role which was continuing (Salisbury et al., 2009). Similar findings are available when post-separation parenting orders are examined in both Australia (Bagshaw et al., 2011) and the United Kingdom (Humphreys and Harrison, 2003). These data reflect the shifting discourse in fathering in which a range of groups from the progressive to the radical have actively asserted that children need fathers, in some cases regardless of issues of safety and well-being (Edleson and Williams, 2007). The groups are particularly active in relation to the rights of fathers post separation and divorce. The upshot of this advocacy has been that many men with histories of domestic violence have contact with the children, much of which is unsupervised.

Comparatively little attention has been given to research on the attitudes and behaviour of domestic violence perpetrators towards their children. What research there is suggests cause for concern. In the study by Salisbury et al. (2009), the majority of arrested and convicted men acknowledged the children had witnessed the violence and abuse towards the children's mother but few perceived that the children were affected. This is a similar finding to Scott and Crooks (2007), who found that men referred to the Caring Dads programme for issues of child maltreatment, much of which occurred in the context of domestic violence, reported little or no understanding of the impact of the abuse on their children. The study by Scott and Crooks also validated previous research which found that a significant group of domestic violence perpetrators had poor parenting skills resulting from the men's sense of entitlement, self-centred attitudes and over-controlling behaviour (Bancroft and Silverman, 2002; Harne, 2011; Scott and Crooks, 2004). Earlier studies indicate that violent fathers are less likely to be involved in raising their children and more likely to use physical forms of discipline (smacking) when compared with non-violent fathers (Fox and Benson, 2004; Holden and Ritchie, 1991). They are more likely to be angry with their children (Holden et al., 1998) and to hold unrealistic expectations and poor understanding of child development (Fox and Benson, 2004; Harne, 2011).

However, Scott and Crooks (2007) also highlighted a sub-group of domestic violence perpetrators who had developed a relatively responsive relationship with their children and were in touch with their children's lives (e.g. health and education needs) but who actively manipulated and undermined the mother–child relationship, sometimes inciting the children against their mothers. In this sense, the domestic violence took the form of an attack on the mother–child relationship (Humphreys et al., 2006). Again, the men showed little or no awareness of the negative impact of this behaviour on their children.

Children's views of fathers who are violent and abusive towards their mothers are under-researched. Perspectives from children in some studies show that they are unequivocal in their attitudes to their father's violence towards their mothers and are clear about their fear and distress (Mullender et al., 2002; Radford and Hester, 2006). In post-separation decision making, children tend to be believed when they want to see their fathers and not believed when they don't (Humphreys and Harrison, 2003). Some studies, such as that by Peled of 14 pre-adolescent children, showed that they were conflicted in their loyalty towards their mothers and fathers: their mother's pain and suffering raised their empathy, but siding with the person with power and control in the family was also attractive (1998: 27). Other studies, including an online survey of 105 children whose parents were divorced, also highlighted that a group of children were ambivalent about their fathers and their violence, particularly post separation, but who identified a continued lack of a sense of safety, even if conflict (abuse) between their mothers and fathers had subsided (Bagshaw et al., 2010).

A number of issues arise for social workers when engaging with the issue of men who use violence as fathers. It is clear that post-separation violence is common and that many children may be less protected rather than more fully protected by separation (Bagshaw et al., 2011; Jaffe et al., 2003a; Radford and Hester, 2006), with child contact and shared parenting arrangements being used to continue power and control over both children and the ex-partner (Bancroft and Silverman, 2002). In extreme situations, children have been killed as an act of retaliatory violence by the perpetrator towards their mother (Kirkwood, 2012). Moreover, the significance of the social work role in gathering evidence and advocacy for protection for children is ongoing and will continue following separation. A number of criteria have been developed in the assessment of the perpetrators of domestic violence to explore whether contact is in the best interests of their children (Bancroft and Silverman, 2002; Sturge and Glaser, 2000; Sullivan, 2007). These criteria (which have been summarized and conflated) are also useful in directing the work with men about their fathering issues and what could be expected of a programme for fathers who have used violence and abuse with their children. The issues include:

- full acknowledgement of the violence and abuse perpetrated and that it was a chosen action over which he has control
- acceptance of responsibility for the violence and abuse, recognition that it is unacceptable behaviour, and acknowledgement of its consequences for children and the child's mother
- a wish to make reparation for the harm that has been done, support for the child's healing both in the short and long term, and willingness to help the child recognize the inappropriateness of violent and abusive behaviour
- a genuine interest in the child's welfare and commitment to their well-being (without conditions)
- acceptance of the consequences of his behaviour, which may mean that the child does not wish to see him either immediately or in the long term
- a commitment not to repeat abusive behaviours and that this may be a long-term process of ongoing learning for which he needs support, and for which the system of intervention will appropriately hold him accountable for any recidivism. (Sturge and Glaser, 2000: 624; Sullivan, 2007: 139–140)

In their Expert's Report to the Official Solicitor for England, Sturge and Glaser (2000) recommended that, without basic criteria being met about taking responsibility for past violence and future healing, there was little to suggest that direct contact in which the child has an opportunity to develop a meaningful relationship with their fathers was in the child's best interests.

In short, men who use violence and abuse towards the child's mother are by definition poor fathers (Bancroft and Silverman, 2002; Radford and Hester, 2006). Nevertheless, the majority of these men are in fathering roles with their birth or step children (Salisbury et al., 2009). Pragmatically, directions for work with men in their fathering role need to be tackled with clear ideas about assessment and intervention processes. Standard parenting programmes are contraindicated as they do not engage with the responsibility taking, healing and reparation issues required from men who use violence (Scott and Crooks, 2007). However, as yet there is little evidence about the positive impact of customized parenting programmes for men who use violence (Safe Horizon, 2008; Scott and Crooks, 2007) and social workers are right to be encouraging but wary about the effectiveness of this work.

The Role of Men's Behaviour Change Programmes

One of the most contentious areas of debate in the domestic violence field centres on the role and effectiveness of men's behaviour change programmes. Points of debate have centred on the place and utility of work with individual men for what is seen as a social problem, rather than one of a few deviant men; the effectiveness of these programmes and how this is best assessed; and more recently, whether the most common model of these programmes, a psycho-educational approach informed by a feminist perspective, should be replaced with a more therapeutic approach based on the individual psychological profile and history of each man (Curwood et al., 2011; Gondolf, 2011).

Methodologies for evaluating the outcomes of men's behaviour change programmes have become more sophisticated over time. There is agreement that men's self-report is an inadequate measure of outcomes. Most evaluations combine official data on re-offending, which will only identify incidents of violence constituting criminal offences which come to official notice, with reports of victims/survivors. Westmarland and Kelly argue that a focus on cessation or reduction in physical violence is too narrow and fails to link outcomes of perpetrator programmes to the core domestic violence dynamic of coercive control: 'For female ex/partners, success is about so much more, encompassing their freedom and ability to live life to the full, have a respectful relationship, and share positive and safe parenting' (2012: 17).

An examination of the evidence base reveals that a series of outcome studies using an experimental design have not demonstrated that men's behaviour change programmes reduce re-offending (Dunford, 2000; Feder and Dugan, 2002; Labriola et al., 2008). A meta-analysis of evaluation studies found only a small treatment effect for men's programmes, concluding that the current interventions have a minimal impact on reducing recidivism beyond the effect of being arrested (Babcock et al., 2004).

In contrast, several quasi experimental studies, using comparison groups rather than random allocation to the intervention or other conditions, have found more promising outcomes. A Scottish study found no difference in criminal recidivism between two groups – men who participated in a programme compared to those receiving other criminal sanctions, such as a fine or imprisonment. However, the partners of the men in the programme group reported significantly fewer violent incidents at three and 12 months' follow up and significant reductions in controlling behaviours (Dobash et al., 2000). Gondolf's (2002) quasi experimental, multi-site study had strengths in its large sample size, long follow-up period (48 months) and the use of multiple outcome measures, including interviews with partners every three months. While almost half the sample committed at least one re-assault, the results showed that, over time, there was de-escalation in the rates of assault, with almost 90 per cent of the men not having re-assaulted their partner or new partner in the previous year by the 48-month point in the follow up. Women also reported declines in other forms of abuse, but at much lower rates than the decline in physical assault.

Perhaps the most important finding from Gondolf's study, based on differences across programmes and on an examination of those cases in which men continued to abuse their partners at serious levels, is that 'the system matters' (2002: 199). Gondolf argues that perpetrator programmes, on their own, cannot offer a safe and effective solution to domestic violence; they must be part of an integrated system that holds perpetrators accountable for their violence and which maintains a central focus on the safety of women and children:

> Batterer programs are not by themselves a cure but serve as a reinforcing component to a coordinated community response … They add to the message from the courts that men must and can stop their abuse of women or will face consequences. (2002: 86)

This means that men mandated to a programme by the criminal justice, child protection or Family Law systems need to be monitored and sanctioned if they fail to carry through with their commitment to participate in the programme or if they re-offend. Often, however, accountability is not monitored and sanctions for failure to attend are weak or inconsistently applied (Gondolf, 2011; Palmer et al., 1992).

The intervention system is a critical source for both safety and accountability.

The principle of attending to the safety of women and children in interventions with men is crucial when men are offered intervention in a behaviour change program. For this reason, men's programmes need to develop a system of accountability and safety to the partners of men in the programme (Research and Education Unit on Gendered Violence, 2003). However, the available evidence indicates that the quality of this attention to women's safety is variable. Austin and Dankwort (1999) interviewed partners of men in a programme and found that the programme was experienced as a positive resource by the women, even if their partners made few, if any, changes towards non-violence. They attributed this to the fact that programme staff actively worked with them on safety issues, provided information and were unequivocal about their partner's sole responsibility for the abuse. However, a similar study in a different context found that a narrow focus on safety did not meet women's wider needs for support (Madoc-Jones and Roscoe, 2010). Active outreach to women partners of men in programmes can reach many women who have not had prior contact with domestic violence services, provided that adequate resources are allocated to this aspect of the work (Power and Kowanko, 2001). This is an important area for policy advocacy where the focus on women's safety and well-being must be kept in focus, even though the direct intervention addresses men's use of violence. Ensuring that men's programmes are part of the multi-agency response to domestic violence is critical to maintaining this focus on safety.

The impact of perpetrator programmes in women's lives can be powerful, beyond the changes that their partners may make. For example, women who have been holding onto hope for change in their partner receive new information about his commitment to taking responsibility through the quality of his participation in the programme. For some women, the support offered to their partner by the programme provides a 'breathing space' in which to consider their needs and to take stock of the relationship. In some cases, this may provide a way to leave the relationship more safely (Shaw et al., 1999). Social workers with understanding of these wider aspects of men's behaviour change programmes can assist women to take these into account in their ongoing safety planning. In this way, practice with men and with women comes together to enhance the focus on safety.

Attention to Diversity and Cultural Location

The opening scenario with Tom and Daniel raises issues about the appropriateness of men's behaviour change programmes for men from diverse backgrounds. Questions should be raised about how comfortable Daniel might feel as the only gay man within a predominately heterosexual men's behaviour change group. Limitations of such options can serve to further entrap victims and fail to address the accountability of the perpetrator.

Although there is widespread agreement about the need to develop culturally-specific programmes for men from marginalized groups, there is as yet little available evidence about the outcomes of these programmes (Gondolf, 2011). However, this is a field in which there are some developments that are consistent with the emphasis in this book on considerations of social location in developing practice responses to domestic violence. Each of the three examples that will be discussed has in common an effort to widen the frame of intervention beyond the intimate partner relationship. This broader framing is shaped by recognition of the importance of simultaneously tackling domestic violence and wider forms of oppression such as racism and the legacies of colonial dispossession that are experienced daily by marginalized groups. Almeida and Lockard (2005) argue that this broader frame opens up possibilities for intervention and system change because the focus of change is on both the intimate partner violence and on creating communities that do not support violence and other forms of oppression. In a sense, these approaches capture some of the early community base of the movement against domestic violence, which, it has been argued, has been lost to more institutionalized, mainstream responses (Goodman and Epstein, 2008). Post-colonial and intersectional perspectives (the latter discussed in Chapter 2) underpin these approaches. In this context, a post-colonial analysis is a perspective that provides 'The simultaneous accounting for the historical and current impact of oppressive social forces, including sexism, racism, homophobia, and classism' (Hernandez et al., 2005: 107).

In thinking about the role of domestic violence perpetrator programmes, much of the debate has been about at which level intervention to reduce domestic violence should be addressed: at the individual man (education/treatment), or at the wider socio-political level that supports violence and discrimination against women (prevention). The Cultural Context Model (CCM) (Almeida and Dolan-Del Vecchio, 1999; Font et al., 1998; Hernandez et al., 2005), in contrast, addresses both levels of intervention but begins with the socio-political. Socio-education is the focus of initial interventions. Drawing on Friere's (1972) concept of critical consciousness, separate 'culture circles' for men and women are used to challenge taken-for-granted notions around gender, race, culture and sexual orientation, prior to couple counselling about domestic violence. Within the CCM, the notion of accountability is central, but is much broader than the usual sense in which the term has become used in domestic violence intervention. In the CCM approach, Almeida and Lockard emphasize that accountability means:

> [A] patterned way of relating to others that challenges the rigid norms of masculine and feminine behavior, and locates collaboration and respect as central norms. In our definition, accountability is broader than links to the criminal justice system and/or battered women's shelters. It includes men and women in the community within which the batterer lives and works who hold him accountable for his violence. (2005: 312)

In their work with Latin Americans living in North America, Colorado et al. (2003) see dominant, Western intervention models, developed from positions of social privilege, as inappropriate because they ignore the impacts of colonization and dislocation on Latino people and stereotype them as inherently violent. In common with the cultural context model, they believe that work with domestic violence must be contextualized within the broader violence and oppression experienced by the Latino community in North America. In this approach, domestic violence is addressed as a community issue through the medium of community meetings:

> Within Latino cultures there is a great diversity of ways of being. Cultural histories including both pro-violence and pro-respect messages can be found ... We propose the reclaiming of enriching cultural stories that promote respect among family members. We seek to create a context in which the liberatory elements of Latino culture can be built upon to foster the creation of respectful relationships. (Colorado et al., 2003: 141)

The approach draws on narrative therapy techniques such as externalizing conversations that encourage participants to join together to resist the problem (White and Epston, 1989) and on cultural ceremonies, stories and music. It exposes the harmful cultural distortions ('pseudo-culture') that have been promoted by the dominant North American culture. Although the intervention occurs in a community context, women's safety is attended to by the use of gender-specific groups and by not obliging women to share experiences, a practice that could jeopardize their safety. This approach and the CCM represent a way of bringing violence committed within the privacy of the family into the public sphere that is an alternative to the dominant approach of criminalizing domestic violence as the methodology of making the private public.

In common with both of these approaches, the practice developed in the Just Therapy Team in New Zealand addresses the unfairness and injustice that are grounded in the histories and ongoing legacies of colonization of Maori and Pacific Islander peoples and the economic injustices, the patriarchal structure and market capitalism of Western societies. It can be understood as an application to practice of the intersectional theoretical perspective that we have discussed throughout this book. Waldegrave explains that a 'Just Therapy' is 'one that takes into account the gender, cultural, social and economic context of the persons seeking help' (2003: 4).

In this approach, work with families from cultures that are significantly different from the majority culture is led by therapists from the same cultural group. This counters practices in which Western meaning structures are imposed on clients, a practice that is seen as racist and as reproducing the injustices imposed outside of therapy by the dominant cultural group. It also challenges the hegemony of Western social science. Similarly, with problems involving gender issues, such as domestic violence, male and female therapists take particular roles: male workers share the story told by the person who abuses, while female workers share the story of the woman who has experienced the abuse. While the man's story is told in its broader context, the therapy focuses primarily on the abuse, its consequences for the woman and others harmed, and works toward freeing them from this abuse. None of the three approaches described here attempts to 'adapt' mainstream approaches; rather they have been developed from the recognition of the social location of the participants.

Working with Men as Victims

In this section, we look first at issues in working with gay men before discussing practice with heterosexual male victims. Both are underserved groups, and further practice development is required.

Gay Men

As discussed in Chapter 2, the available evidence suggests that rates of domestic violence in gay and lesbian relationships are similar to those in heterosexual relationships (Donovan et al., 2006). In a similar pattern to the development of practice with heterosexual domestic violence, considerable activity has occurred in recent years to 'break the silence' about the existence of domestic violence in the same sex community. The case vignette of Daniel and Tom highlights that the context of domestic violence for gay men, while similar, is not the same. Almeida et al. (1994) argue that, while early second-wave feminism exposed privatization as a key tool of patriarchal oppression, this analysis was limited to the experience of White, heterosexual intimate relationships and is therefore inadequate for understanding violence within relationships of marginalized groups. They contend that it is essential to understand violence within homosexual relationships within the larger context of homophobia which devalues and renders invisible same sex intimate relationships:

> [R]acial and homosexual oppression begin as public events ... Subjected to public displays of humiliation, marginalization, bigotry and hatred, the intimate relationships of heterosexuals of color and homosexuals of all races are undermined and rendered invisible by public policies and the absence of supports. Domestic violence enacted in response to public violence often is used as evidence by the dominant culture to support notions of the 'other's' inherent inferiority. (1994: 102)

The wider context of homophobia frames the context for disclosure of domestic violence. An example of the ways in which these challenges have been tackled is the work of the Same Sex Domestic Violence Interagency (SSDVI)* in Sydney, Australia. Established over a decade ago in recognition of the lack of specialist services for gay male victims of domestic violence in the inner city, this coalition includes workers from diverse government and non-government agencies including health, housing, police, Aids Council of NSW (ACON), women's groups and queer advocates (Duffy, 2011). In an example of the importance of cross-agency collaboration in domestic violence work, the SSDVI group has undertaken a range of projects to raise awareness about violence in same sex relationships in the community and among service providers. The resource booklet 'Another Closet' (SSDVI, 2009) provides comprehensive information for people experiencing domestic violence within same sex relationships, including a series of personal accounts of living with domestic violence. These accounts and the other information in the booklet highlight the commonality of coercive control as the core dynamic across domestic violence in both heterosexual and homosexual relationships, in addition to the specificity of the tactics of control that can be deployed in the context of same sex relationships, such as 'outing' as a form of control and the tactics of abuse when one or other of the partners has a chronic illness such as HIV. For example, an abuser may threaten to or actually disclose their partner's health status to others, or withhold access to treatment and medications. If the abuser has a chronic illness, he may use this to induce guilt as a form of manipulation or threaten to infect the partner (SSDVI, 2009). The availability of information and accounts of the many forms that coercive control can take within same sex relationships can enable men who may have previously understood domestic violence to encompass solely physical abuse (Donovan et al., 2006) to name their experiences as domestic violence.

---

*More recently re-named the LGBTIQ Domestic Violence Interagency.

The SSDVI's approach to the development of a state-wide community awareness campaign *There's No Pride in Domestic Violence* demonstrates the complexity of such an endeavour in relation to a group that may be further marginalized by making visible the existence of domestic violence. The campaign was developed with an awareness of this risk, seeking to avoid reinforcing negative stereotypes about same sex relationships:

> The campaign title *There's No Pride In Domestic Violence* ... juxtaposed the concept of community 'pride' with 'domestic violence,' and stated that the two were mutually exclusive. The opening line in the main text stated that 'most gay and lesbian relationships are based on love and respect. Some are based on abuse and control.' This aimed to show that while the majority of relationships were healthy and positive, some were not. (Duffy, 2011: 497)

The activities of the SSDVI – raising awareness about domestic violence in same sex relationships with the gay community and service providers – provides an example of a collaboration to establish safety for victims to name their experiences and to seek help. The experience of the Dyn Project indicates that when gay men are supported to name their experiences of domestic violence, they accepted the services offered to them more frequently than did heterosexual men referred to the project. They were more likely to accept longer periods of support, more referrals to a variety of services, and face-to-face appointments (Robinson and Rowlands, 2006).

Heterosexual Men

Information about practices with heterosexual male victims of domestic violence is more limited. Again the Dyn Project, discussed earlier in this chapter, provides one of the few sources of information. The Dyn evaluation report highlights the centrality of thorough assessment of claims of victimization by heterosexual men, since the majority of men presenting as victims had past or current histories of violence perpetration, either as primary aggressors or as part of a pattern of common couple (situational) violence (Johnson, 1995, 2010). The smaller group of men who were assessed as victims of domestic violence rarely accepted services offered (Robinson and Rowlands, 2006). The reasons for this are unknown. We could speculate that perhaps the form of service delivery developed out of practice with women victims does not meet the specific needs of this population; or perhaps that domestic violence against heterosexual men does not result in the same constellation of physical and mental health impacts that lead many women victims to seek help.

Drawing on the typology of domestic violence that was discussed in Chapter 2 (Johnson, 1995, 2010), the authors draw from the findings of the Dyn Project to suggest a three-group typology of heterosexual men who experience domestic violence:

- Men who do not perpetrate domestic abuse and who have been assaulted by their female partners, yet who do not designate themselves as 'victims' and who desire few services
- Men involved in 'common couple violence' which require an informed and co-ordinated approach between men's and women's projects to produce an effective response
- Men who might be engaged in 'patriarchal terrorism' against their female partners yet who are attempting to manipulate the system in their favour and thus surveillance of this group is vital. (Robinson and Rowlands, 2006: 60)

The work of the Dyn Project with men experiencing domestic violence provides a beginning road map for the development of services for this population. It appears that the dynamics of abuse and response to services are different for gay and heterosexual men and that consequently they may benefit from separate service pathways. As already discussed, work with heterosexual men needs to employ a clear screening protocol. As in work with women victims, risk assessment and multi-agency work are crucial to addressing the safety of men, current or former partners and children. The Dyn Project also demonstrates the importance of developing a programme for men in concert with a women's service, so that essential information for assessing safety is available (Robinson and Rowlands, 2006).

> Men who are assessed as victims of violence will require support and advocacy, safety planning and multi-agency work.

It is clear that there is much scope for further development of practice with men who present as victims of domestic violence. The longstanding contestation over patterns of gender and perpetration of domestic violence has not been helpful in progressing this work. In moving forward, we suspect that both commonalities and differences in the experiences and challenges faced by male and female victims of domestic violence will become better understood. For example, both men and women face challenges in naming their experiences as domestic violence. However, the experiences of these challenges are shaped by their gendered locations. For women, ideas about women's responsibility for the success of family relationships can build a strong barrier of shame to disclosing abuse; for men, ideas about men as strong and powerful can build similar barriers of shame that inhibit disclosure and help-seeking. Both men and women may be motivated to act because of concerns for children's safety and well-being.

Conclusion

In this chapter, we have canvassed the complex issue of practices with men in the context of domestic violence. In comparison to practices with women and children, this work is less well developed. This is partly because of the historical development of the field, but also because of practitioners' reluctance to tackle the complex issues that arise. We hope that the issues addressed in this chapter equip social workers to tackle this aspect of practice as they come into contact with men involved in domestic violence through their work in many and varied fields of practice.

Summary Points

- Practices with men where there is domestic violence need to begin with an understanding of the knowledge base about gendered patterns of victimization and perpetration.
- Risk assessment and risk management underpin the work with men who use violence. This informs not only safety planning for victims but also for workers.
- Assessment is complex but is always the starting point when men present as victims of violence.
- Few men attend specialist men's behaviour change programmes and therefore workers across sectors such as AOD, mental health, aged care and child protection will be working with men who use violence and need to understand the principles of domestic violence intervention.
- 'The system matters' – individual or group work with perpetrators of violence is evaluated to be most effective where there are appropriate, timely and consistent responses to violence and abuse within the intervention system. Workers therefore need to be well connected to the broader justice and interagency context.
- There are particular issues to be addressed in holding men accountable for violence in their intimate relationships when they are simultaneously victimized because of their social location.
- The role of men as fathers is one that is frequently ignored. It is of particular pertinence when men have undermined and abused their relationship with their children through their use of violence towards the child's mother.
- When men are perpetrators of violence, social workers require specialist training and supervision to redirect their practice to work with mandated clients and to keep the safety of women and children at the forefront of the intervention even when the man is the presenting client.
- Where men are assessed as victims of violence, the general principles of safety planning, multi-agency work, advocacy and support underpin the approach.
- Gay men who are victims of domestic violence appear to engage with services more readily than do male heterosexual victims.

Reflective Questions for Practice

- If Tom and Daniel arrive together for the appointment with the social worker, what considerations could inform the ways in which the social worker manages the session?
- Tom and Daniel are adamant that they want couple counselling. What questions could the social worker ask to assess the risks and safety issues in this course of action?

- What different approaches could the social worker take in the event that Daniel was/was not able to acknowledge that his behaviour was abusive?
- How might the social worker engage Daniel in an exploration of his behaviour and assess his motivation to work towards accountability?

Further reading

Robinson, A. L. and Rowlands, J. (2006). The Dyn Project: supporting men experiencing domestic abuse. Final evaluation report. Available at www.cardiff.ac.uk/socsi/resources/Dyn_Final_Evaluation_Report.pdf.

The Dyn Project is one of the first attempts to systematically tackle the complex assessment and information gathering required to work with men who present at a service for male victims of violence.

Gondolf, E. W. (2002). *Batterer Intervention Systems: Issues, Outcomes and Recommendations*. Thousand Oaks, CA: Sage.

A seminal work that addresses the complexities of evaluating the effectiveness of men's behaviour-change programmes. It provides comprehensive information about the relationship between the courts, men's programmes and women's safety.

Donovan, C., Hester, M., Holmes, J. and McCarry, M. (2006). Comparing domestic abuse in same sex and heterosexual relationships. Available at www.bris.ac.uk/sps/research/projects/completed/2006/rc1307/rc1307finalreport.pdf.

This report provides knowledge for practice with gay men and lesbians affected by domestic violence.

Day, A., O'Leary:, Chung, D. and Justo, D. (2009). *Domestic Violence: Working with Men*. Leichhardt, NSW: The Federation Press.

This edited book draws together research and practice to provide a comprehensive picture of working with men within well-structured multi-agency environments.

7
Multi-agency Work: Collaborating for Women's and Children's Safety

Philomena, aged in her late 50s, has had multiple psychiatric hospitalizations for clinical depression and suicide attempts. She migrated to Australia from Greece with her husband as a young woman and raised four children. As she never worked outside the home, Philomena has had little opportunity to become proficient in English, but can communicate with the hospital staff on a limited basis. Her husband appears loving and concerned, and has been more than willing to interpret when Philomena talks with her doctors. At the time of her latest admission, the psychiatric unit had introduced a policy of routine inquiry about domestic violence, using structured screening questions. Following the new protocol, an interpreter is arranged and Philomena is asked the screening questions in a private space on the ward when her husband has left for the day. In response to sensitive inquiry, Philomena discloses a history of severe, controlling domestic violence. At times she has been locked out of the house, naked, and has slept in the dog's kennel. She describes how she and her children have lived in fear of her husband and how the children left home as soon as possible to escape him. Philomena says that she has dreamt of escape but has no money and is terrified of her husband's reaction. The staff are shocked that a patient that they knew 'so well' has disclosed a lifetime of abuse and violation, and feel ill equipped to help her. Her case manager contacts the specialist domestic violence service that recently provided training for their team. The domestic violence worker assists the case manager to develop a safety plan for Philomena on the ward and arranges to come in to meet with Philomena, her case manager and an interpreter so that Philomena can explore the options available to her.

In this chapter, we begin by defining collaboration and then exploring the essential elements of successful collaboration including developing a shared sense of purpose. We also examine the challenges of establishing this when many players view domestic violence through very different lenses. These include the lenses of criminal justice and women's advocacy, child protection and health. We place collaborative efforts to address domestic violence in their historical context and look briefly at the tensions that have arisen as an array of new players have become involved in responding to domestic violence. The chapter concludes with an example of using social work action research to enhance collaboration between two sectors that have not historically worked together: domestic violence and mental health services.

Clearly no sole agency can respond to the multiple effects of domestic violence on the safety, health and well-being of victims, nor provide assistance across the many domains – such as legal, health, housing, immigration and income support – where resources and action may be required to ensure victim safety and to hold offenders accountable. However, while the potential benefits of multi-agency work are clear, there are numerous challenges involved in achieving effective cross-agency collaboration. Some of these are common to all efforts in collaborating to address complex social problems; others stem from the nature and complexity of domestic violence itself.

In the preceding chapters, we have seen that definitions and understandings of domestic violence are contested. Domestic violence work has moved over time from being primarily situated in the community based women's sector to involving an increasing array of 'mainstream' agencies. Each views domestic violence through a different lens, shaped by factors such as its organizational remit, knowledge base and organizational culture. From these different perspectives, different aspects of domestic violence come more sharply into focus, bringing an array of ideas about how to tackle it. Through different lenses, domestic violence can be simultaneously framed as:

- a gender-based violation of human rights, grounded in social inequalities
- a crime
- a public health issue
- a child protection issue
- a personal/relationship issue – a violation of trust enacted against a woman by a man who claims, or claimed, to love her.

These different perspectives bring both benefits and challenges to multi-agency work with domestic violence.

Philomena's story highlights the benefits for victims/survivors that can flow when agencies work together to co-ordinate their responses to complex and potentially life-threatening situations. Leaving or attempting to leave a relationship characterized by controlling violence is a time when the risks of violence, including lethal violence, can escalate for women and children (Campbell et al., 2007). In this situation, the domestic violence service was able to help colleagues in the mental health service to respond to Philomena's immediate safety needs and by working together, provide Philomena with information about resources and options available to her.

A key point to keep in mind throughout this discussion is that collaboration is not the ultimate goal, but rather a means to achieving the key goals of domestic violence intervention: that is, enhancing the safety and autonomy of victims/survivors and holding perpetrators accountable (Shepard and Pence, 1999). We argue that it is important to think about collaboration as a *process*, rather than as an outcome in itself. This leaves open the possibility that there may be other ways to achieve these goals that could be more or less useful in any particular context. The evidence of the crucial role of independent women's advocates in maintaining a focus on these goals will also be highlighted.

> Collaboration is not the ultimate goal, but rather a process for achieving the key goals of domestic violence intervention.

Defining Collaboration

Many terms are used interchangeably when talking about multi-agency work: integration, co-ordination and 'joined-up' working. Multi-agency work is often conceptualized as lying along a continuum where the dimensions differ according to the degree to which the boundaries of the participating organizations are maintained or become permeable; in other words, the extent to which each retains organizational autonomy. Horwath and Morrison (2007: 56), for example, identify five levels of collaboration that range along a continuum from communication, through co-operation, co-ordination, coalition and integration.

For our purposes in this chapter, the more generic term 'collaboration' is preferred because it reflects our focus on process. Wood and Gray define it as:

> Collaboration occurs when a group of autonomous stakeholders of a problem domain engage in an interactive process, using shared rules, norms, and structures, to act or decide on issues related to that domain. (1991: 146)

The earliest efforts at multi-agency domestic violence work were initiated at local level by women's domestic violence services in Australia through local domestic violence committees and in the United Kingdom through borough (local government area) domestic violence forums. Large-scale government approaches to multi-agency collaboration, often termed 'whole-of-government' approaches, represent more recent systematic efforts by governments to respond to the widespread and intractable nature of domestic violence (Ross et al., 2011).

While the involvement of government and government agencies is essential to tackling domestic violence, the involvement of groups that have not historically been major players in responding to domestic violence has resulted in tensions for domestic violence advocates. For example, in the United Kingdom, New Labour's emphasis on whole-of-government approaches provided a statutory requirement that police and local authorities work together to reduce crime, including domestic violence, thus formalizing local collaborative initiatives (James-Hanmer, 2000). Ironically, this boost in recognizing the importance of domestic violence as a social issue was seen by some to have resulted in marginalization of the refuge sector, which had been the driving force in getting domestic violence onto the social agenda (Hague and Malos, 1998). Newer entrants into the collaborative response to domestic violence – often better resourced than women's services – have not always recognized and valued the expertise of the non-government women's sector. An example of the tensions that can arise when mainstream agencies enter the field can be seen in the initial reaction of women's advocates to the way in which a new domestic violence service, charged with building interagency collaboration, was established by several government agencies in Sydney, NSW:

> [F]or the NGOs [non-government organizations] in this area and particularly women's services who for years had been trying to get money and services and input, suddenly DoCS [statutory child protection] and Health had got this money, have consulted nobody and have set up this service down there … I don't think the [initial planning] process was respectful in some ways and it did create some conflict. (Laing et al., 2005: 59)

A source of tension for women's advocates is that service provision is not the sole goal of the domestic violence movement – broad social change to redress women's inequality in all aspects of social life is equally important. This creates a tension for women's services which both need to engage with the state to improve women's safety and to hold perpetrators accountable, yet wish to challenge the inequality structured within state institutions around differences such as gender, 'race', cultural background and ability. The rhetoric of collaboration and partnerships or unresolved conflicts over core issues such as whether domestic violence is gendered can limit the extent to which multi-agency forums actually promote changes that increase women's safety and autonomy, or become mere 'talking shops' (Patel, 2003). Recounting the withdrawal by Southall Black Sisters from an interagency project, Black activist Rahila Gupta provides an example of the this tension, arguing that continuing to participate 'would have severely compromised our autonomous voice, especially in relation to the state's failures' (2003: 21).

Essential Elements of Effective Collaboration

Considerable effort has been made to identify the key factors that facilitate effective multi-agency collaboration by human services organizations in responding to complex social issues. Three elements – leadership, power and a shared purpose – recur throughout the literature. Leadership that is fair (Wood and Gray, 1991) and which creates an inclusive climate that invites contributions from all stakeholders is vital (Allen, 2006). An essential part of creating a fair and inclusive climate involves tackling differences in power between participating agencies (Banks et al., 2008) so that the agenda of more powerful or higher-status agencies does not marginalize other voices. For example, organizations with greater power and resources can triage referrals (through a process of 'gate-keeping'), and this can promote conflict when other agencies with lower thresholds for intervention are unable to access resources for their clients (Scott, 2005). The development of a shared understanding of the nature of the problem being addressed and of the purpose of the collaboration are also core requirements (Horwath and Morrison, 2007; Wood and Gray, 1991). Appreciation of the culture of the participating organizations, including the constraints to their operations, is also very important (Johnson et al., 2003). Banks et al. (2008) describe this as a process of developing 'institutional empathy', which they argue is essential if the partner agencies are to have realistic expectations of what each is able to contribute to the collaboration. Adequate resources are also required if collaborative efforts are to be successful (Johnson et al., 2003).

> It is important for social workers to try to develop an understanding of the culture of the various participating organizations, including the constraints on their operations.

Multi-agency collaborations typically undertake a range of activities such as joint training, community education, developing joint policies and protocols, including for information exchange, establishing specialist positions and undertaking multidisciplinary case reviews. Multidisciplinary case reviews often focus on risk assessment and safety planning to co-ordinate agencies' action in high-risk situations, as, for example, in Multi-Agency Risk Assessment Conferences (MARAC) in the United Kingdom (Robinson, 2006). The Greenbook Project, a large, five-year study of collaboration across the domestic violence, courts and child protection systems in the United States, found that specialist positions were regarded by participants as one of the most influential factors in promoting system change. Examples were domestic violence advocates located within the child protection and the judicial systems. From the perspectives of participants, these positions 'were particularly important for engaging frontline workers in the collaboration, forming a bridge and supporting institutional empathy across systems' (Banks et al., 2008: 899). Involving frontline workers becomes more difficult as governments have become involved in developing complex, whole-of-government policy responses to domestic violence, a 'top-down' approach to developing co-ordinated or integrated responses, in comparison to the locally based efforts that characterized the earliest approaches to multi-agency work (Ross et al., 2011).

Horwath and Morrison (2007) caution that too great a focus on the establish-ment of collaborative structures and systems at the expense of attending to 'peo-ple issues' or the *process* of change involved in developing improved collaboration can result in failure. Building trusting cross-agency relationships takes time and requires ongoing work, but is essential if core differences in approach are to be faced and resolved rather than avoided. Inclusive, neutral leadership alongside specialist positions were found to be pivotal to addressing the volatile issues that arose in the Greenbook Project (Banks et al., 2008). Horwath and Morrison (2007) also note that the central focus of collaborative endeavours is typically on the promotion of multi-agency working relationships per se, rather than on ensur-ing that service users are placed at the centre of the process. As discussed at the beginning of this chapter, it is essential that women and children's safety be held as the focus of domestic violence collaborations. This highlights the importance of including the voices of survivors in multi-agency policy development (Hague and Mullender, 2006).

The role of women's domestic violence advocates is also crucial. Advocates can bring to the work of collaborative groups the first-hand experience of women liv-ing with domestic violence as well as their experiences of barriers and problems encountered in help-seeking. Since all well-intentioned policies and practices can have unintended consequences for the women and children they hope to assist, this information about women's experiences is invaluable data for the ongoing refine-ment of collaborative efforts. Drawing on their experience in the Duluth Abuse Intervention Project (DAIP), Pence and McDonnell argue that 'Victim advocates are obviously going to be your most vocal critics, but they can tell you where the problems exist' (1999: 61).

Ensure that women and children's safety and the accountability of perpetra-tors are held at the centre of domestic violence collaborations.

In some instances, independent women's advocates play a formal role as part of the collaborative system, as in the case with Independent Domestic Violence Advi-sors (IDVAs) who work with women assessed to be at high risk of harm or homicide in the context of the MARACs in the United Kingdom. They offer intensive short- to medium-term support with an emphasis on mobilizing multiple resources and co-ordinating the response of a wide range of agencies, but are independent of any single agency (Howarth et al., 2009). An evaluation of the IDVAs found that 57 per cent of victims experienced a cessation in the abuse following intervention by the IDVA; that intensive support was associated with greater likelihood of cessation of abuse; and that receiving multiple forms of support was also associated with increased chances of positive changes in victims' safety and well-being (Howarth, et al., 2009).

These findings are consistent with findings from an earlier American study of the association between advocacy that empowers women to access resources and improved safety and mental health (Sullivan and Bybee, 1999). They reflect a model of work developed over 30 years in the women's community based domestic violence sector that has been called 'community based advocacy', that is, interventions that 'help survivors of domestic violence navigate the systems involved in the community response as they attempt to acquire needed resources' (Allen et al., 2004: 1017). This approach has also been termed 'woman-defined advocacy' (Davies et al., 1998) or, more recently, 'relationship centred advocacy' (Goodman et al., 2009) and requires advocates 'to reach across silos and systems, crossing organizational cultures to respond to the survivor and her needs as she frames them' (2009: 320).

Given their client-centred approach to practice, we argue that social workers with a good understanding of domestic violence, no matter what their agency designation, are well placed to work with domestic violence advocates to ensure that multi-agency work maintains its focus on the safety and autonomy of the victim/survivor and accountability of the perpetrator. As domestic violence is increasingly recognized as underlying the presentations of many women, children and men to a range of agencies, social workers will be required to incorporate the skills of domestic violence advocacy into their practice. One approach is to build networks with specialist domestic violence services. For example, the mental health social worker was able to call on the skills of specialist colleagues to address the complexities of Philomena's situation.

Developing a Shared Purpose: The Struggle Over Meaning

One of the biggest challenges in working collaboratively is for the various participants to develop a shared understanding about the nature of the problem that is being addressed. Without such a shared understanding, it is not possible to build the essential sense of purpose that guides and gives meaning to collaborative efforts and motivates the various players. As each potential partner to the collaboration brings its unique perspective, tackling these differences in understanding can be one of the most challenging aspects of collaborative efforts. Core differences of philosophy and understanding about domestic violence, such as whether it is gendered and whether men and women's use of violence is different, can make it difficult to develop a shared purpose. For example, in a study of the effectiveness of a new, co-ordinated approach to domestic violence initiated by health and child protection services in Sydney, NSW, women's domestic violence services described struggles over philosophy:

> I guess there have been some serious conflicts around philosophy ... like taking out 'woman' and putting in 'family'. Philosophically there were some barriers there to achieving the greatest outcomes ... for them to take 'women' out of the aims and objectives was incredible to us. (Laing et al., 2005: 64)

At some stages in the movement against domestic violence, domestic violence advocates have framed domestic violence through particular lenses to build strategic partnerships with other agencies in order to further the goals of enhancing victim safety and perpetrator accountability. However, this strategy requires the various participants to negotiate shared understandings about the nature of domestic violence and the goals of intervention, and can result in tensions and challenges to building solid collaborative relationships. The following section of the chapter provides some examples of these challenges.

The Criminal Justice Lens and Women's Advocacy

At first sight, there appears to be an excellent 'fit' between a criminal justice response to domestic violence and the early call by feminist activists for violence committed in the privacy of the home to be treated in the same way by the criminal law as violence committed in public. As discussed in Chapter 3, this has resulted in the adoption of policies such as mandatory or preferred arrest, 'no drop' prosecution and 'zero tolerance' of violence. The success of advocating that domestic violence be seen through the lens of criminal justice is shown in the federal Violence Against Women legislation in the United States that prioritized criminal justice responses to domestic violence.

However, responding to domestic violence solely through the lens of criminal justice has resulted in some unanticipated consequences, such as women being arrested (often when using violence in self-defence) and women being forced to testify against their wishes in criminal proceedings against their partners when they may believe that this will increase, rather than decrease, the risks to their safety and well-being. Arrest of women can have far-ranging effects that can undermine their future efforts to establish a violence-free life. For example, it can disadvantage them in family law proceedings, and can exclude them from employment in some fields. Other women may fear that their partner receiving a criminal conviction will lead to the loss of his job, with subsequent impact on the family's financial security. Given the over-representation of Indigenous Australians in the criminal justice system and the history of Aboriginal deaths in custody, Indigenous women may fear that policies which centralize criminal justice responses place them in an invidious position where seeking assistance for domestic violence compromises their loyalty to their communities. These brief examples illustrate some of the ways in which framing domestic violence solely as a crime cannot capture the complexity of women's situations.

For the purposes of this discussion about collaboration, this example illustrates the difficulties that women's advocates, police and prosecutors may have in coming to a common understanding of what constitutes domestic violence and what the goals of legal intervention should be. The criminal justice system's goals of prosecution, punishment, deterrence and rehabilitation traditionally focus on offenders; this does not necessarily guarantee the victim's safety from future violence. Domestic violence advocates may highlight the fact that some criminal justice policies may, in fact, undermine the autonomy of a woman who has already suffered attacks to her autonomy through the coercive control exercised by her ex/partner. Dilemmas such as these in using the criminal law to respond to domestic violence are discussed in more detail in Chapter 3, together with some approaches that are being implemented to make the legal system more victim-focused.

The Child Protection Lens

Recognition of the harmful effects of living with domestic violence on children has resulted in the need to build collaboration between child protection and women's domestic violence services. These services have different histories, knowledge bases and service philosophies that shape the different lenses of each service. These can be described as 'child focused' on one hand and 'woman focused' on the other. Fleck-Henderson (2000) has described the necessary adjustments that are required to bring these two fields of practice together as 'seeing double' if a common purpose is to be established that focuses on the safety of both women and children. This issue is discussed in detail in Chapter 5.

The Health Lens

In comparison to the criminal justice sector, the health sector has been a relatively late entrant into the collaborative response to domestic violence. Advocates have drawn strategically on the extensive research evidence about the short- and long-term effects of domestic violence on women's physical and mental health (e.g. Bonomi et al., 2009; Campbell et al., 2002; Roberts et al., 2006; World Health Organization, 2005) to call for health services to become better at identifying the victims of domestic violence who remain largely invisible within health services. The evidence about the prevalence of domestic violence during pregnancy and its harmful effects on the mother and unborn child has further highlighted the importance of health services becoming involved in addressing domestic violence (Gartland et al., 2011; Taillieu and Brownridge, 2010). The key study by the Victorian Health Promotion Foundation (2004), which showed that domestic violence makes a greater contribution to the morbidity and mortality of women aged under 45 than the more commonly recognized risks such as obesity, smoking and high blood pressure, has been pivotal in providing an authorizing environment for greater health involvement in domestic violence intervention.

A health service may be the sole place that a woman might legitimately avoid the controlling presence of an abusive partner and safely disclose (Taft, 2003). Identification of domestic violence as a factor underlying women's presentation to health services can have the benefit of ensuring that the health response deals with the underlying issue rather than just the symptoms, such as depression (Astbury and Cabral, 2000). Disclosure also enables the women to be referred to domestic violence services. For these reasons, although the evidence is contested (Ramsay et al., 2002; Spangaro et al., 2009), some health services have introduced the policy of routine inquiry or 'screening' for domestic violence. Screening involves asking all women, or women attending health services such as mental health services and antenatal clinics where rates of domestic violence are known to be high, a series of questions that provide a woman with the opportunity to disclose that she is experiencing domestic violence. It was through a screening pro-gramme within the mental health service that domestic violence was identified as a previously invisible contributor to Philomena's depression.

Nevertheless, some advocates argue that the dominant biomedical model within health services, with its emphasis on diagnosis and on the expertise of the health care provider, pathologizes and individualizes what is essentially a social problem, and in some ways the survivor/health care provider relationship can replicate the power imbalance that women experience in relation to their abuser (Lavis et al., 2005). Wom-en's reactions to living with violence, including the development of symptoms of post-traumatic stress disorder (PTSD) such as hyper vigilance, fighting back or adopting a stance of 'passivity' are understood by advocates as the best coping actions available to a woman at a particular time, given the behaviour of the perpetrator and the relative availability of informal and formal sources of support. Through a medical lens, how-ever, they may be seen as indicative of the woman's pathology and the problem may come to be seen as lying within the woman. This can result in the woman being blamed for choosing not to disclose to the health care provider in response to screening ques-tions, stigmatized or disadvantaged in family law proceeding through receipt of a mental health diagnosis or labelled as 'non-compliant' for failing to follow the recom-mended 'treatment'(which may be simply advice that she must leave the relationship).

Collaboration is essential if the potential of better identification of domestic violence by health services is to be realized, because most of the resources that women require to deal with domestic violence lie outside the health system. To be effective, however, collaborative endeavours need to find ways to bridge the different understandings that shape the work of each sector. An example of collaboration across the domestic vio-lence and mental health sectors is described in the next section of this chapter.

These examples highlight one of the core requirements of successful collabora-tions, which is the development of a shared understanding of the nature of the prob-lem. Without such shared understandings, women's encounters with mainstream agencies can be potentially more harmful rather than helpful. For example, women may be blamed and treated with disrespect for their reluctance to proceed with a partner's prosecution, to leave a violent partner at the behest of child protection services, or for their reluctance to disclose violence to a health care provider.

Using Social Work Action Research to Enhance Collaboration

The Towards Better Practice (TBP) research project[*] was initiated in 2004 by a team of social work researchers, domestic violence and mental health workers in the state of New South Wales (NSW), Australia. Impetus for the research came

[*]The research project was funded through an Australian Research Council Linkage Grant (LP0562636) and four partner organizations: Transcultural Mental Health Centre and Education Centre Against Violence (NSW Health), Joan Harrison Support Services for Women, Inc. (shelter, outreach and advocacy services) and Fairfield/Liverpool Mental Health Service.

from recognition of the complex links between domestic violence and women's mental health. For example, when compared with women who have not experienced domestic violence, victims/survivors experience higher rates of depression, anxiety, post-traumatic stress disorder, alcohol and substance abuse and suicidality (Bonomi et al., 2009; Golding, 1999; World Health Organization, 2005). In addition, women living with a diagnosed serious mental illness such as schizophrenia or bi-polar disorder face increased risk of domestic violence (Howard et al., 2010). However, these links between domestic violence and women's mental health are often not recognized by mental health services, resulting in inappropriate health intervention that can compound women's suffering and compromise their safety (Humphreys and Thiara, 2003a). Even when the links are recognized, mental health assessment and treatment plans typically do not address the domestic violence (e.g. by including safety planning) or result in referrals to domestic violence services (Howard et al., 2010). In Philomena's case, the pervasiveness but invisibility of domestic violence in her life undermined the assessment and the efficacy of her mental health intervention.

From the perspective of domestic violence services, many women seeking assistance are experiencing mental health issues that require specialist mental health services. As a consequence, refuge cannot always be provided to women with a mental illness who are escaping domestic violence (Chung, et al., 2000). This increases the risk of homelessness, escalation of health issues and increases the risk that children will be removed from women's care.

A second important impetus to the research project was the broader policy context. In 2003, following the evaluation of a pilot screening programme (Irwin and Waugh, 2001), NSW Health issued a revised domestic violence policy which included the mandatory requirement that routine screening for domestic violence be carried out in all antenatal, mental health, drug and alcohol and early childhood services (NSW Department of Health, 2003). Implementation of the policy was supported by comprehensive training, an implementation protocol, the use of short, scripted screening questions, a data collection process and an unobtrusive, wallet-sized information card that was provided to all women, regardless of their response to screening (Spangaro, 2007). In mental health services, the domestic violence screening questions were integrated into the existing assessment protocol, the Mental Health Outcomes Assessment Tool (MH-OAT) (Spangaro, 2007). This domestic violence policy gave a clear message to health workers that domestic violence was very much part of the 'business' of public health services.

The Towards Better Practice research comprised a series of independent but related studies. The first was a series of in-depth interviews with 33 women from diverse cultural backgrounds that explored their experiences of attempting to navigate the mental health and domestic violence service systems (Laing et al., 2010b). While the women described how they came to recognize the links between their experiences of abuse at the hands of their partners and mental health impacts such as anxiety and depression, they found that mental health workers generally failed to ask about violence or to believe them if they disclosed it. For example,

Denise* was diagnosed with schizophrenia at age 22 and had experienced violence from three partners while receiving mental health treatment, but she noted:

> They never asked me about my relationships and stuff like that. They never asked me anything about that, like how my living standards were or anything. They just came and gave me my injection and my tablets and that was it. (Laing et al., 2010b: 12)

The women also reported that their partners were able to interfere with their treatment, particularly in the case of women whose first language was not English. For example, Bahar and her children endured 25 years of severe physical and emotional abuse, despite her attempts to get help:

> I went to doctors, I tried to get help, I tried hard to get help but my husband was interpreting ... and he was undermining my efforts to get help to improve my situation. (Laing et al., 2010b:14)

The second study involved a series of separate focus groups with domestic violence and mental health workers in a range of urban and rural locations at which the barriers and facilitators of collaboration were discussed. Each group described examples of failed efforts to get help for clients from the other sector, often due to unclear or confusing eligibility conditions and referral pathways, different models of assessment and different thresholds for intervention. For example:

> [O]ften women are abused but they don't qualify to go into the refuge. So [there are] others that fall through the gap – they might not have children or – I'm not sure what the criteria is but they just don't meet that so you've just got to send them back [to the abuse]. (Rural mental health worker in Laing et al., 2012b: 48)

The focus group participants at each location were then invited to participate in a meeting to receive feedback together with their colleagues from the other sector about the findings from the focus groups. While the ensuing discussion raised many barriers to collaboration and many examples of problems were described, this opportunity to begin a dialogue was appreciated by many participants. For example, one mental health worker commented: 'The most important thing you have done is get us together and open dialogue ... Initiating this conversation has created a lot of opportunities' (Laing et al., 2012b). Participants also discovered that they faced many common challenges in their work, such as inadequate resources, particularly in rural areas. Other examples of the process of beginning to find some 'common ground' were also seen. For example, domestic violence workers had commonly expressed concern about the impact on women of receiving a mental health diagnosis, fearing that this would result in women being blamed for their victimization, rather than responsibility being attributed to the perpetrator. They

---

*This is a pseudonym, as are the others in reported research.

discovered that some mental health workers were also concerned about the ways in which the perpetrator of violence could use the metal health system to hide their abuse by having their victim labelled as mentally ill:

> Perpetrators are sometimes so convincing that I have seen a woman recently who for four years was given medication injections for schizophrenia, until she came to the hospital two months ago and the doctor who looked after her said 'no this is a case of domestic violence.' She ceased all medication and she was discharged and she was asked to go to a refuge and she did. So this woman was treated for four years for schizophrenia with injections. (Mental health focus group participant in Laing et al., 2012b: 52)

Participants were invited by the research team to enter the third study where, using an action research approach, the researchers aimed to discover whether, and how, collaboration could be improved between the two service sectors. Action research is an approach that seeks to simultaneously produce knowledge and to implement change through continuous cycles of planning, acting, systematic observation and reflection (Craig, 2009). Through a participatory process, practitioners were engaged as co-researchers with the aim of improving practice.

Two action research groups in different geographical locations joined this study. The groups met monthly for a year, engaging in the cyclic process of reflection, planning, action and evaluation. Participants included domestic violence workers from shelters and community based outreach services and mental health practitioners from inpatient, crisis and outpatient teams. Both groups developed training strategies to share skills, knowledge and information about referral processes across the sectors. Beyond this, although each group identified similar broad strategies in response to barriers to collaboration identified in the focus groups, the actions implemented at the two locations were different, reflecting the strength of action research in responding to the specificity of local contexts of practice. For example, one group prioritized embedding change within a formal service agreement between the mental health service and three domestic violence services so that changes would not be lost with turnover of personnel. The service agreement includes an agreed definition of domestic violence, acknowledges the links between domestic violence and mental health and outlines specific procedures for a range of situations, such as clients of domestic violence services with a newly identified mental health concern; women using domestic violence services who are also active consumers of the mental health service; new consumers who present to the mental health service and are identified as victims of domestic violence (e.g. through routine screening); and actual or suspected perpetrators of domestic violence within the health service. The research group monitored the day-to-day implementation of the service agreement to ensure that it was a 'living' document, contributing to achieving enhanced collaborative practices. With support from their mental health colleagues, the domestic violence workers also successfully lobbied for funding to establish a new, specialist domestic violence/mental health outreach position. Based in a domestic violence service, this specialist worker had a brief to take referrals from the mental health service and to promote continuing cross-sector collaboration and training. This brought the skills of domestic violence advocacy that were discussed earlier to women in the mental health system.

Qualitative interviews were conducted with participants in the action research at this location at the mid-way (six months) and conclusion (12 months) of the action research, to explore what participants identified as contributing to the successful collaboration. Recognizing the commitment of each partner to the collaboration was the most important contributor from the perspective of both mental health and domestic violence workers:

> Having an awareness now that the mental health service is as committed as we (DV) are, has given us a different perspective on referring to them and dealing with them. We have still had some difficulties with different clients, but the people in mental health have been very positive and as committed as we are. (DV worker, Time 1) (Laing et al., 2012a: 126)

Building personal relationships, establishing a shared sense of purpose, developing 'institutional empathy', committed and inclusive leadership and having sufficient time to implement change, were other aspects that participants identified as contributing to the collaboration.

In the second location, the action research group established a joint mental health and domestic violence assessment process for women who disclosed domestic violence within the mental health service. This provided the opportunity for workers from the two sectors to work jointly with women, sharing skills and developing expertise on a case-by-case basis. This joint assessment process has continued beyond the conclusion of the action research, with participants jointly presenting their model of practice to other practitioners at seminars and conferences.

However, the test of any collaborative effort is the outcomes that flow to women. In both locations, interviews with participating staff identified ways in which they were now able to better assist victims/survivors. The greatest benefit reported by domestic violence workers was that they could now access mental health services for women, while mental health workers described changes in practices that stemmed from their new understanding about domestic violence and about the services available to women. For example, mental health workers reported that they were now more committed to screening women for domestic violence because they were confident that could offer something positive if women disclosed. Some reported that they were alert to the reality of domestic violence in the lives of the women using the mental health service:

> Before, when we did an assessment and there were some issues of domestic violence, the clinician was more inclined to think that it was part of the mental illness, that it wasn't really a reality, that it was a delusion. But now people are more thinking into like, no it can be possible it's not just a delusion it can be possible that there is domestic violence. (Mental health worker) (Laing et al., 2012a : 129)

Conclusion

In this chapter, we have attempted to move beyond the rhetoric that urges workers to collaborate, but that frequently underestimates the complexity and challenges of this endeavour. Drawing on research with domestic violence and mental health workers who had participated in an endeavour aimed at improving collaboration, we have heard from the people who have to make collaboration 'work', and what they saw as the keys to successful multi-agency work. At this point it is important to again emphasize that collaboration is not an end in itself, but an approach that can enhance women's safety and perpetrator accountability. However, without active domestic violence advocacy (provided in the action research example by the women's domestic violence services), even the best-intentioned collaborations can inadvertently harm women, for example by undermining rather than enhancing their autonomy or by blaming them for failing to adopt 'solutions' shaped by others. It is also important to be aware that no amount of collaboration can address issues such as inadequate resources or poor policy. The successful action research project, for example, was implemented against a background of systemic support through a comprehensive health service domestic violence policy. It demonstrated that collaboration through a problem-solving framework that keeps women's safety central can be a powerful approach to system change.

Summary Points

- No agency can tackle domestic violence alone, so multi-agency collaborative work is essential.
- Collaboration is a process rather than an outcome in itself.
- The goals of collaboration are enhancing the safety of women and children; enhancing women's autonomy; and holding perpetrators of violence accountable.
- Domestic violence advocates, including social workers, play a crucial role in ensuring that collaborative efforts remain focused on these goals.
- A key challenge to collaboration is developing a shared understanding of the nature of domestic violence and a shared sense of purpose for the collaborative efforts.
- Successful collaborations require:

  - fair and inclusive leadership;
  - that power differences are addressed;
  - realistic expectations of each agency;
  - adequate resources, including time;
  - attention to both collaborative structures and building relationships.

- Social workers can use action research to engage practitioners in efforts to build collaborative practices.

Reflective Questions for Practice

The mental health team and the domestic violence service that has worked with them to assist Philomena belong to the local domestic violence multi-agency forum. They are aware that clients such as Philomena have needs that are beyond the remit and resources of their respective agencies, such as access to legal advice and protections, safe housing and income support. However, one key agency persistently fails to turn up to the multi-agency forum. A lot of the group's time is spent grumbling about this problem and criticizing the absent organization. The mental health and domestic violence representatives realize that this situation is a barrier to effective multi-agency work in their local area and decide to work together to try to change the situation.

- What ideas in this chapter might be helpful to them in working out how to tackle this situation?
- What questions might they ask themselves about the ways in which power is operating in the forum and how this might be affecting attendance?
- What factors might they identify as possibly getting in the way of this agency's participation?
- What strategies might they come up with to tackle this problem and build a stronger collaboration?

Further Reading

Banks, D., Dutch, N. and Wang, K. (2008). Collaborative efforts to improve system response to families who are experiencing child maltreatment and violence. *Journal of Interpersonal Violence*, 23(7): 876–902.

This reports the findings of a major study of efforts to enhance collaboration between domestic violence, child protection and the courts at six sites over five years in the United States. It provides comprehensive analysis of the facilitators and enablers of collaboration.

Shepard, M. and Pence, E. (1999). *Coordinating Community Responses to Domestic Violence: Lessons from Duluth and Beyond*. Thousand Oaks, CA: Sage.

This is a foundational source on co-ordinated community responses to domestic violence. It remains a key text in this area for good reasons, providing a distillation of years of practice experience and efforts to implement systems change.

(Continued)

(Continued)

Robinson, A. L. (2006). Reducing repeat victimization among high-risk victims of domestic violence: the benefits of a co-ordinated community response in Cardiff, Wales. *Violence Against Women*, 12(8): 761–788.

An example of effective, evaluated multi-agency practice which provided the basis for the Multi-agency Risk Assessment Conferences that are now widely available in the United Kingdom.

8

Concluding Reflections

> *Faiza is an 18-year-old woman who has grown up in England. She has strong connections with the drop-in centre in her local neighbourhood, which has a particular focus and activities for young people with a South Asian background. Faiza has recently been for a holiday in Pakistan to visit her extended family. After a long absence from the drop-in centre, she arrives one day, obviously physically unwell, with a fever, asking to see Nada, the community development/youth worker who facilitates the programme for young people. Faiza is tearful and clearly distressed. Nada notices that she now wears a wedding ring. On initial questioning about her physical well-being, Nada suspects that Faiza has a serious urinary tract infection which needs immediate medical intervention. Further questioning also brings to light that Faiza is now married to an older man. She is clearly deeply distressed by her current circumstances but is reticent to disclose details of what is happening for her. However, the focus on responding to the possible urinary tract infection brings to light the fear and distress she is experiencing about her recent marriage, which she says occurred against her will. This is the first time that she has been able to speak to anyone about her changed circumstances.*

To hold traumatic reality in consciousness requires a social context that affirms and protects the victim and which joins victim and witness in common alliance. For the individual victim, this social context is created by relationships with friends, lovers and family. For the larger society, the social context is created by political movements that give voice to the disempowered. (Herman, 1992: 9)

In considering future developments in the interface between social work and domestic violence, the comment from Judith Herman is as relevant today as it was in 1992. A social movement which continues to name and respond with passion to the victims of intimate partner violence is an essential backdrop for effective intervention. A number of strategies may be of importance in shaping the future, though there is no crystal ball to predict what issues may be pivotal. In the 1970s, for example, could we have predicted that the issues for children living with domestic violence would have become 'hitched' to the child protection agenda, or that the issues of divorce and separation would have brought such a widespread backlash against women naming the violence they and their children have experienced as a reason for separation? As we write, the shape of social work is also shifting as the configuration of human services changes and the role of social workers moves from generic work, to specialization and back again. Some trends in domestic violence work are currently evident and therefore invite some concluding reflections.

We begin this chapter by focusing on two important trends: a broader engagement of the domestic violence field with the **many forms that violence against women and their children can take**; and the momentum gathering around **prevention and earlier intervention strategies**. These issues connect with areas where social work may not be central, but where the ramifications for practice will be experienced if these areas of work continue to develop. We conclude by providing **a framework for ongoing critical reflection and action** by social workers about their practice, highlighting three themes that have emerged consistently throughout the book: **secrecy, responsibility and protection/loyalty**.

Violence Against Women and their Children

In many western nations, services for sexual assault and domestic violence developed separately even though early feminist research stressed the continuities across the many forms of violence against women and girls (Kelly, 1988; Russell, 1984). The increasing adoption of a human rights framework to underpin action on violence against women (Kelly, 2005) has increased calls to develop policy responses that include multiple forms of gender-based violence: domestic violence; female genital mutilation; forced and child marriage; 'honour' crimes; rape and sexual assault; stalking, sexual abuse and sexual exploitation of girls; sexual harassment including through the Internet; trafficking in women and exploitation in the sex industry (Kelly and Lovett, 2005). England and Wales and Scotland now have strategic plans for addressing all forms of violence against women (HM Government, 2011, 2012; The Scottish Government, 2009). The Australian Government's National Plan, although less comprehensive, does address both sexual and domestic violence (National Council to Reduce Violence Against Women and their Children, 2009).

There are clear advantages in such comprehensive approaches. Almost 50 per cent of women are estimated to experience at least one form of gender-based violence in their lifetime and many women experience multiple and overlapping forms of violence (Heise et al., 1999; Kelly, 1988; Walby and Allen, 2004). These can compound and exacerbate the effects on women's physical and mental health and life chances. Such an approach enables consideration of both the continuities in the forms that gendered violence takes and the specificity of forms of abuse stemming from each woman's social location, without simply ascribing these to static factors such as culture or disability. Although our focus is on domestic violence, we believe that as part of the efforts to 'widen the frame', keeping in mind the intersection of domestic violence with other forms of violence against women should form part of the critical reflection that social workers undertake in their work with domestic violence (Nixon and Humphreys, 2010).

Within the United Kingdom, the work of Liz Kelly has been instrumental in drawing attention to the interconnections in the violence against women arena and the common impacts and consequences of violence against women, which include:

- longstanding myths and stereotypes that have served to justify or excuse abuse and/or to blame victims
- the dynamics of power and control underlying abuse
- the social organization of gender which produces the distribution of victimization and perpetration
- high levels of under-reporting
- the justice gap in relation to prosecutions and convictions
- the long-term psychological, social and economic impacts and consequences
- the extent of repeat victimization, both by the same and different perpetrators
- a historic failure of state agencies to respond appropriately. (Kelly and Lovett, 2005: 5)

Taken together, there is more commonality than difference in the many forms that violence against women and girls takes. Situating the work within a wider frame highlights the issue as not only a personal problem for individual women and girls, but also draws attention to the social context which makes these experiences of abuse widespread and indicative of a major social problem in which governments, organizations, professionals and individuals all have responsibility for intervention. Conceptualizing domestic violence using the violence against women frame also highlights the constellation of patterns and forms that violence against women can take while ensuring that the movement makes room for the voices of marginalized women (Nixon and Humphreys, 2010). In an increasingly globalized world, social workers are frequently working with refugees and immigrants from diverse cultural backgrounds and in different settings across the world, where knowledge of the many forms of gender-based violence is essential.

The confluence of issues that are impacting on Faiza in the opening scenario provides an example of the complex intervention which may be needed to respond to her. Violence against women brings a wide range of inter-related health and mental health impacts (Heise et al., 1999), and Faiza's experience suggests that she may well be both physically and emotionally affected by forced sex as an aspect of forced marriage. Further information would be needed to establish that this was the case. However, for social workers working in this area, effective intervention will need to be cognizant of the health impacts of violence. From a comprehensive review of research on the health impacts of gender-based violence, Astbury and Cabral concluded that:

Women who have experienced violence, whether in childhood or adult life, have increased rates of depression and anxiety, stress related syndromes, pain syndromes, phobias, chemical dependency, substance use, suicidality, somatic and medical symptoms, negative health behaviours, poor subjective health and changes to health service utilization. (2000: 75)

The wide range of health impacts highlights that violence against women is a major issue of gender-based health inequality. This conceptualization is supported by other research studies, such as the Australian study (Victorian Health Promotion Foundation, 2004) which found that the highest risk factor in determining the physical health of women under 45 years of age was whether they had experienced intimate partner violence. The health burden contributed by intimate partner violence was significantly greater than any other risk factor (2004: 25). This finding is similar to the assertion made by the World Health Organization report (Krug et al., 2002), namely that experiences of violence are the biggest contributor to women's poor physical and mental health, and unsurprisingly, that those exposed to chronic and severe gender-based violence are those at most risk of these health problems.

There are clearly many advantages that flow from widening the frame to address more broadly the issues of violence against women, such as better responding to the holistic needs and experiences of women and girls. However, as with any conceptualization, the inclusions and exclusions will always be problematic. Clearly, the emphasis on violence against women excludes male victims of domestic and sexual violence. This is not an insignificant issue and illustrates the complexity of naming and framing in this area. A reflection would be that while embracing the turn to the wider framing of 'violence against women', more active attention will need to be simultaneously given to men who are victims, recognizing in the process that 'men as victims' is a complex area in itself (see Chapter 6).

Prevention and Earlier Intervention

As the 'wicked problem' (Rittel and Webber, 1973) of domestic violence continues to emerge with all its problems of definition, different perspectives, undefined boundaries, complex and changing approaches to intervention, increasing attention is being given to the prevention agenda (HM Government, 2011). It is clear that there is no easy way to 'treat' our way out of the problem. It is far better to prevent rape and coercive control in an intimate relationship, to eradicate a problem through tackling its root causes, than to intervene once the problem has occurred. Faiza would not be facing her current crisis if she had not been forced into a marriage in the first place.

The prevention field is dynamic and changing. Generally, the prevention field draws on public health models which designate inter-related primary, secondary and tertiary dimensions to a prevention strategy (Ellis, 2008; VicHealth, 2007). Primary domestic violence prevention focuses on not only changing individual behaviour, knowledge and skills, but also the structural, cultural and social contexts in which violence occurs, fostered by relationships of inequality and violence (Hester and Westmarland, 2005; VicHealth, 2007).

The World Health Organization's *World Report on Violence and Health* (Krug et al., 2002) provides the basis from which many national prevention strategies have drawn. An ecological model which recognizes the multiple and interacting levels of influence provides the foundation for strategic thinking. VicHealth (2007: 13), for instance, has adapted the model to build a strategic framework for action based on a comprehensive evidence base. Three broad themes for action are identified: promoting equal and respectful relationships between men and women; promoting non-violent norms and reducing the effects of prior exposure to violence; and improving access to resources and systems of support. Much of the public health model focuses particularly on the first theme of promoting respectful relationships between men and women. Internationally recognized campaigns such as White Ribbon (e.g. Flood, 2010) or Reclaim the Night (see www.reclaimthenight.org) exemplify the primary prevention focus through a targeted and co-ordinated strategy. Campaigns such as these seek to make small changes in large populations of people (Ellis, 2008), drawing attention to the broader issue rather than responding to the individuals involved.

Schools have also been a site for a strategic focus on primary prevention (Ellis et al., 2006). While this strategy is far from straightforward within an over-crowded curriculum, the opportunity to reach children and young people in the general population and engage them in the establishment of positive cultural norms to promote respectful and equal relationships is considered a significant point of change. National violence prevention strategies consistently highlight the foundational nature of this work (Council of Australian Governments, 2011). However, a national audit of prevention programmes in schools undertaken in England pointed to the complexity of the issues involved (Ellis, 2004). While there was a wide spread of school-based prevention programmes at that time, without a coherent national strategy and resource base the work was fragmented and short term. On average, programmes were lasting no more than two years and were strongly dependent on whether the work was supported in a multi-agency context. The content and structure of the curricula varied significantly from minimal 20-minute 'talks' in school assemblies to embedding programmes in a whole-of-school approach to respectful relationships. The most common programmes were six hours delivered across six sessions. Evaluation was constrained by resources and small programmes and so it was difficult to establish effectiveness (Ellis, 2004). Thus, while school-based programmes are considered to provide rich opportunities for the prevention agenda, national political will is required to both resource and prioritize this strategy.

A Frame for Critical Reflection and Action

We began this chapter with a comment from Judith Herman, which emphasized the importance of a social movement in creating a context in which the voices of victims/survivors of sexual and domestic violence can be heard and responded to through the types of policies and practices that have been discussed in this book: those that centralize the safety of women, children and some men who experience violence and abuse; that partner with survivors to enhance their autonomy; that respond to the complexity of the survivors' social locations; and that recognize the necessity of multi-agency work.

Ensuring that this space remains open for recognition and response to victims/ survivors also depends on practitioners and policy workers, such as social workers, who continue to name violence, resisting the very real and persistent pressure to look the other way, or to accept the perpetrators' views that blame the victim (Herman, 1992). This is not an easy task in a context of limited and diminishing resources and increased and often contradictory demands on the profession.

Throughout the book, we have emphasized the importance of critical reflection by social workers as a core element of engaging with the complexities and challenges of domestic violence work. To draw together the key ideas in this book we identify here some recurring themes that reflect the dynamics of domestic violence as well as the wider forms of violence against women. We suggest that these three themes can provide social workers with a framework or lens for critically reflecting on their practice with domestic violence and a touchstone for evaluating and developing new policy approaches. These themes are:

- secrecy
- responsibility
- protection/loyalty.

We argue that these dynamics operate not only in the immediate context of the relationship between the victim and perpetrator, but also at the broader socio-political level where patterned gender inequalities intersect with other inequalities such as those based on 'race', class, ability and sexuality.

Secrecy

We saw in Chapter 2 in the discussion of the historical context of the 'discovery' of domestic violence, that silence and secrecy enabled the abuse of women and children to continue for centuries, yet to be effectively invisible. Perpetrators invariably attempt to silence their victims through tactics such as fear or threats because secrecy enables both the ongoing abuse of power within intimate relationships and the evasion of accountability. However, the key to the effectiveness of the silencing tactics of perpetrators lies in the reluctance of institutions and the broader society to acknowledge the prevalence and devastating effects of intimate partner violence, a reluctance that speaks not merely to the attitudes of individuals but to deeply entrenched patterns of gender inequality, cultural supports for violence against women and girls and the ongoing legacies of colonization, war and slavery (Nixon and Humphreys, 2010; Waldegrave, 2003).

We also saw in Chapter 2 how challenging secrecy by naming the formerly silenced experiences of violence promoted major social change and the development of institutional responses to domestic violence. We saw the benefits as well as the risks for victims/survivors of violence in breaking that silence and secrecy. Disclosure or breaking the silence is an act of enormous courage, and if responded to with support and validation can form the cornerstone of recovery from the effects of living with violence and abuse. In Chapter 3 we discussed how the core skills and values of social work, together with understanding of the unique aspects of work with victims/survivors of domestic violence, positioned social workers to make an important contribution to advocacy work with domestic violence, both with individual victims/survivors and at the policy level.

We also reviewed evidence that a significant proportion of women who challenge secrecy by naming their experiences of violence report that they received no useful assistance from either formal or informal sources of support. Responses to disclosures that reflect disbelief, that suggest that victims/survivors are lying or exaggerating, that blame or stigmatize them for their victimization, or that question their motives for telling, perpetuate secondary victimization which compounds the harm of the abuse itself and can further entrap victims within a relationship of coercive control. This highlights the important continuing role for social workers and other advocates in community education about domestic violence so that friends, family and work colleagues are better resourced to support victims/survivors who reach out for help. It also illustrates the importance of social workers being aware of the ways in which domestic violence may present in their particular agency context, whether this be mental health, child protection or aged care, to name a few. Sensitive inquiry in a safe and confidential environment can provide a bridge to disclosure and to safety. Particular attention to the possibility that domestic violence may be occurring will be required when powerful discourses allow little space for the disclosure of experiences of violence. For example, we discussed in Chapter 5 the ways in which the current ideological commitment to shared parenting in the Family Law system can silence women about the domestic violence or can cast suspicion and disbelief on disclosures made in the context of separation. In contexts such as these, social workers with knowledge of the domestic violence evidence base are well placed to challenge efforts to silence women (e.g. through simplistic constructions of them as 'alienating mothers').

Responsibility

Misplaced responsibility is at the core of domestic violence and all other forms of violence against women. Perpetrators typically deny, minimize and excuse their violence and its effects on both women and children. They are active in blaming their victim whose failure to conform to their (usually ever shifting) demands is portrayed as the cause of the violence. Blaming the victim and excusing the perpetrator of violence is still unfortunately a common response by both informal networks and service providers, exacerbating the pain and self-blame experienced by victims/survivors. Studies of community attitudes to domestic violence indicate that, while some attitudes have changed over time in response to educational activities, some remain deeply entrenched. There remains, for example, limited empathy for the entrapment of victims of domestic violence. A comprehensive national survey of community attitudes to violence against women in Australia found that just half of the respondents believed that a woman could leave a violent relationship if she really wanted to (Victorian Health Promotion Foundation, 2009), suggesting that women are seen to hold considerable responsibility for ending domestic violence.

We have explored many examples of misplaced responsibility for domestic violence in this book. Most obvious is the historical pattern of statutory child protection services placing responsibility onto women rather than onto the perpetrator for the exposure of children to domestic violence, which was discussed in Chapter 5, along with suggestions for shifting the policy and practice response to one that is both more just and more able to acknowledge and protect the adult and child victims of domestic violence. In addition, throughout the book, we have encouraged the practice of critical reflection by social workers and other service providers to avoid women being inappropriately held accountable for the shortcomings of service delivery and policies. We have argued that social workers with a good understanding of domestic violence dynamics and victims/survivors' safety planning and risk management strategies are well placed to advocate for them in multi-agency contexts in which their failure to follow 'worker led' or 'system prescribed' solutions may otherwise result in their being subjected to victim-blaming attitudes and behaviours that discourage, rather than encourage, future help-seeking. We contend that accountability in policy and practice requires an equal focus on the readiness of the service system to change, rather than a sole focus on the readiness of victims/survivors to undertake the complex and challenging process of change in the context of domestic violence (Humphreys et al., 2011).

Protection/Loyalty

As a result of the misplaced responsibility for domestic violence, victims are often burdened not only with the abuse and its effects on their lives and relationships, but also with the responsibility for taking care of others, often at the risk to their own safety and well-being. Women may excuse their partner's behaviour, for example, because they feel responsible to help overcome the effects of his difficult childhood; they may struggle with a sense of responsibility for depriving their children of a father if they end the relationship; they may feel responsible for making a success of the marriage. In some communities, women may carry a heavy load of loyalty to family and community, because ending a relationship engenders shame for their extended family. Women from minoritized communities and gay male victims of domestic violence may feel that seeking safety from domestic violence through the use of the law is an act of disloyalty, one that may increase racism and homophobia towards their communities. Effective work in these situations is not possible through the imposition of worker-led solutions that fail to acknowledge the complexities of victims/survivors' responses to domestic violence. Returning to our opening scenario, the dangers for Faiza are evident in speaking to someone about her 'forced marriage': an action in which she is putting her own emotional and physical survival above that of family loyalty and secrecy. The utmost sensitivity will be required to work at Faiza's pace and build the necessary alliances professionally and personally that would support her through a potentially dangerous situation.

Conclusion

In this book we have argued that, while most social workers will not be involved in specialist roles in responding to domestic violence, all social workers need to have a framework of understanding that they can draw on when they inevitably encounter domestic violence in their work. Knowledge of the evidence base in this field and the capacity for critical reflection on policy and practice are crucial to an effective response. We suggest that attention to the ways in which the dynamics of secrecy, responsibility and protection/loyalty are operating can provide a productive starting point for critical reflection and informed action.

References

Abrahams, C. (1994). *Hidden Victims*. London: NCH Action for Children.

Abrahams, H. (2010). *Rebuilding Lives after Domestic Violence: Understanding Long-Term Outcomes*. London: Jessica Kingsley.

Adams, R., Dominelli, L. and Payne, M. (eds) (2002). *Social Work: Themes, Issues and Critical Debates* (2nd ed.). Basingstoke: Palgrave Macmillan.

Ainsworth, F. and Hansen, P. (2006). Five tumultuous years in Australian child protection: little progress. *Child and Family Social Work*, 11(1), 33–41.

Allen, N. E. (2006). An examination of the effectiveness of domestic violence coordinating councils. *Violence Against Women*, 12(1), 46–67.

Allen, N. E., Bybee, D. I. and Sullivan, C. M. (2004). Battered women's multitude of needs: evidence supporting the need for comprehensive advocacy. *Violence Against Women*, 10(9), 1015–1035.

Almeida, R. V. and Dolan-Del Vecchio, K. (1999). Addressing culture in batterers intervention: the Asian Indian community as an illustrative example. *Violence Against Women*, 5(6), 654–683.

Almeida, R. V. and Durkin, T. (1999). The cultural context model: therapy for couples with domestic violence. *Journal of Marital and Family Therapy*, 25, 313–324.

Almeida, R. V. and Lockard, J. (2005). The cultural context model: a new paradigm for accountability, empowerment and the development of critical consciousness against domestic violence. In N. J. Sokoloff (ed.), *Domestic Violence at the Margins: Readings on Race, Class, Gender and Culture* (pp. 301–320). New Brunswick: Rutgers University Press.

Almeida, R. V., Woods, R., Messineo, T., Font, R. J. and Heer, C. (1994). Violence in the lives of the racially and sexually different: a public and private dilemma. *Journal of Feminist Family Therapy*, 5(3/4), 99–126.

Alston, M. and Bowles, W. (2003). *Research for Social Workers. An Introduction to Methods* (2nd ed., pp. 1–26). Sydney: Allen and Unwin.

Anderson, D. K. and Saunders, D. G. (2003). Leaving an abusive partner: an empirical review of predictors, the process of leaving and psychological well-being. *Trauma, Violence and Abuse*, 4(2), 163–191.

Anitha, S. (2011). Legislating gender inequalities: the nature and patterns of domestic violence experienced by South Asian women with insecure immigration status in the United Kingdom. *Violence Against Women*, 17(10), 1260–1285.

Archer, J. (2000). Sex differences in aggression between heterosexual partners: a meta-analytic review. *Psychological Bulletin*, 126(5), 651–680.

Arney, F. and Scott, D. (2010). *Working with Vulnerable Families – A Partnership Approach*. Melbourne: Cambridge University Press.

Astbury, J. and Cabral, M. (2000). *Women's Mental Health: An Evidence Based Review*. Retrieved 16 July 2006 from www.who.int/mental_health/media/en/67.pdf.

Atkinson, J. (2002). *Trauma Trails, Recreating Song Lines: The Transgenerational Effects of Trauma in Indigenous Australia*. Melbourne: Spinifex.

Austin, J. B. and Dankwort, J. (1999). The impact of a batterers' program on battered women. *Violence Against Women, 5*(1), 25–42.

Australian Bureau of Statistics (1996). *Women's Safety Australia* Cat. 4128.0. Canberra: Australian Bureau of Statistics.

Australian Bureau of Statistics (2005). *Personal Safety Survey*. Canberra: Australian Bureau of Statistics.

Babcock, J. C., Green, C. E. and Robie, C. (2004). Does batterers' treatment work? A meta-analytic review of domestic violence treatment. *Clinical Psychology Review, 23*(8), 1023–1053.

Bagshaw, D. and Chung, D. (2000). *Men, Women and Domestic Violence*. Canberra: Commonwealth of Australia.

Bagshaw, D., Brown, T., Wendt, S., Campbell, A., McInnes, E., Tinning, B., Batagol, B., Sifris, A., Tyson, D., Baker, J. and Arias, P. F. (2010). *Family Violence and Family Law in Australia: The Experiences and Views of Children and Adults from Families who Separated Post-1995 and Post-2006* (Vol. 1). Retrieved 6 December 2011 from www.ema.gov.au/www/agd/rwpattach. nsf/VAP/%289A5D88DBA63D32A661E6369859739356%29~FLB+-+Monash+Family+Vi olence+Research+-+FINAL+REPORT+Volume+1+-+April+2010.pdf/$file/FLB+-+Monash+F amily+Violence+Research+-+FINAL+REPORT+Volume+1+-+April+2010.pdf.

Bagshaw, D., Brown, T., Wendt, S., Campbell, A., McInnes, E., Tinning, B., Batagol, B., Sifris, A., Tyson, D., Baker, J. and Arias, P. F. (2011). The effect of family violence on post-separation parenting arrangements: the experiences and views of children and adults from families who separated post-1995 and post-2006. *Family Matters,* (86), 49–61.

Baker, P. (1997). And I went back: battered women's negotiation of choice. *Journal of Contemporary Ethnography, 26*(1), 55–74.

Bancroft, L. and Silverman, J. G. (2002). *The Batterer as Parent*. Thousand Oaks: Sage.

Banks, D., Dutch, N. and Wang, K. (2008). Collaborative efforts to improve system response to families who are experiencing child maltreatment and violence. *Journal of Interpersonal Violence, 23*(7), 876–902.

Belknap, J., Melton, H. C., Denney, J. T., Feury-Steiner, R. E. and Sullivan, C. M. (2009). The levels and roles of social and institutional support reported by survivors of intimate partner abuse. *Feminist Criminology, 4*(4), 377–402.

Bell, M. E. and Goodman, L. A. (2001). Supporting battered women involved with the court system: an evaluation of a law school-based advocacy intervention. *Violence Against Women, 7*(12), 1377–1404.

Bell, M. and McGoren, J. (2003) *Domestic Violence Risk Assessment Model*. Ulster, Northern Ireland: Barnardo's.

Bell, M. E., Perez, S., Goodman, L. A. and Dutton, M. A. (2011). Battered women's perceptions of civil and criminal court helpfulness: the role of court outcome and process. *Violence Against Women, 17*(1), 71–88.

Bennett, L., Goodman, L. A. and Dutton, M. A. (1999). Systemic obstacles to the criminal prosecution of a battering partner: a victim perspective. *Journal of Interpersonal Violence, 14*(7), 761–772.

Blagg, H., Ray, D., Murray, R. and Macarthy, E. (2000). *Crisis Intervention in Aboriginal Family Violence*. Canberra: Department of Prime Minister and Cabinet.

Bograd, M. (1999). Strengthening domestic violence theories: intersections of race, class, sexual orientation and gender. *Journal of Marital and Family Therapy, 25*(3), 275–289.

Bograd, M. and Mederos, F. (1999). Battering and couples therapy: universal screening and selection of treatment modality. *Journal of Marital and Family Therapy, 25*(3), 291–312.

Bonomi, A. E., Anderson, M. L., Reid, R. J., Rivara, F. P., Carrell, D. and Thompson, R. S. (2009). Medical and psychosocial diagnoses in women with a history of intimate partner violence. *Archives of Internal Medicine*, 169(18), 1692–1697.

Bonomi, A. E., Anderson, M. L., Rivara, F. P. and Thompson, R. S. (2007). Health outcomes in women with physical and sexual intimate partner violence exposure. *Journal of Women's Health*, 16(7), 987–997.

Braaf, R. and Barrett Meyering, I. (2011). Seeking security: women's economic wellbeing during and following domestic violence. *Research Report*. Retrieved 13 July 2011 from www.adfvc.unsw.edu.au/PDF%20files/Seeking%20Security%20Report%20WEB.pdf.

Brandon, M., Belderson, P., Warren, C., Gardner, R., Howe, D., Dodsworth, J. and Black, J. (2008a). The preoccupation with thresholds in cases of child death or serious injury through abuse and neglect. *Child Abuse Review*, 17(5), 313–330.

Brandon, M., Belderson, P., Warren, C., Howe, D., Gardner, R., Dodsworth, J. and Black, J. (2008b). Analysing child deaths and serious injury through abuse and neglect: what can we learn? A biennial analysis of serious case reviews 2003–2005. *Research Report No DCSF-RR023*. London: Department of Children, Skills and Families.

Branigan, E. (2007). 'Who pays in the end?' The personal and political implications of financial abuse of women in intimate partner relationships. *Just Policy*, 44, 31–36.

Breckenridge, J. and James, K. (2010). Thinking about homicide risk: a practice framework for counselling. *Stakeholder Paper 9*. Australian Domestic and Family Violence Clearinghouse Available from www.adfvc.unsw.edu.au/PDF%20files/Stakeholder%20Paper_9.pdf.

Bromfield, L. and Miller, R. (2009). *Cumulative Harm: A Practice Guide*. Victoria: Department of Human Services. Retrieved 3 February 2012 from www.aifs.gov.au/nch/pubs/presentations/cumulativeharm.ppt#256,1.

Buchanan, A., Hunt, J., Bretherton, H. and Bream, V. (2001). *Families in Conflict*. Bristol: Policy Press.

Buchanan, F. (2008). Mother and infant attachment theory and domestic violence: crossing the divide. *Stakeholder Paper 5*. Retrieved 13 July 2011 from www.adfvc.unsw.edu.au/PDF%20files/Stakeholder%20Paper_5.pdf.

Bunston, W. and Heynatz, A. (eds) (2006). *Addressing Family Violence Programs: Groupwork Interventions for Infants, Children and their Parents*. Melbourne: The Royal Children's Hospital Mental Health Service.

Burman, E. and Chantler, K. (2005). Domestic violence and minoritisation: legal and policy barriers facing minoritized women leaving violent relationships. *International Journal of Law and Psychiatry*, 28(1), 59–74.

Campbell, J. (1986). Nursing assessment for risk of homicide with battered women. *Advances in Nursing*, 8(4), 36–51.

Campbell, J. (2004). Helping women understand their risk in situations of intimate partner violence. *Journal of Interpersonal Violence*, 19(12), 1464–1477.

Campbell, J. C. and Dienemann, J. D. (2001). Ethical issues in research on violence against women. In C. Renzetti, J. L. Edleson and R. K. Bergen (eds), *Sourcebook on Violence Against Women* (pp. 57–72). Thousand Oaks, CA: Sage.

Campbell, J. C. and Soeken, K. (1999). Forced sex and intimate partner violence: effects on women's risk and women's health. *Violence Against Women*, 5, 1017–1035.

Campbell, J., Glass, N., Sharps, P. W., Laughon, K. and Bloom, T. (2007). Intimate partner homicide: review and implications of research and policy. *Trauma Violence and Abuse*, 8(3), 246–269.

Campbell, J., Jones, A., S., Dienemann, J., Kub, J., Schollenberger, J., O'Campo, P., Carlson Gielen, A. and Wynne, C. (2002). Intimate partner violence and physical health consequences. *Archives of Internal Medicine*, 162(10), 1157–1163.

Campbell, J., Rose, L., Kub, J. and Nedd, D. (1998). Voices of strength and resistance: a contextual and longitudinal analysis of women's responses to battering. *Journal of Interpersonal Violence*, 13(6), 743–762.

Campbell, J., Webster, D. W. and Glass, N. (2009). The danger assessment: validation of a lethality risk assessment instrument for intimate partner femicide. *Journal of Interpersonal Violence*, 24(4), 653–674.

Carlson, B. (2000). Children exposed to intimate partner violence: research findings and implications for intervention. *Trauma, Violence and Abuse*, 1(4), 321–340.

Casey, E. A. and Nurius, P. S. (2005). Trauma exposure and sexual revictimization risk: comparisons across single, multiple incident and multiple perpetrator victimizations. *Violence Against Women*, 11(4), 505–530.

Cattaneo, L. B. and Goodman, L. A. (2010). Through the lens of therapeutic jurisprudence: the relationship between empowerment in the court system and well-being for intimate partner violence victims. *Journal of Interpersonal Violence*, 25(3), 481–502.

Cavanagh, K. (2003). Understanding women's responses to domestic violence. *Qualitative Social Work*, 2(3), 229–249.

Cavanagh, K., Dobash, R. E., Dobash, R. P. and Lewis, R. (2001). 'Remedial work': men's strategic responses to their violence against intimate female partners. *Sociology*, 35(3), 695–714.

Cawson, P. (2002). *Child Maltreatment in the Family: The Experience of a National Sample of Young People*. London: NSPCC.

Chang, J. C., Dado, D., Ashton, S., Hawker, L., Patricia, A. C., Buranosky, R. and Scholle, S. H. (2006). Understanding behavior change for women experiencing intimate partner violence: mapping the ups and downs using the stages of change. *Patient Education and Counseling*, 62(3), 330–339.

Chantler, K. (2006). Independence, dependency and interdependence: struggles and resistances of minoritized women within and on leaving violent relationships. *Feminist Review*, (82), 26–48.

Chantler, K., Gangoli, G. and Hester, M. (2009). Forced marriage in the UK: religious, cultural, economic or state violence? *Critical Social Policy*, 29(4), 587–612.

Chung, D., Kennedy, R., O'Brien, B., Wendt, S. and Cody, S. (2000). *Home Safe Home: The Link Between Domestic and Family Violence and Women's Homelessness*. Canberra: Commonwealth of Australia.

Cohen, M. and Mullender, A. (eds) (2003). *Gender and Groupwork*. London: Routledge.

Coker, A. L., Smith, P. H., Thompson, M. P., McKeown, R. E., Bethea, L. and Davis, K. E. (2002). Social support protects against the negative effects of partner violence on mental health. *Journal of Women's Health and Gender-Based Medicine*, 11(5), 465–476.

Coker, D. (2001). Crime control and feminist law reform in domestic violence law: a critical review. *Buffalo Criminal Law Review*, 4(2), 801–860.

Coker, D. (2004). Race, poverty and the crime-centred response to domestic violence. *Violence Against Women*, 10(11), 1331–1353.

Colorado, A., Montgomery, P. and Taylor, J. (2003). Creating respectful relationships in the name of the Latino family: a community approach to violence. In Dulwich Centre (ed.), *Responding to Violence: A Collection of Papers Relating to Child Sexual Abuse and Violence in Intimate Relationships* (pp. 139–159). Adelaide: Dulwich Centre Publications.

Community Care Division Victorian Government Department of Human Services (2004). Women's journey away from family violence: framework and summary. Retrieved 23 June 2012 from www.cyf.vic.gov.au/__data/assets/pdf_file/0020/16715/fcs_womens_journey.pdf.

Cook, D., Burton, M., Robinson, A. L. and Vallely, C. (2004). *Evaluation of Specialist Domestic Violence Courts/Fast Track Systems*. Retrieved 29 September 2011 from http://wlv.openrepository.com/wlv/bitstream/2436/22612/1/Cook%20et%20al%20%282004%29.pdf.

Cooley, B. and Frazer, C. (2006). Children and domestic violence: a system of safety in clinical practice. *Australian Social Work*, 59(4), 462–473.

Council of Australian Governments (2011). *National Plan to Reduce Violence Against Women and their Children*. Canberra: COAG.

Craig, D. V. (2009). *Action Research Essentials* (pp. 1–28). San Francisco, CA: Jossey-Bass.

Crenshaw, K. W. (1991). Mapping the margins: intersectionality, identity politics and violence against women of color. *Stanford Law Review*, 43, 1241–1299.

Cresswell, J. and Plano Clark, V. (2011). *Designing and Conducting Mixed Methods Research* (2nd ed.). Thousand Oaks, CA: Sage.

Crinall, K. and Hurley, J. (2009). Responding to family violence and preventing homelessness: what is required for effective implementation of 'safe at home' programs? *Parity*, 22(10), 40–41.

Crockenberg, S. and Langrock, A. (2001). The role of specific emotions in children's responses to interparental conflict: a test of the model. *Journal of Family Psychology*, 15(2), 163–182.

Curwood, S., DeGreer, I., Hymmen, P. and Lehmann, P. (2011). Using strength-based approaches to explore pretreatment change in men who abuse their partners. *Journal of Interpersonal Violence*, 26(13), 2698–2715.

Davies, J., Lyon, E. and Monti-Catania, D. (1998). *Safety Planning with Battered Women: Complex Lives/Difficult Choices*. Thousand Oaks, CA: Sage.

Davies, M. and Mouzos, J. (2007). Homicide in Australia 2005–2006: National Homicide Monitoring Program Annual Report. *Research and Public Policy Series Number 77*. Canberra: Australian Insititute of Criminology.

Davis, R. C. and Auchter, B. (2010). National Institute of Justice funding of experimental studies of violence against women: a critical look at implementation issues and policy implications. *Journal of Experimental Criminology*, 6(4), 377–395.

Day, A., O'Leary, P., Chung, D. and Justo, D. (2009). *Domestic Violence: Working with Men*. Leichhardt, NSW: The Federation Press.

de Bocanegra, H. T., Rostovtseva, D. P., Khera, S. and Godhwani, N. (2010). Birth control sabotage and forced sex: experiences reported by women in domestic violence shelters. *Violence Against Women*, 16(5), 601–612.

DeKeseredy, W. S. and Schwartz, M. D. (1998). Measuring the extent of woman abuse in intimate heterosexual relationships: a critique of the conflict tactics scales. *VAWnet Applied Research Papers*. Retrieved 5 January 2012 from www.vawnet.org/Assoc_Files_VAWnet/AR_ctscrit.pdf.

Denborough, D. (Ed.) (2006). *Trauma: Narrative Responses to Traumatic Experience*. Adelaide: Dulwich Centre Publications.

Department of Health (2002). *Women's Mental Health: Into the Mainstream*. London: The Stationery Office.

Department of Human Services Victoria (2007). *Family Violence Risk Assessment and Risk Management: Supporting an Integrated Family Violence Service System*. Retrieved 2 August 2011 from www.dpcd.vic.gov.au/__data/assets/pdf_file/0008/39662/FinalRiskAssessmentandRiskManagementFramework.pdf.

Dickens, J. (2012). The definition of social work in the United Kingdom, 2000–2010. *International Journal of Social Welfare*, 21, 34–43.

Dobash, R. E. and Dobash, R. P. (1979). *Violence Against Wives: A Case Against the Patriarchy*. New York: Free Press.

Dobash, R. E., Dobash, R. P., Cavanagh, K. and Lewis, R. (eds) (2000). *Changing Violent Men*. Thousand Oaks, CA: Sage.

Dobash, R. P., Dobash, R. E., Wilson, M. and Daly, M. (1992). The myth of sexual symmetry in marital violence. *Social problems*, 39(1), 71–91.

Dolan, F. E. (2003). Battered women, petty traitors and the legacy of coverture. *Feminist Studies*, 29(2), 249–277.

Donnelly, D., Cook, K., Van Ausdale, D. and Foley, L. (2005). White privilege, color blindness and services to battered women. *Violence Against Women*, 11(1), 6–37.

Donovan, C., Hester, M., Holmes, J. and McCarry, M. (2006). *Comparing Domestic Abuse in Same Sex and Heterosexual Relationships*. Retrieved 12 January 2012 from www.bris.ac.uk/sps/research/projects/completed/2006/rc1307/rc1307finalreport.pdf.

Douglas, H. and Walsh, T. (2010). Mothers, domestic violence and child protection. *Violence Against Women*, 16(5), 489–508.

Duffy, K. (2011). There's no pride in domestic violence: the Same Sex Domestic Violence Interagency, Sydney, Australia. In J. L. Ristock (ed.), *Intimate Partner Violence in LGBTQ Lives* (pp. 487–515). NY: Routledge.

Dunford, F. W. (2000). The San Diego Navy experiment: an assessment of interventions for men who assault their wives. *Journal of Consulting and Clinical Psychology*, 68(3), 468–476.

Durfee, A. (2009). Victim narratives, legal representation and domestic violence civil protection orders. *Feminist Criminology*, 4(1), 7–31.

Dutton, M. A. (1996). Battered women's strategic response to violence: the role of context. In J. L. Edleson and Z. C. Eisikovits (eds), *Future Interventions with Battered Women and their Families*. Thousand Oaks, CA: Sage.

Dutton, M. A. and Goodman, L. A. (2005). Coercion in intimate partner violence: toward a new conceptualization. *Sex Roles*, 52(11–12), 743–756.

Edleson, J. L. (1999a). Children's witnessing of adult domestic violence. *Journal of Interpersonal Violence*, 14(8), 839–870.

Edleson, J. L. (1999b). The overlap between child maltreatment and woman battering. *Violence Against Women*, 5(2), 134–154.

Edleson, J. L. (2004). Should childhood exposure to domestic violence be defined as child maltreatment under the law? In P. Jaffe, P. L. Baker and A. Cunningham (eds), *Protecting Children from Domestic Violence: Strategies for Community Intervention* (pp. 1–17). New York: Guilford Press.

Edleson, J. L. and Bible, A. (2001). Collaborating for women's safety: partnerships between research and practice. In C. Renzetti, J. L. Edleson and R. K. Bergen (eds), *Sourcebook on Violence Against Women* (pp. 73–95). Thousand Oaks, CA: Sage.

Edleson, J. L. and Malik, N. M. (2008). Collaborating for family safety: results from the *Greenbook* multisite evaluation. *Journal of Interpersonal Violence*, 23(7), 871–875.

Edleson, J. L. and Williams, O. J. (eds) (2007). *Parenting by Men Who Batter: New Directions for Assessment and Intervention*. New York: Oxford University Press.

Edleson, J. L., Gassman-Pines, J. and Hill, M. B. (2006). Defining child exposure to domestic violence as neglect: Minnesota's difficult experience. *Social Work*, 51(2), 167–174.

Edleson, J. L., Mbilinyi, J. F., Beeman, S. K. and Hagemeister, A. K. (2003). How children are involved in adult domestic violence – results from a four-city telephone survey. *Journal of Interpersonal Violence*, 18(1), 18–32.

Edwards, R. (2004a). *Staying Home Leaving Violence: Promoting Choices for Women Leaving Abusive Partners*. Retrieved 17 October 2011 from www.austdvclearinghouse.unsw.edu.au/PDF%20files/SHLV.pdf.

Edwards, R. (2004b). *Violence Excluded: A Study into Exclusion Orders in South East Sydney: Final Report* (No. 0734728271). Sydney: Attorney General's Department of NSW.

Edwards, R. (2011). *Staying Home Leaving Violence: Listening to Women's Experiences.* Retrieved 22 June 2012 from www.sprc.unsw.edu.au/media/File/SPRC_report_411.pdf.

Ellis, J. (2004). *Preventing Violence Against Women and Girls: A Study of Educational Programmes for Children and Young People.* London: WOMANKIND Worldwide.

Ellis, J. (2008). Primary prevention of domestic abuse through education. In C. Humphreys, C. Houghton and J. Ellis (eds), *Literature Review: Better Outcomes for Children and Young People Experiencing Domestic Abuse –Directions for Good Practice.* Edinburgh: The Scottish Government.

Ellis, J., Stanley, N. and Bell, J. (2006). Prevention programs of children and young people. In C. Humphreys and N. Stanley (eds), *Domestic Violence and Child Protection: Directions for Good Practice* (pp. 69–81). London: Jessica Kingsley.

Ellsberg, M. and Heise, L. (2005). *Researching Violence Against Women: A Practical Guide for Researchers and Activists.* Retrieved 17 January 2012 from www.path.org/publications/files/GBV_rvaw_complete.pdf.

Ellsberg, M., Jansen, H. A. F. M., Heise, L., Watts, C. H. and García-Moreno, C. (2008). Intimate partner violence and women's physical and mental health in the WHO multi-country study on women's health and domestic violence: an observational study. *The Lancet, 371*(9619), 1165–1172.

Epstein, D., Bell, M. and Goodman, L. A. (2003). Transforming aggressive prosecution policies: prioritizing victims' long-term safety in the prosecution of domestic violence cases. *American University Journal of Gender Social Policy and the Law, 11*(2), 465–498.

Erez, E. and Belknap, J. (1998). In their own words: battered women's assessment of the criminal processing system's response. *Violence and Victims, 13*(3), 251–268.

Fanslow, J. L. and Robinson, E. M. (2010). Help-seeking behaviors and reasons for help seeking reported by a representative sample of women victims of intimate partner violence in New Zealand. *Journal of Interpersonal Violence, 25*(5), 929–951.

Farmer, E. and Pollock, S. (1998). *Substitute Care for Sexually Abused and Abusing Children.* Chichester: Wiley.

Featherstone, B. and Trinder, L. (1997). Familiar subjects: domestic violence and child welfare. *Child and Family Social Work, 2,* 147–160.

Featherstone, B., Hooper, C.-A., Scourfield, J. and Taylor, J. (eds) (2010). *Gender and Child Welfare in Society.* Chichester and Hoboken, NJ: Wiley-Blackwell.

Feder, L. and Dugan, L. (2002). A test of the efficacy of court-mandated counseling for domestic violence offenders: the Broward Experiment. *Justice Quarterly, 19*(2), 343–375.

Feder, L., Niolon, P. H., Campbell, J., Wallinder, J., Nelson, R. and Larrouy, H. (2011). The need for experimental methodology in intimate partner violence: finding programs that effectively prevent IPV. *Violence Against Women, 17*(3), 340–358.

Fileborn, B. (2011). Sexual assault laws in Australia. *Australian Centre for the Study of Sexual Assault Resource Sheet.* Retrieved 23 January 2012 from www.aifs.gov.au/acssa/pubs/sheets/rs1/rs1.pdf.

Fineman, M. A. and Mykitiuk, R. (eds) (1994). *The Public Nature of Private Violence: The Discovery of Domestic Abuse.* New York: Routledge.

Finkelhor, D., Ormrod, R. and Turner, H. (2009a). Lifetime assessment of poly-victimization in a national sample of children and young people. *Child Abuse and Neglect, 33,* 403–411.

Finkelhor, D., Ormrod, R., Turner, H. and Holt, M. (2009b). Pathways to poly-victimization. *Child Maltreatment, 14*(4), 316–329.

Fisher, S. (2011). *From Violence to Coercive Control: Renaming Men's Abuse of Women.* White Ribbon Research Series: No. 3. Retrieved 29 January 2012 from www.whiteribbon.

org.au/uploads/media/449%20White%20Ribbon%20-%20Policy%20Report%20 Fisher%20%28web%29%20-%2011220.pdf.

Fisher, T. and Somerton, J. (2000). Reflection on action: the process of helping social work students to develop their use of theory in practice. *Social Work Education*, *19*(4), 387–401.

Fitzgerald, J. and Weatherburn, D. (2002). Aboriginal victimisation and offending: the picture from police records. *Aboriginal and Islander Health Worker Journal*, *26*(4), 26–28.

Fleck-Henderson, A. (2000). Domestic violence in the child protection system: seeing double. *Children and Youth Services Review*, *22*(5), 333–354.

Fleury, R. E., Sullivan, C. M., Bybee, D. I. and Davidson II, W. S. (1998). 'Why don't they just call the cops?': reasons for differential police contact among women with abusive partners. *Violence and Victims*, *13*(4), 333–346.

Fleury-Steiner, R. E., Bybee, D., Sullivan, C. M., Belknap, J. and Melton, H. C. (2006). Contextual factors impacting battered women's intentions to reuse the criminal legal system. *Journal of Community Psychology*, *34*(3), 327–342.

Flood, M. (2010). Where men stand: men's roles in ending violence against women. *White Ribbon Prevention Research Series, No. 2*. Broadway, NSW: White Ribbon Foundation.

Font, R. V., Dolan-Del Vecchio, K. and Almeida, R. V. (1998). Finding the words: instruments for a therapy of liberation. *Journal of Feminist Family Therapy*, *10*(1), 85–97.

Fook, J. (1996). The reflective researcher: developing a reflective approach to practice. In J. Fook (ed.), *The Critical Researcher* (pp. 1–8). Sydney: Allen and Unwin.

Fook, J. and Askeland, G. A. (2007). Challenges of critical reflection: 'nothing ventured, nothing gained'. *Social Work Education*, *26*(5), 520–533.

Ford, D. A. (1991). Prosecution as a victim power resource: a note on empowering women in violent conjugal relationships. *Law and Society Review*, *25* (2, Special Issue on Gender and Sociolegal Studies), 313–334.

Ford, D. A. and Regoli, M. J. (1993). The criminal prosecution of wife assaulters: process, problems and effects. In N. Z. Hilton (ed.), *Legal Responses to Wife Assault: Current Trends and Evaluation* (pp. 127–164). Newbury Park, CA: Sage.

Forrester, D. and Harwin, J. (2006). Parental substance misuse and child care social work: findings from the first stage of a study of 100 families. *Child and Family Social Work*, *11*, 325–335.

Foucault, M. (1980). Two lectures. In C. Gordon (ed.), *Michel Foucault: Power/Knowledge*. London: Harvester Wheatsheaf.

Fox, G. and Benson, M. (2004). Violent men, bad dads? Fathering profiles of men involved in intimate partner violence. In R. Day and M. Lamb (eds), *Violent Men, Bad Dads? Fathering Profiles of Men Involved in Intimate Partner Violence*. Hillsdale, NJ: Lawrence Erlbaum.

Frederick, L. (2008). Questions about family court domestic violence screening and assessment. *Family Court Review*, *46*(3), 523–530.

Friere, P. (1972). *Pedagogy of the Oppressed*. New York: Herder and Herder.

Gadd, D., Farrall, S., Dallimore, D. and Lombard, N. (2002). *Domestic Abuse Against Men in Scotland*. Retrieved 10 January 2012 from www.scotland.gov.uk/Resource/ Doc/46737/0030602.pdf.

Galvani, S. (2006). Alcohol and domestic violence: women's views. *Violence Against Women*, *12*(7), 641–662.

Ganley, A. and Schechter, S. (1996). *Domestic Violence: A National Curriculum for Children's Protective Services*. San Francisco, CA: Family Violence Prevention Fund.

Garner, J. H. and Maxwell, C. D. (2000). What are the lessons of the police arrest studies? In S. K. Ward and D. Finkelhor (eds), *Program Evaluation and Family Violence Research*. New York: The Haworth Maltreatment and Trauma Press.

Gartland, D., Hemphill, S. A., Hegarty, K. L. and Brown, S. J. (2011). Intimate partner violence during pregnancy and the first year postpartum in an Australian pregnancy cohort study. *Maternal and Child Health Journal, 15*(5), 570–578.

Gillingham, P. and Humphreys, C. (2010). Child protection practitioners and decision-making tools: observations and reflections from the front line. *British Journal of Social Work, 40*(8), 2598–2616.

Gioia, D. (2012). Book review: Hesse-Biber, S. (2010) 'Mixed methods research: merging theory and practice', New York, Guilford Press. *Qualitative Social Work, 11*(2), 220–225.

Goddard, C. and Bedi, G. (2010). Intimate partner violence and child abuse: a child-centred perspective. *Child Abuse Review, 19*(1), 5–20.

Golding, J. M. (1999). Intimate partner violence as a risk factor for mental disorders: a meta analysis. *Journal of Family Violence, 14*(2), 99–132.

Gondolf, E. W. (2001). Limitations of experimental evaluation of batterer programs. *Trauma Violence and Abuse, 2*(1), 79–88.

Gondolf, E. W. (2002). *Batterer Intervention Systems: Issues, Outcomes and Recommendations.* Thousand Oaks, CA: Sage.

Gondolf, E. W. (2011). The weak evidence for batterer program alternatives. *Aggression and Violent Behavior, 16*(4), 347–353.

Gondolf, E. W. and Fisher, E. R. (1988). *Battered Women as Survivors: An Alternative to Treating Learned Helplessness.* Lanham, MD: Lexington Books.

Goodman, L. A. and Epstein, D. (2008). *Listening to Battered Women: A Survivor-Centred Approach to Advocacy, Mental Health and Justice.* Washington, DC: American Psychological Association.

Goodman, L. A., Bennett, L. and Dutton, M. A. (1999). Obstacles to victims' cooperation with the criminal prosecution of their abusers: the role of social support. *Violence and Victims, 14*(4), 427–444.

Goodman, L. A., Fels Smyth, K., Borges, A. M. and Singer, R. (2009). When crises collide: how intimate partner violence and poverty intersect to shape women's mental health and coping. *Trauma Violence and Abuse, 10*(4), 306–329.

Gordon, L. (1988). *Heroes of their Own Lives: The Politics and History of Family Violence, Boston, 1880–1960.* New York: Viking.

Graham-Bermann, S. A. and Levendosky, A. A. (1998). Traumatic stress symptoms in children of battered women. *Journal of Interpersonal Violence, 13*(1), 111–128.

Graham-Bermann, S. A., Lynch, S., Banyard, V., Devoe, E. R. and Halabu, H. (2007). Community-based intervention for children exposed to intimate partner violence: an efficacy trial. *Journal of Consulting and Clinical Psychology, 75*(2), 199–209.

Grealy, C., Humphreys, C., Milward, K. and Power, J. (2008). *Practice Guidelines: Women and Children's Family Violence Counselling and Support Program.* Victoria: Department of Human Services.

Greer, P. and Laing, L. (2001). Pathways to safety: an interview about indigenous family violence. *Issues Paper.* Retrieved 16 October 2006 from www.austdvclearinghouse.unsw. edu.au/PDF%20files/Issuespaper5.pdf.

Guille, L. (2004). Men who batter and their children: an integrated review. *Aggression and Violent Behavior, 9*(2), 129–163.

Gupta, R. (2003). Some recurring themes: Southall Black Sisters, 1979–2003 – and still going strong. In R. Gupta (ed.), *From Homebreakers to Jailbreakers: Southall Black Sisters* (pp. 1–27). London: Zed Books.

Hague, G. and Malos, E. (1998) Inter-agency approaches to domestic violence and the role of social services. *British Journal of Social Work. 28* (3), 369–386.

Hague, G. and Mullender, A. (2006). Who listens? – The voices of domestic violence survivors in service provision in the United Kingdom. *Violence Against Women*, 12(6), 568–587.

Hague, G., Mullender, A. and Aris, R. (2003). *Is Anyone Listening? Accountability and Women Survivors of Domestic Violence*. New York: Routledge.

Hague, G., Thiara, R. and Mullender, A. (2011). Disabled women, domestic violence and social care: the risk of isolation, vulnerability and neglect. *British Journal of Social Work*, 41(1), 148–165.

Haller, B. (2005). *The Austrian Legislation Against Domestic Violence. Brief Summary of the Key Aspects of the Legislation and the Judiciary System Relevant to Protection of Women and Children*. Report written for the Coordination Action against Human Rights Violations. Retrieved 26 August 2012 from www.ikf.ac.at/english/austrian_legislation_against_domestic_violence.pdf.

Hamby, S. (2009). Battered women's protective strategies. *VAWnet Applied Research Forum*. Retrieved July 6, 2011 from www.vawnet.org/Assoc_Files_VAWnet/AR_BWProtStrat.pdf.

Hanna, C. (1996). No right to choose: mandated victim participation in domestic violence prosecutions. *Harvard Law Review*, 109(8), 1849–1910.

Harne, L. (2011). *Violent Fathering and the Risks to Children: The Need for Change*. Bristol: Policy Press.

Harris, J. (2003). *The Social Work Business*. London: Routledge.

Hartley, C. (2004). Severe domestic violence and child maltreatment: considering child physical abuse, neglect and failure to protect. *Children and Youth Services Review*, 26, 373–392.

Healey, L., Howe, K., Humphreys, C., Jennings, C. and Julian, F. (2008). *Building the Evidence: A Report on the Status of Policy and Practice in Responding to Violence Against Women with Disabilities in Victoria*. Melbourne: Victorian Women with Disabilities Network Advocacy Information Service.

Healey, L., Humphreys, C. and Howe, K. (2013, forthcoming). Inclusive domestic violence standards, codes and guidelines: a strategy for improving service responses to women with disabilities. *Violence and Victims*, 28(1).

Hegarty, K. L., Bush, R. and Sheehan, M. (2005). The composite abuse scale: further development and assessment of reliability and validity. *Violence and Victims*, 20(5), 529–547.

Hegarty, K. L., O'Doherty, L. J., Gunn, J., Pierce, D. and Taft, A. J. (2008). A brief counselling intervention by health professionals utilising the 'readiness for change' concept for women experiencing intimate partner abuse: the Weave Project. *Journal of Family Studies*, 14(2–3), 376–388.

Heise, L. and Garcia-Moreno, C. (2002). Violence by intimate partners. In E. G. Krug, L. L. Dahlberg, J. A. Mercy, A. Zwi and R. Lozano (eds), *World Report on Violence and Health* (pp. 87–121). Geneva: World Health Organization.

Heise, L., Ellsberg, M. and Gottemoeller, M. (1999). *Ending Violence Against Women: Population Reports, Series L, No. 11*. Baltimore: Johns Hopkins University School of Public Health.

Hendricks, J., Kaplan, T. and Black, D. (1993). *When Father Kills Mother: Guiding Children through Trauma and Grief*. London: Routledge.

Herman, J. L. (1992). *Trauma and Recovery*. New York: Basic Books.

Herman, J. L. (2005). Justice from the victim's perspective. *Violence Against Women*, 11(5), 571–602.

Hernandez, P., Almeida, R. V. and Dolan-Delvecchio, K. (2005). Critical consciousness, accountability and empowerment: key processes for helping families heal. *Family Process*, 44(1), 105–119.

Hesse-Biber, S. (2010). *Mixed Methods Research: Merging Theory and Practice*. New York: Guilford Press.

Hester, M. (2006a). Asking about domestic violence: implications for practice. In C. Humphreys and N. Stanley (eds), *Domestic Violence and Child Protection: Directions for Good Practice* (pp. 97–109). London: Jessica Kingsley.

Hester, M. (2006b). Making it through the Criminal Justice system: attrition and domestic violence. *Social Policy and Society*, 5(1), 79–90.

Hester, M. (2011). The three planet model: towards an understanding of contradictions in approaches to women and children's safety in contexts of domestic violence. *British Journal of Social Work*, 41(5), 837–853.

Hester, M. and Pearson, C. (1998). *From Periphery to Centre: Domestic Violence in Work with Abused Children*. Bristol: Policy Press.

Hester, M. and Westmarland, N. (2005). *Tackling Domestic Violence: Effective Interventions and Approaches – Home Office Research Study 290*. London: Home Office Research, Development and Statistics Directorate.

Hester, M., Hanmer, J., Coulson, S., Morahan, M. and Razak, A. (2003). *Domestic Violence: Making it Through the Criminal Justice System*. Retrieved 30 September 2011 from www.nr-foundation.org.uk/wp-content/uploads/2011/07/dv-attrition-report.pdf.

Hester, M., Pearson, C., Harwin, N. and Abrahams, H. (2006). *Making an Impact: A Reader*. London: Jessica Kingsley.

HM Government (2011). *Call to End Violence Against Women and Girls: Action Plan*. Retrieved 22 July 2011 from www.homeoffice.gov.uk/publications/crime/call-end-violence-women-girls/vawg-action-plan?view=Binary.

HM Government (2012). *Call to End Violence Against Women and Girls: Taking Action – The Next Chapter*. Retrieved 7 April 2012 from www.homeoffice.gov.uk/publications/crime/call-end-violence-women-girls/action-plan-new-chapter?view=Binary.

Hobart, M. (2004). *Advocates and Fatality Reviews*. Retrieved 27 June 2012 from www.wscadv.org/resourcesAlpha.cfm?aId=CF8A7A0A-C298–58F6–074F7EB90E9413FB.

Holden, G. W. and Ritchie, K. L. (1991). Linking extreme marital discord, child rearing and child behavior problems: evidence from battered women. *Child Development*, 62(2), 311–327.

Holden, G. W., Stein, J. D., Ritchie, K. L., Harris, S. D. and Jouriles, E. N. (1998). Children exposed to marital violence: theory, research and applied issues. In G. W. Holden, R. Geffner and E. N. Jouriles (eds), *Children Exposed to Marital Violence: Theory, Research and Applied Issues* (pp. 289–334). Washington, DC: American Psychological Association.

Holder, R. (2001). Domestic and family violence: criminal justice interventions. *Issue Paper No. 3*. Retrieved 4 September 2006 from www.austdvclearinghouse.unsw.edu.au/PDF%20files/issuespaper3.pdf.

Holder, R. (2007). Police and domestic violence: an analysis of domestic violence incidents attended by police in the ACT and subsequent actions. *Research Report*. Retrieved 5 January 2012 from www.austdvclearinghouse.unsw.edu.au/PDF%20files/Robyn_Holder_Research_Report.pdf.

Holt, S. (2003). Child protection social work and men's abuse of women: an Irish study. *Child and Family Social Work*, 8(1), 53–65.

Holt, S., Buckley, H. and Whelan, S. (2008). The impact of exposure to domestic violence on children and young people: a review of the literature. *Child Abuse and Neglect*, 32(8), 797–810.

Home Office (2011). *Multi-agency Statutory Guidance for the Conduct of Domestic Homicide Reviews*. Retrieved 22 June 2012 from www.homeoffice.gov.uk/publications/crime/DHR-guidance?view=Binary.

hooks, b. (1981). *Ain't I a Woman: Black Women and Feminism*. Boston, MA: South End Press.

hooks, b. (1984). *Feminist Theory: From Margin to Center*. Boston, MA: South End Press.

Horwath, J. and Morrison, T. (2007). Collaboration, integration and change in children's services: critical issues and key ingredients. *Child Abuse and Neglect*, 31, 55–69.

Houghton, C. (2006). Listen louder: working with children and young people. In C. Humphreys and N. Stanley (eds), *Domestic Violence and Child Protection: Directions for Good Practice* (pp. 82–94). London: Jessica Kingsley.

Howard, L. M., Trevillion, K., Khalifeh, H., Woodall, A., Agnew-Davies, R. and Feder, G. (2010). Domestic violence and severe psychiatric disorders: prevalence and interventions. *Psychological Medicine*, 40(6), 881–893.

Howarth, E., Stimpson, L., Barran, D. and Robinson, A. L. (2009). *Safety in Numbers: A Multi-site Evaluation of IDVA Services*. London: The Hestia Fund, The Sigrid Rausing Trust and The Henry Smith Charity.

Howe, D. (1997). Psychosocial and relationship-based theories for child and family social work: politics, philosophy, psychology and welfare practice. *Child and Family Social Work*, 2, 162–169.

Hoyle, C. and Sanders, A. (2000). Police response to domestic violence: from victim choice to victim empowerment. *British Journal of Criminology*, 40, 14–36.

Hughes, H. M. and Luke, D. A. (1998). Heterogeneity in adjustment among children of battered women. In G. W. Holden, R. Geffner and E. N. Jouriles (eds), *Children Exposed to Marital Violence: Theory, Research and Applied Issues* (pp. 185–221). Washington, DC: American Psychological Association.

Hughes, H. M., Graham-Bermann, S. and Gruber, G. (2001). Resilience in children exposed to domestic violence. In S. Graham-Bermann and J. L. Edleson (eds), *Domestic Violence in the Lives of Children: The Future of Research, Intervention and Social Policy* (pp. 67–90). Washington, DC: American Psychological Association.

Humphreys, C. (2007). Domestic violence and child protection: exploring the role of perpetrator risk assessments. *Child and Family Social Work*, 12(4), 360–369.

Humphreys, C. (2008). Problems in the system of mandatory reporting of children living with domestic violence. *Journal of Family Studies*, 14(2–3), 228–239.

Humphreys, C. (2010). Crossing the great divide: response to Douglas and Walsh. *Violence Against Women*, 16(5), 509–515.

Humphreys, C. and Absler, D. (2011). History repeating: child protection responses to domestic violence. *Child and Family Social Work*, 16(4), 464–473.

Humphreys, C. and Harrison, C. (2003). Focusing on safety: domestic violence and the role of Child Contact Centres. *Child and Family Law Quarterly*, 15(3), 237–253.

Humphreys, C. and Holder, R. (2004). A plea for evidence. *Safe: Domestic Abuse Quarterly*, 9(Spring), 10–12.

Humphreys, C. and Kertesz, M. (2012). Personal identity records to support young people in care. *Adoption and Fostering*, 36(1): 31.

Humphreys, C. and Stanley, N. (2006). *Domestic Violence and Child Protection: Directions for Good Practice*. London: Jessica Kingsley.

Humphreys, C. and Thiara, R. K. (2003a). Mental health and domestic violence: 'I call it symptoms of abuse'. *British Journal of Social Work*, 33, 209–226.

Humphreys, C. and Thiara, R. K. (2003b). Neither justice nor protection: women's experiences of post-separation violence. *Journal of Social Welfare and Family Law*, 25(3), 195–214.

Humphreys, C., Mullender, A., Thiara, R. K. and Skamballis, A. (2006). Talking to my mum: developing communication between mothers and children in the aftermath of domestic violence. *Journal of Social Work*, 6(1), 53–64.

Humphreys, C., Thiara, R. K. and Skamballis, A. (2011). Readiness to change: mother–child relationship and domestic violence intervention. *British Journal of Social Work*, 41(1), 166–184.

Hunter, R. (2002). Border protection in law's empire: feminist explorations of access to justice. *Griffith Law Review*, 11(2), 263–285.

Indermaur, D. (2001). Young Australians and domestic violence. *Trends and Issues in Crime and Criminal Justice, No 195*. Canberra: Australian Institute of Criminology.

International Federation of Social Work (2000). Definition of social work. Retrieved 30 January 2009 from www.ifsw.org/f38000138.html.

Irwin, J. and Waugh, F. (2001). *Unless They're Asked: Routine Screening for Domestic Violence in NSW Health. An Evaluation Report of the Pilot Project*. Sydney: NSW Health Department.

Irwin, J. and Waugh, F. (2007). Domestic violence: a priority in child protection in New South Wales, Australia? *Child Abuse Review*, 16(5), 311–322.

Irwin, J., Waugh, F. and Wilkinson, M. (2002). *Domestic Violence and Child Protection: A Research Report*. Sydney: Department of Social Work, Social Policy and Sociology, University of Sydney.

Ison, R. L. and Blackmore, C. P. (2010). *Managing Systemic Change: Getting Started. Study Guide Block 1. Managing Systemic Change: Inquiry, Action and Interaction (TU812)*. Milton Keynes, UK: The Open University.

Jacob, A. and Fanning, D. (2006). *Report on Child Protection Services in Tasmania*. Retrieved 2 February 2012 from http://dhhs.tas.gov.au/__data/assets/pdf_file/0009/32967/child_protection_report_6_October.pdf.

Jaffe, P. G. and Juodis, M. (2006). Children as victims and witnesses of domestic homicide: lessons learned from domestic violence death review committees. *Juvenile and Family Court Journal*, 57(3), 13–28.

Jaffe, P. G., Crooks, C. V. and Poisson, S. E. (2003a). Common misconceptions in addressing domestic violence in child custody disputes. *Juvenile and Family Court Journal*, 54(4), 57–67.

Jaffe, P. G., Lemon, N. K. D. and Poisson, S. E. (2003b). *Child Custody and Domestic Violence: A Call for Safety and Accountability*. Thousand Oaks, CA: Sage.

Jaffe, P. G., Wolfe, D. and Wilson, S. (1990). *Children of Battered Women*. Thousand Oaks, CA: Sage.

James-Hanmer, D. (2000). Enhancing multi-agency work. In J. Hanmer and C. Itzin (eds), *Home Truths About Domestic Violence: Feminist Influences on Policy and Practice: A Reader* (pp. 269–286). London: Routledge.

Jenkins, A. (2009). *Becoming Ethical: A Parallel Political Journey with Men Who Have Abused*. Lyme Regis: Russell House.

Johnson, H. (1996). *Dangerous Domains: Violence Against Women in Canada* (pp. 23–51). Toronto: Nelson.

Johnson, H. (2006). *Measuring Violence Against Women: Statistical Trends*. Ottawa: Statistics Canada.

Johnson, H., Ollus, N. and Nevala, S. (2008). *Violence Against Women: An International Perspective*. New York: Springer.

Johnson, L. J., Zorn, D., Kai Yung Tam, B., Lamontage, M. and Johnson, S. A. (2003). Stakeholders' views of factors that impact successful interagency collaboration. *Exceptional Children*, 69(2), 195–209.

Johnson, M. P. (1995). Patriarchal terrorism and common couple violence: two forms of violence against women. *Journal of Marriage and the Family*, 57, 283–294.

Johnson, M. P. (2005). Domestic violence: it's not about gender – or is it? *Journal of Marriage and the Family*, 67(5), 1126–1130.

Johnson, M. P. (2010). Langhinrichsen-Rolling's confirmation of the feminist analysis of intimate partner violence: comment on 'Controversies involving gender and intimate partner violence in the United States'. *Sex Roles*, 62(3–4), 212–219.

Johnson, M. P. and Leone, J. M. (2005). The differential effects of intimate terrorism and situational couple violence: findings from the national violence against women survey. *Journal of Family Issues*, 26(3), 322–349.

Jordan, C. E., Pritchard, A. J., Duckett, D. and Charnigo, R. (2010). Criminal offending among respondents to protective orders: crime types and patterns that predict victim risk. *Violence Against Women*, 16(12), 1396–1411.

Kanuha, V. (1996). Domestic violence, racism and the battered women's movement in the United States. In J. L. Edleson and Z. Eisikovits (eds), *Future Interventions with Battered Women and their Families*. Thousand Oaks, CA: Sage.

Kapur, N. and Windish, D. (2011). Optimal methods to screen men and women for intimate partner violence: results from an internal medicine residency continuity clinic. *Journal of Interpersonal Violence*, 26(12), 2335–2352.

Kelleher, K. J., Hazen, A. L., Coben, J. H., Wang, U., Geehan, J., Kohl, P. and Gardner, W. (2008). Self-reported disciplinary practices among women in the child welfare system: association with domestic violence victimization. *Child Abuse and Neglect*, 32(8), 811–818.

Kellogg, N. D. and Menard, S. W. (2003). Violence among family members of children and adolescents evaluated for sexual abuse. *Child Abuse and Neglect*, 27(12), 1367–1376.

Kelly, L. (1988). *Surviving Sexual Violence*. Oxford: Polity Press.

Kelly, L. (2002). From commonality to difference and back again?: reflections on international efforts to challenge violence against women. *Expanding Our Horizon: Understanding the Complexities of Violence Against Women: Meanings, Cultures, Difference*. Retrieved 12 December 2011 from www.adfvc.unsw.edu.au/Conference%20 papers/Exp-horiz/Kelly.pdf.

Kelly, L. (2005). Inside outsiders: Mainstreaming violence against women into human rights discourse and practice. *International Feminist Journal of Politics*, 7(4), 471–495.

Kelly, L. and Lovett, J. (2005). *What a Waste: The Case for an Integrated Violence Against Women Strategy*. Retrieved 27 January 2012 from www.thewnc.org.uk/pubs/whatawaste.pdf.

Kelly, U. A. (2009). 'I'm a mother first': the influence of mothering in the decision-making processes of battered immigrant Latino women. *Research in Nursing and Health*, 32(3), 286–297.

Keys Young (1998). *Against the Odds: How Women Survive Domestic Violence*. Canberra: Office of the Status of Women, Department of Prime Minister and Cabinet.

Kirkwood, D. (2012). *'Just Say Goodbye': Parents Who Kill their Children in the Context of Separation*. Melbourne: Domestic Violence Resource Centre Victoria.

Kitzmann, K., Gaylord, N., Holt, A. and Kenny, E. (2003). Child witnesses to domestic violence: a meta-analytic review. *Journal of Consulting and Clinical Psychology*, 71(2), 339–352.

Krug, E. G., Dahlberg, L. L., Mercy, J. A., Zwi, A. and Lozano, R. (2002). *World Report on Violence and Health*. Geneva: World Health Organization.

Labriola, M., Rempel, M. and Davis, R. C. (2008). Do batterer programs reduce recidivism? Results from a randomized trial in the Bronx. *Justice Quarterly*, 25(2), 252–282.

Laing, L. (2000). Children, young people and domestic violence. *Issues Paper 2*. Retrieved 30 June 2009 from http://pandora.nla.gov.au/pan/34659/20030410–0000/issuespaper2.pdf.

Laing, L. (2008). A perilous journey: seeking protection in the aftermath of domestic violence. *Communities, Children and Families Australia*, 3(2), 19–29.

Laing, L. (2010). No way to live: women's experiences of negotiating the family law system in the context of domestic violence. Retrieved 6 May 2011 from http://hdl.handle.net/2123/6255.

Laing, L. (2012). *'It's Like this Maze': Women's Experiences of Seeking an ADVO in NSW*. Sydney: NSW Law and Justice Foundation.

Laing, L., Irwin, J. and Kennaugh, C. (2005). *Evaluation of the Green Valley Domestic Violence Service (GVDVS): Final Report*. Retrieved 31 May 2010 from http://hdl.handle.net/2123/6108.

Laing, L., Irwin, J. and Toivonen, C. (2010a). Women's stories of collaboration between domestic violence and mental health services. *Communities Children and Families Australia*, 5(2), 16–28.

Laing, L., Irwin, J. and Toivonen, C. (2012a). Across the divide: using research to enhance collaboration between mental health and domestic violence services. *Australian Social Work*, 65(1), 120–135.

Laing, L., Toivonen, C., Irwin, J. and Napier, L. (2010b). *'They Never Asked Me Anything About That': The Stories of Women who Experience Domestic Violence and Mental Health Concerns/Illness*. Retrieved 12 September 2010 from http://hdl.handle.net/2123/6535.

Laing, L., Toivonen, C., Irwin, J. and Napier, L. (2012b). *Towards Better Practice: Final Project Report*. Sydney: University of Sydney.

Landenburger, K. (1989). A process of entrapment in and recovery from an abusive relationship. *Issues in Mental Health Nursing*, 10(3–4), 209–227.

Lapierre, S. (2010). Are abused women 'neglectful' mothers? A critical reflection based on women's experiences. In B. Featherstone, C.-A. Hooper, J. Scourfield and J. Taylor (eds), *Gender and Child Welfare in Society*. Chichester and Hoboken, NJ: Wiley-Blackwell.

Lavis, V., Horrocks, C., Kelly, N. and Barker, V. (2005). Domestic violence and health care: opening Pandora's box – challenges and dilemmas. *Feminism and Psychology*, 15(4), 441–460.

Lempert, L. B. (1996). Women's strategies for survival: developing agency in abusive relationships. *Journal of Family Violence*, 11(3), 269–289.

Levendosky, A. A., Huth-Bocks, A. C., Shapiro, D. L. and Semel, M. A. (2003). The impact of domestic violence on the maternal–child relationship and preschool-age children's functioning. *Journal of Family Psychology*, 17(3), 275–287.

Lewis, R., Dobash, R. P., Dobash, R. E. and Cavanagh, K. (2000). Protection, prevention, rehabilitation or justice? Women's use of the law to challenge domestic violence. *International Review of Victimology*, 7(1,2,3 special issue: Domestic Violence: Global Responses), 179–205.

Lieberman, A. F., Ippen, C. G. and Van Horn, P. (2006). Child–parent psychotherapy: 6-month follow-up of a randomized controlled trial. *Journal of the American Academy of Child and Adolescent Psychiatry*, 45(8), 913–918.

Lipchik, E., Sirles, E. A. and Kubicki, A. D. (1997). Multifaceted approaches in spouse abuse treatment. *Journal of Aggression, Maltreatment and Trauma*, 1(1), 131–148.

Littlechild, B. and Bourke, C. (2006). Men's use of violence and intimidation against family members and child protection workers. In C. Humphreys and N. Stanley (eds), *Domestic Violence and Child Protection: Directions for Good Practice* (pp. 203–215). London: Jessica Kingsley.

Logan, T. K. and Walker, R. (2009). Civil protective order outcomes: violations and perceptions of effectiveness. *Journal of Interpersonal Violence, 24*(4), 675–692.

Loosely, S., Drouillard, D., Ritchie, D. and Abercromby, S. (2006). *Groupwork with Children Exposed to Woman Abuse: Concurrent Groupwork Program for Children and Their Mothers, Children's Program Manual.* London: The Children's Aid Society of London and Middlesex.

Lumby, B. and Farrelly, T. (2009). Family violence, help-seeking and the close-knit aboriginal community: lessons for mainstream service provision. *Issues Paper 19.* Retrieved 8 December 2011 from www.austdvclearinghouse.unsw.edu.au/PDF%20files/Issues%20 Paper_19.pdf.

Lutze, F. E. and Symons, M. L. (2003). The evolution of domestic violence policy through masculine institutions: from discipline to protection to collaborative empowerment. *Criminology and Public Policy, 2*(2), 319–328.

Macy, R. J. (2008). A research agenda for sexual revictimization: priority areas and innovative statistical methods. *Violence Against Women, 14*(10), 1128–1147.

Madoc-Jones, I. and Roscoe, K. (2010). Women's safety service within the Integrated Domestic Abuse Programme: perceptions of service users. *Child and Family Social Work, 15* (2), 155–164.

Magen, R. H. (1999). In the best interests of battered women: reconceptualizing allegations of failure to protect. *Child Maltreatment, 4*(2), 127–135.

Mann, S. (2006). 'How can you do this work?' Responding to questions about the experience of working with women who were subjected to child sexual abuse. In D. Denborough (ed.), *Trauma: Narrative Responses to Traumatic Experience* (pp. 1–24). Adelaide: Dulwich Centre Publications.

Mama, A. (1989). Violence against black women: gender, race and state responses. *Feminist Review, 32*(Summer), 30–48.

Margolin, G. and Gordis, E. B. (2004). Children's exposure to violence in the family and community. *Current Directions in Psychological Science, 13*(4), 152–155.

Margolin, G., Gordis, E. B., Medina, A. M. and Oliver, P. H. (2003). The co-occurrence of husband-to-wife aggression, family-of-origin aggression and child abuse potential in a community sample: implications for parenting. *Journal of Interpersonal Violence, 18*(4), 413–440.

Mathias, J. L., Mertin, P. and Murray, A. (1995). The psychological functioning of children from backgrounds of domestic violence. *Australian Psychologist, 30*(1), 47–56.

McCloskey, L., Figueredo, A. and Koss, P. (1995). The effects of systemic family violence on children's mental health. *Child Development, 66*(5), 1239–1261.

McDermott, J. M. and Garofalo, J. (2004). When advocacy for domestic violence victims backfires. *Violence Against Women, 10*(11), 1245–1266.

McFarlane, J. M., Groff, J. Y., O'Brien, J. A. and Watson, K. (2003). Behaviors of children who are exposed and not exposed to intimate partner violence: an analysis of 330 black, white and Hispanic children. *Pediatrics, 112* (3), e202 -e207.

McFerran, L. (2009). The disappearing age: a discussion paper on a strategy to address violence against older women. *Topic Paper No. 18.* Retrieved 25 June 2012 from www. austdvclearinghouse.unsw.edu.au/PDF%20files/Topic%20Paper%20Disappearing%20 Age.pdf.

Meltzer, H., Doos, L., Vostanis, P., Ford, T. and Goodman, R. (2009). The mental health of children who witness domestic violence. *Child and Family Social Work, 14*(4), 491–501.

Mendes, P. (1996). The historical and political context of mandatory reporting and its impact on child protection practice in Victoria. *Australian Social Work, 49*(4), 25–32.

Merritt-Gray, M. and Wuest, J. (1995). Counteracting abuse and breaking free: the process of leaving revealed through women's voices. *Health Care for Women International*, 16(5), 399–412.

Mertin, P. and Mohr, P. (2000). Incidence and correlates of post-traumatic stress disorder in Australian victims of domestic violence. *Journal of Family Violence*, 15(4), 411–422.

Miller, S. L. (2001). The paradox of women arrested for domestic violence: criminal justice professionals and service providers respond. *Violence Against Women*, 7(12), 1339–1376.

Miller, S. L. and Smolter, N. L. (2011). 'Paper abuse': when all else fails, batterers use procedural stalking. *Violence Against Women*, 17(5), 637–650.

Mills, L. G. (2003). *Insult to Injury: Rethinking Our Responses to Intimate Abuse*. Princeton, NJ: Princeton University Press.

Ministry of Children and Family Development (2010). Best practice approaches: child protection and violence against women. Retrieved 1 February 2012 from www.mcf.gov. bc.ca/child_protection/pdf/best_practice_approaches_nov2010.pdf.

Moore, T. and Pepler, D. (1998). Correlates of adjustment in children at risk. In G. W. Holden, R. Geffner and E. N. Jouriles (eds), *Children Exposed to Marital Violence*. Washington, DC: American Psychological Association.

Morgan Disney and Associates (2000). *Two Lives – Two Worlds: Older People and Domestic Violence* (Vol. 1). Canberra: Partnerships Against Domestic Violence.

Mouzos, J. and Makkai, T. (2004). Women's experiences of male violence: findings from the Australian component of the International Violence Against Women Survey (IVAWS). *Research and Public Policy Series, Number 56*. Canberra: Australian Institute of Criminology.

Mullender, A. and Morley, S. (eds) (1994). *Children Living with Domestic Violence*. London: Whiting and Birch.

Mullender, A., Hague, G., Imam, U., Kelly, L., Malos, E. and Regan, L. (2002). *Children's Perspectives on Domestic Violence*. London: Sage.

Munro, E. (2011). *The Munro Review of Child Protection Final Report: A Child-Centred System*. London: Stationery Office.

Murray, S. and Powell, A. (2011). *Domestic Violence: Public Policy in Australia*. Melbourne: Australian Scholarly Publishing.

National Council to Reduce Violence Against Women and their Children (2009). *Time for Action: The National Council's Plan for Australia to Reduce Violence Against Women and Their Children, 2009–2021*. Canberra: Department of Families, Housing, Community Services and Indigenous Affairs. Retrieved 26 August 2012 from www.fahcsia.gov.au/ sites/default/files/documents/05_2012/the_plan.pdf.

Nixon, J. and Humphreys, C. (2010). Marshalling the evidence: using intersectionality in the domestic violence frame. *Social Politics*, 17(2), 137–158.

NSW Department of Health (2003). *Policy and Procedures for Identifying and Responding to Domestic Violence*. Sydney: NSW Department of Health.

NSW Government (2009). *Report of the NSW Domestic Violence Homicide Advisory Panel*. Retrieved 22 June 2012 from http://lawlink.nsw.gov.au/lawlink/Corporate/ll_corporate. nsf/vwFiles/251109_domestic_violence.pdf/$file/251109_domestic_violence.pdf.

NSW Ombudsman (2006). *Domestic Violence: Improving Police Practice*. Sydney: NSW Ombudsman.

O'Hara, M. (1994). Child deaths in the context of domestic violence: implications for professional practice. In A. Mullender and S. Morley (eds), *Children Living with Domestic Violence*. London: Whiting and Birch.

O'Keefe, M. (1995). Predictors of child abuse in maritally violent families. *Journal of Interpersonal Violence*, 10(1), 3–25.

Office of Women's Policy Victoria (2005). *Reforming the Family Violence System in Victoria. Report of the Statewide Steering Committee to Reduce Family Violence*. Melbourne: Department of Victorian Communities.

Osofsky, J. D. (2003). Prevalence of children's exposure to domestic violence and child maltreatment: implications for prevention and intervention. *Clinical Child and Family Psychology Review*, 6(3), 161–170.

Palmer, S. E., Brown, R. A. and Barrera, M. E. (1992). Group treatment for abusive husbands: long-term evaluation. *American Journal of Orthopsychiatry*, 62(2), 276–283.

Parton, N. and O'Byrne, P. (2000). *Constructive Social Work: Towards a New Practice*. Basingstoke: Macmillan.

Patel, P. (2003). The tricky blue line: black women and policing. In R. Gupta (ed.), *From Homebreakers to Jailbreakers: Southall Black Sisters* (pp. 160–187). London: Zed Books.

Patton, M. Q. (1990). *Qualitative Evaluation and Research Methods* (2nd ed.). Newbury Park, CA: Sage.

Patton, S. (2003). *Pathways: How Women Leave Violent Men*. Retrieved 21 November 2006 from www.women.tas.gov.au/resources/padv/pathways.pdf.

Paymar, M. (2000). *Violent No More: Helping Men End Domestic Abuse* (2nd ed.). Alameda, CA: Hunter House.

Peirce, J. (2005). 'Family violence and the law: putting 'private' violence on the public agenda'. Paper presented at the Families Matter: 9th Australian Institute of Family Studies Conference, Melbourne.

Peled, E. (1998). The experience of living with violence for preadolescent children of battered women. *Youth and Society*, 29, 395–430.

Pence, E. L. and McDonnell, C. (1999). Developing policies and protocols. In M. F. Shepard and E. L. Pence (eds), *Coordinating Community Responses to Domestic Violence: Lessons from Duluth and Beyond* (pp. 41–64). Thousand Oaks, CA: Sage.

Perry, B. (1997). Incubated in terror: neurodevelopment factors in the 'cycle of violence'. In J. Osofsky (ed.), *Children, Youth and Violence: The Search for Solutions* (pp. 124–248). New York: Guildford Press.

Pochaska, J. O. and DiClemente, C. C. (1983). Stages and processes of self-change of smoking: toward an integrative model of change. *Journal of Consulting and Clinical Psychology*, 51(3), 390–395.

Power, C. and Kowanko, I. (2001). *Just Don't Give Up on Us: An Evaluation of the Central and Northern Violence Intervention Programs*. Adelaide: Central Violence Intervention Program.

Quinlivan, J. and Evans, S. (2005). Impact of domestic violence and drug abuse in pregnancy on maternal attachment and infant temperament in teenage mothers in the setting of best clinical practice. *Archives of Women's Mental Health*, 8(3), 191–199.

Radford, L. and Hester, M. (2006). *Mothering Through Domestic Violence*. London: Jessica Kingsley.

Radford, L. and Tsutsumi, K. (2004). Globalization and violence against women: inequalities in risks, responsibilities and blame in the UK and Japan. *Women's Studies International Forum*, 27(1), 1–12.

Radford, L., Blacklock, N. and Iwi, K. (2006). Domestic abuse risk assessment and safety planning in child protection: assessing perpetrators. In C. Humphreys and N. Stanley (eds), *Domestic Violence and Child Protection: Directions for Good Practice* (pp. 171–189). London: Jessica Kingsley.

Rajah, V., Frye, V. and Haviland, M. (2006). 'Aren't I a victim?' Notes on identity challenges relating to police action in a mandatory arrest jurisdiction. *Violence Against Women*, 12(10), 897–916.

Ramsay, J., Richardson, J., Carter, Y. H., Davidson, L. L. and Feder, G. (2002). Should health professionals screen women for domestic violence? Systematic review. *British Journal of Criminology*, 325, 314–318.

Raphael, J. (2004). Rethinking Criminal Justice responses to intimate partner violence. *Violence Against Women*, 10(11), 1354–1366.

Rees, S., Silove, D., Chey, T., Ivancic, L., Steel, Z., Creamer, M., Teesson, M., Bryant, R., McFarlane, A. C., Mills, K. L., Slade, T., Carragher, N., O'Donnell, M. and Forbes, D. (2011). Lifetime prevalence of gender-based violence in women and the relationship with mental disorders and psychosocial function. *JAMA*, 306(5), 513–521.

Research and Education Unit on Gendered Violence (2003). *A Comparative Assessment of Good Practice in Programs for Men Who Use Violence Against Female Partners*. Canberra: Office of the Status of Women, Department of the Prime Minister and Cabinet.

Riggs, D. S., Caulfield, M. B. and Street, A. E. (2000). Risk for domestic violence: factors associated with perpetration and victimization. *Journal of Clinical Psychology*, 56(10), 1289–1316.

Rittel, H. W. J. and Webber, M. M. (1973). Dilemmas in a general theory of planning. *Policy Sciences*, 4(2), 155–169.

Roberts, G., Hegarty, K. L. and Feder, G. (eds) (2006). *Intimate Partner Abuse Health Professionals: New Approaches to Domestic Violence*. Edinburgh: Churchill Livingstone Elsevier.

Robertson, N., Busch, R., D'Souza, R., Lam Sheung, F., Anand, R., Balzer, R., Simpson, A. and Paina, D. (2007). *Living at the Cutting Edge: Women's Experiences of Protection Orders*. Retrieved 1 October 2011 from http://hdl.handle.net/10289/450.

Robinson, A. L. (2003). *The Cardiff Women's Safety Unit: A Multi-agency Approach to Domestic Violence. Final Evaluation Report*. Retrieved 30 September, 2011 from www.cardiff.ac.uk/socsi/resources/robinson-WSU-final-evaluation-report.pdf.

Robinson, A. L. (2006). Reducing repeat victimization among high-risk victims of domestic violence: the benefits of a coordinated community response in Cardiff, Wales. *Violence Against Women*, 12(8), 761–788.

Robinson, A. L. and Rowlands, J. (2006). *The Dyn Project: Supporting Men Experiencing Domestic Abuse. Final Evaluation Report*. Retrieved 15 December 2011 from www.cardiff.ac.uk/socsi/resources/Dyn_Final_Evaluation_Report.pdf.

Robinson, A. L. and Stroshine, M. S. (2005). The importance of expectation fulfilment on domestic violence victims' satisfaction with the police in the UK. *Policing: An International Journal of Police Strategies and Management*, 28(2), 301–320.

Robson, C. (2002). *Real World Research*. Oxford: Blackwell.

Ross, S. (1996). Risk of physical abuse to children of spouse abusing parents. *Child Abuse and Neglect*, 20, 589–598.

Ross, S., Frere, M., Healey, L. and Humphreys, C. (2011). A whole of government strategy for family violence reform. *Australian Journal of Public Administration*, 70(2), 131–142.

Rossman, B. B. (2001). Longer term effects of children's exposure to domestic violence. In S. A. Graham-Bermann and J. L. Edleson (eds), *Domestic Violence in the Lives of Children: The Future of Research, Intervention and Social Policy*. Washington, DC: American Psychological Association.

Ruch, G. (2005). Relationship-based practice and reflective practice: holistic approaches to contemporary child care social work. *Child and Family Social Work*, 10(2), 111–123.

Russell, D. E. H. (1984). *Sexual Exploitation: Rape, Child Sexual Abuse and Workplace Harassment*. Beverly Hills, CA: Sage.

Safe Horizon (2008). *Introducing the Impact of Domestic Violence on Children into a Batterer Program Curriculum: Does an Emphasis on the Kids Improve the Response?* Final report for National Institute of Justice, grant number 2003-WG-BX-1005. Washington, DC: US Department of Justice, National Institute of Justice.

Saleebey, D. (1994). Culture, theory and narrative: the intersection of meanings in practice. *Social Work*, 39(4), 351–359.

Saleebey, D. (1996). The strengths perspective in social work practice: extensions and cautions. *Social Work*, 41(3), 296–305.

Saleebey, D. (1997). Introduction: power in the people. In D. Saleebey (ed.), *The Strengths Perspective in Social Work Practice* (2nd ed.; pp. 3–19). New York: Longman.

Salisbury, E. J., Henning, K. and Holdford, R. (2009). Fathering by partner-abusive men: attitudes on children's exposure to interparental conflict and risk factors for child abuse. *Child Maltreatment*, 14(3), 232–242.

Sarantakos, S. (1993). *Social Research*. Melbourne: MacMillan Education Australia.

Saunders, H. (2004). *29 Child Homicides: Lessons Still to Learn on Domestic Violence and Child Protection*. Bristol: Women's Aid Federation.

Saville, H. (1982). Refuges: a new beginning to the struggle. In C. O'Donnell and J. Craney (eds), *Family Violence in Australia*. Melbourne: Longman Cheshire.

Schneider, E. M. (1992). Particularity and generality: challenges of feminist theory and practice in work on woman-abuse. *New York University Law Review*, 67, 520–568.

Schon, D. (1983). *The Reflective Practitioner: How Professionals Think in Action*. New York: Basic Books.

Schore, A. (2003). *Affect Dysregulation and Disorders of the Self*. New York: Norton.

Scott, D. (2005). Inter-organisational collaboration in family-centred practice: a framework for analysis and action. *Australian Social Work*, 58(2), 132–141.

Scott, D. (2006). Towards a public health model of child protection in Australia. *Communities, Children and Families Australia*, 1(1), 9–16.

Scott, K. L. and Crooks, C. V. (2004). Effecting change in maltreating fathers: critical principles for intervention planning. *Clinical Psychology – Science and Practice*, 11(1), 95–111.

Scott, K. L. and Crooks, C. V. (2007). Preliminary evaluation of an intervention program for maltreating fathers. *Brief Treatment and Crisis Intervention*, 7(3), 224–238.

Scottish Executive (2000). *The National Strategy to Address Domestic Abuse in Scotland*. Edinburgh: Scottish Executive.

Scottish Government Statistician Group (2010). Domestic abuse recorded by the police in Scotland, 2009–10. *Statistical Bulletin: Crime and Justice Series*. Retrieved 5 January 2012 from www.scotland.gov.uk/Resource/Doc/330575/0107237.pdf.

Seeley, J. and Plunkett, C. (2002). *Women and Domestic Violence: Standards for Counselling Practice*. Retrieved 13 July 2011 from www.salvationarmy.org.au/salvwr/_assets/main/documents/reports/womenanddomestic_violence_counselling_standards.pdf.

Shaw, E., Bouris, A. and Pye, S. (1999). A comprehensive approach: the family safety model with domestic violence. In J. Breckenridge and L. Laing (eds), *Challenging Silence: Innovative Responses to Sexual and Domestic Violence*. Sydney: Allen and Unwin.

Shepard, M. and Pence, E. (1999). *Coordinating Community Responses to Domestic Violence: Lessons from Duluth and Beyond*. Thousand Oaks, CA: Sage.

Shephard, M. and Raschick, M. (1999). How child welfare workers assess and intervene around issues of domestic violence. *Child Maltreatment*, 4(2), 148–156.

Sherman, L. and Berk, R. A. (1984). The specific deterrent effects of arrest for domestic assault. *American Sociological Review*, 49(2), 261–272.

Smith, K., Coleman, K., Eder, S. and Hall, P. (2011). *Homicides, Firearm Offences and Intimate Violence 2009/10. Supplementary Volume 2 to Crime in England and Wales 2009/10* (2nd ed.). London: Home Office.

Smith, K., Flatley, J., Coleman, K., Osborne, S., Kaiza, P. and Roe, S. (2010). Homicides, firearm offences and intimate violence 2008/09: supplementary volume 2 to crime in England and Wales 2008/09. *Home Office Statistical Bulletin*, Retrieved 5 January 2012 from http://webarchive.nationalarchives.gov.uk/20110218135832/rds.homeoffice.gov.uk/rds/pdfs10/hosb0110.pdf.

Snider, L. (1998). Towards safer societies: punishment, masculinities and violence against women. *The British Journal of Criminology*, 38(1), 1–39.

Sokoloff, N. J. (ed.) (2005). *Domestic Violence at the Margins: Readings on Race, Class, Gender and Culture*. New Brunswick, NJ: Rutgers University Press.

Sokoloff, N. J. and Dupont, I. (2005). Domestic violence at the intersections of race, class and gender: challenges and contributions to understanding violence against marginalized women in diverse communities. *Violence Against Women*, 11(1), 38–64.

Spangaro, J. (2007). The NSW Health routine screening for domestic violence program. *New South Wales Public Health Bulletin*, 18(6), 86–89.

Spangaro, J., Zwi, A. B. and Poulos, R. (2009). The elusive search for definitive evidence on routine screening for intimate partner violence. *Trauma Violence and Abuse*, 10(1), 55–68.

SSDVI (2009). Another closet. Retrieved 4 February 2012 from http://anothercloset.squarespace.com/storage/AVP%20-%20Another%20Closet%20Web.pdf.

Stanley, J. and Goddard, C. (2002). *In the Firing Line: Violence and Power in Child Protection Work*. Chichester: Wiley.

Stanley, N., Miller, P., Richardson Foster, H. and Thomson, G. (2010). *Children and Families Experiencing Domestic Violence: Police and Children's Services Responses*. London: NSPCC.

Stanley, N., Miller, P., Richardson Foster, H. and Thomson, G. (2011a). Children's experience of domestic violence: developing an integrated response from police and child protection services. *Journal of Interpersonal Violence*, 25(12), 2372–2391.

Stanley, N., Miller, P., Richardson Foster, H. and Thomson, G. (2011b). A stop-start response: social services' interventions with children and families notified following domestic violence incidents. *British Journal of Social Work*, 41, 296–313.

Stark, E. (2004). Insults, injury and injustice. *Violence Against Women*, 10(11), 1302–1330.

Stark, E. (2007). *Coercive Control: How Men Entrap Women in Personal Life*. New York: Oxford University Press.

Stella Project (2007). *Stella Project Toolkit (2007): Domestic Violence, Drugs and Alcohol: Good Practice Guidelines* (2nd ed.). Retrieved 12 December 2011 from www.avaproject.org.uk/our-resources/good-practice-guidance--toolkits/stella-project-toolkit-(2007).aspx.

Stewart, J. (2005). *Specialist Domestic/Family Violence Courts within the Australian context. Issues Paper 10*. Retrieved 30 September 2010 from www.adfvc.unsw.edu.au/documents/Issuespaper_10.pdf.

Straus, M. A. (1979). Measuring intrafamily conflict and violence: the conflict tactics (CT) scales. *Journal of Marriage and the Family*, 41(1), 75–88.

Straus, M. A. and Gelles, R. J. (1986). Societal change and change in family violence from 1975–1985 as revealed by two national surveys. *Journal of Marriage and the Family*, 48(3), 465–479.

Sturge, C. and Glaser, D. (2000). Contact and domestic violence: the experts' court report. *Family Law*, 30, 622–623.

Suchting, M. (1999). The case of the too hard basket: investigating the connections between 'ethnicity', 'culture' and 'access' to sexual assault services. In J. Breckenridge and L. Laing (eds), *Challenging Silence: Innovative Responses to Sexual and Domestic Violence* (p. 74). Sydney: Allen and Unwin.

Sullivan, C. (2007). Evaluating parenting programs for men who batter: current considerations and controversies. In J. Eldleson and O. Williams (eds), *Parenting by Men Who Batter* (pp. 137–148). Oxford: Oxford University Press.

Sullivan, C. M. and Bybee, D. I. (1999). Reducing violence using community-based advocacy for women with abusive partners. *Journal of Consulting and Clinical Psychology*, 67(1), 43–53.

Sullivan, C., Nguyen, H., Allen, N., Bybee, D. and Juras, J. (2000). Beyond searching for deficits: evidence that physically and emotionally abused women are nurturing parents. *Journal of Emotional Abuse*, 2(1), 51–71.

Taft, A. (2003). Promoting women's mental health: the challenges of intimate/domestic violence against women. *Issues Paper*. Retrieved 19 October 2006 from www.austdvclearinghouse.unsw.edu.au/PDF%20files/Issues_Paper_8.pdf.

Taillieu, T. L. and Brownridge, D. A. (2010). Violence against pregnant women: prevalence, patterns, risk factors, theories and directions for future research. *Aggression and Violent Behavior*, 15(1), 14–35.

Tamasese, K. (2003). Gender and culture – together. In C. Waldegrave, K. Tamasese, F. Tuhaka and W. Campbell (eds), *Just Therapy – A Journey: A Collection of Papers from the Just Therapy Team New Zealand* (pp. 203–206). Adelaide: Dulwich Centre Publications.

Taylor, B. (2008). '*Dying to be Heard': Domestic and Family Violence Death Reviews*. Discussion Paper. Retrieved 29 March 2012 from www.wlsq.org.au/documents/publicat/cle/dvdrag%20%20ver%202.pdf.

Teicher, M. (2002). The neurobiology of child abuse. *Scientific American*, 286(3), 70.

The Scottish Government (2009). *Safer Lives: Changed Lives – A Shared Approach to Tackling Violence Against Women in Scotland*. Retrieved 6 February 2012 from www.scotland.gov.uk/Resource/Doc/274212/0082013.pdf.

Thiara, R. K. and Gill, A. K. (2010a). Understanding violence against South Asian women. In R. K. Thiara and A. K. Gill (eds), *Violence Against Women in South Asian Communities* (pp. 29–54). London: Jessica Kingsley.

Thiara, R. K. and Gill, A. K. (eds) (2010b). *Violence Against Women in South Asian Communities*. London: Jessica Kingsley.

Thiara, R. K., Hague, G., Ellis, B., Bashall, R. and Mullender, A. (2012). *Disabled Women and Domestic Violence: Responding to the Experiences of Survivors*. London: Jessica Kingsley.

Thompson, N. (2002). *People Skills* (2nd ed.). Basingstoke: Palgrave.

Thompson, N. (2003). *Promoting Equality: Challenging Discrimination and Oppression* (2nd ed.). Houndmills: Palgrave Macmillan.

Thomson and Goodall Associates (2010). *Family Violence Safety Notices Evaluation*. Retrieved 17 October 2011 from www.dvrcv.org.au/wp-content/uploads/FVSN-evaluation-summary.pdf.

Tjaden, P. and Thoennes, N. (2000). Prevalence and consequences of male-to-female and female-to-male intimate partner violence as measured by the National Violence Against Women Survey. *Violence Against Women*, 6(2), 142–161.

United Nations General Assembly (1993). *A/RES/48/104: Declaration on the Elimination of Violence Against Women*. Retrieved 12 December 2010 from www.un.org/documents/ga/res/48/a48r104.htm.

Ursel, J. (2002). 'His sentence is my freedom': processing domestic violence cases in the Winnipeg Family Violence Court. In L. Tutty and C. Goard (eds), *Reclaiming Self: Issues and Resources for Women Abused by Intimate Partners* (pp. 43–63). Halifax: Fernwood.

Van Horn, P. and Groves, B. M. (2006). Children exposed to domestic violence: making trauma-informed custody and visitation decisions. *Juvenile and Family Court Journal*, 57(1), 51–60.

VicHealth (2007). *Preventing Violence Before it Occurs: A Framework and Background Paper to Guide the Primary Prevention of Violence Against Women in Victoria*. Retrieved 30 January 2012 from www.vichealth.vic.gov.au/en/Publications/Freedom-from-violence/Preventing-violence-before-it-occurs.aspx.

Victoria Police (2010). *Code of Practice for the Investigation of Family Violence* (2nd ed.). Retrieved 17 October 2011 from www.police.vic.gov.au/content.asp?Document_ID=288.

Victorian Government Department of Justice (2009). *Victorian Family Violence Database (Vol. 4): Nine-Year Trend Analysis: 1999–2009*. Retrieved 5 January 2012 from www.justice.vic.gov.au/resources/2/e/2ed0e280404a4dec8a04fbf5f2791d4a/vfvd_1999_2008.pdf.

Victorian Health Promotion Foundation (2004). *The Health Costs of Violence: Measuring the Burden of Disease Caused by Intimate Partner Violence: A Summary of Findings*. Melbourne: Victorian Health Promotion Foundation.

Victorian Health Promotion Foundation (2009). *National Survey on Community Attitudes to Violence Against Women 2009: Changing Cultures, Changing Attitudes – Preventing Violence Against Women*. Melbourne: Victorian Health Promotion Foundation.

Virueda, M. and Payne, J. (2010). Homicide in Australia: 2007–08 National Homicide Monitoring Program annual report. *Monitoring Report 13*. Retrieved 5 January 2012 from www.aic.gov.au/documents/8/9/D/%7B89DEDC2D-3349–457C-9B3A-9AD9DAFA7256%7Dmr13_004.pdf.

Vodde, R. and Gallant, J. P. (2002). Bridging the gap between micro and macro practice: large-scale change and a unified model of narrative-deconstructive practice. *Journal of Social Work Education*, 38(3), 439–458.

Wade, A. (1997). Small acts of living: everyday resistance to violence and other forms of oppression. *Contemporary Family Therapy*, 19(1), 23–39.

Wade, A. (2007). Despair, resistance, hope. In C. Flaskas, I. McCarthy and J. Sheehan (eds), *Hope and Despair in Narrative and Family Therapy: Adversity, Forgiveness and Reconciliation*. Hove: Brunner-Routledge.

Walby, S. and Allen, J. (2004). Domestic violence, sexual assault and stalking: findings from the British Crime Survey. *Home Office Research Study 276*. Retrieved 5 January 2012 from http://broken-rainbow.org.uk/research/Dv%20crime%20survey.pdf.

Waldegrave, C. (2003). Just therapy. In C. Waldegrave, K. Tamasese, F. Tuhaka and W. Campbell (eds), *Just Therapy – A Journey: A Collection of Papers from the Just Therapy Team New Zealand* (pp. 3–56). Adelaide: Dulwich Centre Publications.

Walker, L. E. (1977–78). Battered women and learned helplessness. *Victimology*, 2(3–4), 525–534.

Warshaw, C., Gugenheim, M., Moroney, G. and Barnes, H. (2003). Special report – Fragmented services, unmet needs: building collaboration between the mental health and domestic violence communities. *Health Affairs*, 22(5), 230–234.

Weatherburn, D. and Snowball, L. (2006). Indigenous over-representation in prison: the role of offender characteristics. *Crime and Justice Bulletin*. Retrieved 24 September 2011 from www.lawlink.nsw.gov.au/lawlink/bocsar/ll_bocsar.nsf/vwFiles/CJB99.pdf/$file/CJB99.pdf.

Weisz, A. N., Tolman, R. M. and Saunders, D. G. (2000). Assessing the risk of severe domestic violence: the importance of survivors' predictions. *Journal of Interpersonal Violence*, 15(1), 75–90.

Westmarland, N. and Kelly, L. (2012). Why extending measurements of 'success' in domestic violence perpetrator programmes matters for social work. *British Journal of Social Work*, (Advance access), 1–19.

Westmarland, N., Kelly, L. and Chalder-Mills, J. (2010). *What Counts as Success?* London: Respect.

White, M. (2007). *Maps of Narrative Practice*. New York: Norton.

White, M. and Epston, D. (1989). *Literate Means to Therapeutic Ends*. Adelaide: Dulwich Centre Publications.

White, S., Hall, C. and Peckover, S. (2009). The descriptive tyranny of the common assessment framework: technologies of categorization and professional practice in child welfare. *British Journal of Social Work*, 39(7), 1197–1217.

Wilkinson, K. and Davidson, J. (2008). *They've Been my Lifeline: An Evaluation of South Yorkshire's Specialist Domestic Violence Court Initiative: The Independent Domestic Violence Advocacy Service. Project Report.* Retrieved 12 December 2011 from http://shura.shu.ac.uk/994/1/fulltext.pdf.

Williamson, E. (2010). Living in the world of the domestic violence perpetrator: negotiating the unreality of coercive control. *Violence Against Women*, 16(12), 1412–1423.

Women's Aid Federation of England (nd). *What is Domestic Violence?* Retrieved 12 December 2010 from www.womensaid.org.uk/domestic-violence-articles.asp?section=00010001002 200410001anditemid=1272anditemTitle=What+is+domestic+violence.

Women's Health Goulburn North East (2011). *BSAFE Pilot Project 2007–2010*. Wangaratta, Victoria: Women's Health Goulburn North East.

Wood, D. J. and Gray, B. (1991). Toward a comprehensive theory of collaboration. *Journal of Applied Behavioral Science*, 27(2), 139–162.

Wood, J. (2008). *Report of the Special Commission of Inquiry into Child Protection Services in NSW* (Vol. 2). Sydney: State of NSW through the Special Commission of Inquiry into Child Protection Services in NSW.

World Health Organization (2005). *Multi-country Study on Women's Health and Domestic Violence Against Women: Summary Report*. Retrieved 1 August 2010 from www.who.int/gender/violence/who_multicountry_study/summary_report/summary_report_English2.pdf

Zaher, C. (2002). When a woman's marital status determined her legal status: A research guide on the common law doctrine of coverture. *Law Library Journal*, 94(3), 459–486.

Zanoti-Jeronymo, D. (2009). Prevalence of physical abuse in childhood and exposure to parental violence in a Brazilian sample. *Cadernos de Saude Publica*, 25, 2467–2479.

Index

Note: Page numbers in **bold** indicate figures.